AF553813

MARKETING STRATEGY OF LIFE INSURANCE COMPANIES

MARKETING STRATEGY OF LIFE INSURANCE COMPANIES

By

Dr. (Mrs.). S.Lilly Rosari

Associate Professor
Deptt. of Commerce
Holy Cross College
Tiruchirappalli (Tamil Nadu)

&

I.Francis Ganasekar

M.com., B.Ed., M.Phil., M.B.A., Ph.D.
Associate Professor & Head
Deptt. of Commerce
St.Joseph's College
Tiruchirappalli (Tamil Nadu)
(India)

DISCOVERY PUBLISHING HOUSE PVT. LTD.

NEW DELHI-110 002

Published by:
Tilak Wasan
DISCOVERY PUBLISHING HOUSE PVT. LTD.
4383/4B, Ansari Road, Darya Ganj
New Delhi-110 002 (India)
Phone : +91-11-23279245, 43596064-65
Fax : +91-11-23253475
E-mail : discoverypublishinghouse@gmail.com
sales@discoverypublishinggroup.com
parul.wasan@gmail.com
web : www.discoverypublishinggroup.com

First Edition: **2013**

ISBN: 978-93-5056-281-9

Marketing Strategy of Life Insurance Companies

Printed at:
Aditi Fine Art Press
Delhi

The Success of Every Child is a Credit
To the Parents

With Lots of Love and
Hearty Salutations

I Dedicate this Thesis
to my
Beloved Father
SRI K.S. SANTIAGO

Preface

The Life Insurance sector which is booming sector in India has become a very attractive destination for global insurance players. The winds of liberalization and privatization have brought about dynamic and phenomenal changes in the insurance sector. Increased dynamism in the external environment in the form of competition has made it imperative to bring about transformation in the life insurance market. The tremendous growth recorded by Indian in this sector has been driven by liberalisation, with the players both public and private enhancing product awareness and promoting consumer information. Innovative products, attractive pricing strategies, well designed promotional tools and distribution strategies, good quality, customer-centric services have been facilitated by the players. There has been a perceptible shift from the sellers" market to the buyers' market. The Insurance Regulatory Development Authority (IRDA) has evolved stringent norms to enhance quality services and to ensure that the insurance services reach both rural and urban masses effectively.

The book titled "Marketing Strategy of Life Insurance Companies" is an attempt to understand the policyholders' views as regards the marketing efforts implemented by select life insurance companies viz., LIC, Bajaj Allianz Life Insurance Company and ICICI Prudential Life Insurance Company.

The book will be a useful guide to readers and persons interested in insurance policy making/taking. It throws light on:

(*i*) Various aspects of Marketing Mix.

(*ii*) Marketing strategies adopted by the Life Insurance companies.

(*iii*) It also gives an insight into the perception of policy holders towards various attributes of Marketing Mix.

(*iv*) Valuable suggestions have been provided to the insurance companies, Government and to the policy makers.

Authors

Aknowledgements

I thank the *OMNIPOTENT GOD* who is always the source of all knowledge and wisdom for the magnificent presence and strength that has made the study possible.

I offer my profound gratitude and heartfelt thanks to my guide *Dr. I. Francis Gnana Sekar*, M.Com., M.Phil, B.Ed., Ph.D., M.B.A., Reader & Head, Department of Commerce, St. Joseph's College, Tiruchirappalli. I wish to acknowledge his untiring enthusiasm, dynamic guidance, constant motivation and committed help at every stage of the study. The creative insight and sustained interest of my guide were of immense value for the successful accomplishment of the present research.

I wish to express my thanks to *University Grants Commission of India, New Delhi* for providing me a Teacher Fellowship under the Faculty Improvement Programme (FIP) which helped me finish my work in time.

I am very much grateful to the *authorities* of Bharathidasan University for having given me an opportunity to undergo Ph.D. Programme.

I acknowledge my gratefulness to *Dr.(Sr.) Rosy* (Former Principal), *and Dr.(Sr.) Surguna*, Principal and Head of the Department of Commerce, Holy Cross College (Autonomous), Tiruchirappalli for permitting me to undertake this study and also for giving constant support.

I thank the *Management* and the Principal *Dr.(Fr.) Rajaratanam, SJ*, of St. Joseph's College (Autonomous), Tiruchirappalli for allowing me to use the Library and for providing me with all infrastructure facilities.

Thanks are due to Doctoral Committee Members *Dr. Ramachandran and Dr. Srinivasan*, Department of Commerce, National College, Tiruchirappalli, for their inspiring advice and valuable suggestions.

My gratitude is due to *Dr. Stephen Vincent Raj*, Reader, Department of Statistics, St. Joseph's College (Autonomous), Tiruchirappalli, and *Dr. Sam David*, Lecturer, Department of Business Administration, Jamal Mohammed College, Tiruchirappalli for their significant help in the application of statistical analysis at various levels of this thesis.

I express my deep sense of gratitude to *Dr. Valsamma Antony* and *Dr. Pushparani,* the former Heads of the Department of Commerce, Holy Cross College (Autonomous), Tiruchirappalli for their assistance and support in the research endeavour.

I am grateful to the *Librarian*s of St. Joseph's College, Holy Cross College (Autonomous), Tiruchirappalli, IIM Bangalore, International Institute for Insurance and Finance, Hyderabad and IFMR Chennai for the assistance rendered to me in gathering vital information pertaining to my research.

Thanks are extended to *Mrs. S. Mahalakshmi Rajan* for her meticulous typing and compiling of the project report with adequate care and precision.

I wish to thank the *officials* of the Life Insurance Corporation, Bajaj Allianz Life Insurance Company and ICICI Prudential Life Insurance Company, Development Officers and Agents who supported and helped during my data collection. I express my deep sense of gratitude to all the respondents for their co-operation in the process of data collection for the study.

I wish to acknowledge the time and expertise rendered by *Dr. Inez Gonsalvas,* Public Relation Officer, Holy Cross College, Tiruchirappalli who offered help in evaluating the language content of the dissertation and provided valuable suggestions.

Grateful acknowledgement is extended to *Mrs. Mena Seetharaman*, Lecturer, Department of Economics Cross College (Autonomous), Tiruchirappalli for her constant help and encouragement at all the phases of the study.

I thank the *faculty members* of Department of Commerce, Holy Cross College (Autonomous), Tiruchirappalli for their support during my research.

With a grateful heart, I remember my loving family members, my husband *Mr. A. James* and my loving children *J. Jesvine Preetha and J. Joan Cecilia* for their continuous support and co-operation throughout my study.

Last but not the least I owe my heartfelt thanks to all those people who have helped me in a special way.

S. LILLY ROSARI

Contents

Abbreviations

LIC	-	Life Insurance Corporation of India
BAJAJ	-	Bajaj Allianz Life Insurance Company
ICICI	-	ICICI Prudential Life Insurance Company
IRDA	-	Insurance Regulatory Development Authority

1

Introduction

The most important aspect of human life is its uncertainty. In the modern industrialized era, human life and property are inevitably exposed to different kinds and varying degrees of risks and uncertainties. Human beings, to protect themselves and their property from total disaster, resort intelligently to protection coverage extended by the insurance companies which act as a trustee to the amount collected through premiums and provide certainty in the place of uncertainty. A very prominent step taken by human beings to mitigate the eventualities of life is investment in insurance companies which act as protectors of future ambitions and aspirations of the people. Insurance is a co-operative device which safeguards financially both longevity of human life or premature mishaps when man, out of genuine concern for his dependants, insures his life taking into account the various unforeseeable risk factors that are prevalent everywhere. The maturity amount takes care of not only the dependants of the insured, but also of self, when he is neglected or forsaken by his family members. Middle income groups certainly resort to insurance companies for their future financial needs and commitments. The salaried group depends upon insurance for saving for the future as well as for tax purposes.

The proper channelizing of the insurance companies funds have benefited the community at large. The utilization of people's money invested in life insurance for planned economic development has helped the country march forward. The amount amassed through premium is invested in socially desirable and societal- oriented projects like housing, electricity, water drainage systems and infrastructure development (Sajit Ali, *et.al.*, 2007). Capital is provided for capital accumulation, increase in production and job opportunities. The much-needed capital requirements of business and commerce are provided by means of these investments. All these aspects highlight the importance of insurance companies in the modern economic scenario and they are an integral part of our investment portfolio, not only for the salaried class but also for anyone who can pay a minimum premium in his own capacity for his future security. Even the families from the marginalized class now invest in life insurance policies to protect themselves from unwanted mental stress and financial risks. Life insurance facilitates disciplined savings, protects against untimely demise, guarantees asset protection, steady growth of investment and planning for retirement. Life insurance is civilization's partial solution to the problems caused by death (Neera Banzal, 2004).

The insurance companies have come to the doorstep of every family today, especially after the financial sector reforms. With the advent of private sector players in the field, there is great competition in the mode of operation and each company employs its own unique marketing strategy for the best results. As indicated in the report, the insurance companies have started focusing on the rural markets, as competition has become acute in the urban markets. (Thompson report, 2007). There is a felt need to concentrate on the security as well as the health aspect of the policy holders. Moreover, the insurance companies have been concentrating on all sections of society including the marginalized and the destitute irrespective of their status. (NCAER, 2004). The captivating captions of advertisements that promise the fulfillment of various dream visions from rags to riches, illustrate the companies varied marketing strategies.

The elements of marketing strategy adopted by the insurance companies vary considerably and it is worth examining the marketing mix adopted by the insurance companies both in the private and public sectors to analyze and gauge their effectiveness and suggest further modifications needed, for the best results. In addition to product, price, physical distribution and promotion, there are a few more elements such as customer-care and location advantages that comprise the marketing mix. These factors constitute the agents of success for these companies and hence the present study.

Marketing Mix of Insurance Services

Marketing mix is an important tool used by the marketing manager in formulating the marketing planning to suit the requirements of the customers. It is a tool used to ascertain the needs, tastes and preferences of the customers. The term 'marketing mix', was introduced by Prof. N.H.Borden of the Harvard Business School of America. It describes combination of the four inputs which constitute the core of a company's marketing system – the product, the distribution system, the price structure and the promotional activities.

In the words of Borden "Marketing mix refers to the appointment of efforts, the combination, the designing and the integration of the elements of marketing into a programme or mix which, on the basis of an appraisal of the market forces will best achieve an enterprise at a given time". (Pillai, R.S.N. and Bagavathi, 2004).

Jerome McCarthy, defines the term thus : 'Marketing mix is a pack of four sets of variables, namely, product variables, price variables, promotion variables and place variables'. (Varshney, R.L. and Gupta, S.L., 2004).

Services lie at the very centre of economic activity of a society. Since the Second World War there has been a decline in the traditional manufacturing of goods and service based industries have taken up that place. The developed economies also called as service economies reveal that the service sector accounts for more employment, more consumption, and contribution to GDP, as compared to manufactured articles. (Vasanthi Venugopal. and Raghu,V.N., 2006).The contribution of service sector to the GDP has increased from 56.8 per cent in the year 2001-2002 to 60.7 per cent in the year 2005-2006. *(www. indiaonestop.com.).*

Boom and Bitner expanded the marketing mix by adding 3 P's namely people, process and physical evidence. (www.valuebasedmanagement.net).

The services industries at present adopt marketing mix with nine P's namely Product, Price, Promotion, Physical, Distribution, People, Process, Physical Evidence, Packaging and Public Relations. (www.londre marketing.com.)

Considering the nature of services, insurance is one of the essential services categorized under financial services. Along with financial services, real estates and business services insurance contributes nine point seven per cent to the GDP of our country. (www.indiaonestop.com.)

The strategies of marketing mix require some modifications, when applied to service sector undertakings. Due to the special features of the services namely intangibility, inseparability, perishability and heterogeneity. Customer service lies at the heart of service industries and therefore marketing has become far more customer oriented than ever before. The marketing mix of the services industries comprises of nine P's namely Product, Price, Promotion, Physical distribution, People, Process, Physical Evidence, Packaging and Public Relations. (www.londremarketing.com)

Services can be classified on several bases such as nature of service act, type of relationship between the service providers, scope of customization and so on. Considering the nature of services, insurance is one of the essential services categorized under financial services. Along with financial services real estates and business services insurance contributes nine point seven per cent to the GDP of our country. (www.indiaonestop.com.)

According to Hansell, D.S., "Insurance is a contract in which a sum of money is paid by the assured in consideration of insurer's incurring the risk of paying a large sum upon a given contingency."(Motihar, M., 2004).

Insurance services are broadly classified into life insurance and general insurance services. Life insurance aims at providing financial security towards financial losses arising due to the loss of life of the bread winner of the family.

According to Sharma, R.S., "Life Insurance contract may be defined whereby the insurer, in consideration of a premium paid either in lump sum or in periodical installments, undertakes to pay an annuity or a certain sum of money either on death of the insured or on the expiry of certain number of years". (Motihar, M., 2004).

The term insurance marketing refers to the marketing of insurance services with the motto of customer-orientation and profit generation (Jha. S.M., 2003).

Insurance marketing is the adoption of marketing practices to the insurance business. It is concerned with the expansion of insurance business in the best interest of the society and the insurance organizations. Prime focus is made on the policy holders who are the end users of the insurance services. The needs, preferences, motives, perceptions and attitudes are found instrumental in designing the marketing strategies of the life insurance services.

Insurance Origin and Developments

The Biblical story of Joseph during the famine in Egypt has been cited as the first insurance case in recorded history. The Egyptian ruler Pharaoh had a dream one night in which he stood on the bank of the Nile and saw seven fat ant gloss cows coming out of the river followed by another set of seven cows which were lean and hungry. The latter devoured the former. Pharaoh was so disturbed by the experience that he sent for Joseph to interpret the dream. According to Joseph, the seven fat cows represented seven years of good crops and seven lean cows foreboded seven years of famine. He advised Pharaoh to take one-fifth of the crop of each prosperous year to be used in the years of famine. Joseph, himself was entrusted with the implementation of the scheme. (Sesha Iyer, V., 2003).

The story illustrates, though symbolically, the insurance principle of spreading the risk and the wisdom of setting aside some portion of wealth in the prosperous present to care for the needs of an uncertain future.

The ancient Greeks organized a life insurance system. Some temples collected money from their members. If the member paid his dues faithfully, he was given a good burial. The Romans and later the medieval guilds followed the same system. The guilds used the money to take care of the losses from fire and robbery too. Life Insurance in rudimentary form was practised centuries ago. Members in certain communities collected amounts to be paid to the families of those who died during the year. A system akin to the present-day self-insurance was prevalent in the social setup of the Indian community. The institution of joint family which was so widely practised in India afforded protection for its members. Education and marriage of children, taking care of the old and the sick members of the family as well as maintenance of widows were deemed a part of the responsibilities of the other members of the joint family. In ancient India it was a normal practice (prior to proceeding on a holy pilgrimage) for widows to hand over their entire belongings to some rich neighbors, who were willing to pay them a monthly allowance for life. Perhaps, the concept of a life annuity originated from this practice.

The earliest form of insurance was in the nature of marine insurance. The marine insurance business began in North Italy by the end of 12th century. The Italian merchants who came to England brought with them their marine insurance practice. It is said that the first marine insurance policy called 'Poolliza' was issued in 1300 in Italy. In 1300, 'Charter of Insurance' was established in Belgium. The marine insurance was greatly developed during the 14th and 15th centuries. The origin of fire insurance can be traced to the 16th century in Germany. In 1609, in Oldenburg, a scheme was made to indemnify the fire victims by collecting premium. The origin of life insurance took place in England in 16th century, with the issuance of the first life insurance policy on the life of Mr. William Gybbons on 18th June, 1653. (Motihar, M, 2004).

Towards the end of the seventeenth century, the growing importance of London as a center for trade led to rising demand for marine insurance. In the late 1680s, Mr. Edward Lloyd opened a coffee house which became a popular haunt of ship owners, merchants, and ships' captains, and thereby a reliable source of the latest shipping news. It became the meeting place for parties' wishing to insure cargoes and ships, and those willing to underwrite such ventures. Today, Lloyd's of London remains the leading market for marine and other specialist types of insurance, but it works rather differently from the more familiar kinds of insurance. The first policy, providing temporary cover for 12 months was issued as early as 1583 AD. The development of mortality tables was a landmark in the history of life insurance. With this, development life insurance acquired a scientific character. The Equitable Society founded in 1762 was the first to be organized on scientific lines with premiums computed according to age and period of insurance. Actuarial science helped in this process. The concept of a level premium payable from inception for life cover for a number of years or endowment benefits for certain period was put into practice. The human value method of assessing the extent of Life Insurance cover and savings needed by an individual was enunciated by Prof.S.S.Heubner of USA. This along with the needs method is used extensively. (Encyclopedia, 1978).

Since the recent financial meltdown which began in September 2008, a reshuffling of the market value of the world's largest insurance companies has occurred. Below is a list of the top ten insurance companies:

Rank	Company	Market Value($ Billions)	Country
1	American Intl Group	$172.24	United States
2	AXA Group	$66.12	France
3	Allianz Worldwide	$65.55	Germany
4	Manulife Financial	$50.52	Japan
5	Generali Group	$45.45	Italy
6	Prudential Financial	$39.70	United States
7	MetLife	$37.94	United States
8	Aviva	$33.10	United Kingdom
9	Munich Re Group	$30.99	Germany
10	Aegon	$26.40	Netherlands

Fig. 1.11 : Top Ten Global Insurance Companies by Market Value-2009

Source: www.economywatch.com.

Indian Scenario

Life Insurance in its existing form came to India from the United Kingdom with the establishment of a British firm, Oriental Life Insurance Company in Calcutta in 1818 followed by Bombay Life Assurance Company in 1823, the Madras Equitable Life Insurance Society in 1829 and Oriental Government Society Life Assurance Company in 1871.

On January 19, 1956, The Management of the Insurance Business of 245 Indian and foreign insurers and provident societies, then operating in India, was taken over by the Central Government and then nationalized on September 1, 1956. The Life Insurance Corporation (LIC) was formed in September 1956 with a capital contribution rupees five crores from the government. The mission given to Life Insurance Corporation at the time of nationalization can be summarized as follows:

Providing protection of insurance to people in every nook and corner of the country; Mobilizing savings for the development of the country and responding to customer's sensitivity. (www.internationalinsurance.org.).

Some of the important milestones in the life insurance business in India are:

1912 : The Indian Life Assurance Companies Act enacted as the first statute to regulate the life insurance business.

1928 : The Indian Insurance Companies Act enacted to enable the government to collect statistical information about both life and non-life insurance businesses.

1938 : Earlier legislation consolidated and amended by the Insurance Act with the objective of protecting the interests of the insuring public.

1956 : 245 Indian and foreign insurers and provident societies were taken over by the central government and nationalized. Life Insurance Corporation was formed by an Act of Parliament, viz. Life Insurance Corporation Act, 1956, with a capital contribution of Rupees five crores from the Government of India.

In the year 1974, Life Insurance Corporation formulated its objectives with a view to "spread life insurance much more widely and in particular to the rural areas and to the socially and economically backward classes with a view to reaching all insurable persons in the country and providing them a reasonable cover to meet certain contingencies."

Recommendations of Malhotra Committee

With a view to meeting the challenges posed by the emerging and increasing integration of India into the global economy, the Government had set up a committee under the chairmanship of Late Dr. R N Malhotra to study and suggest reforms in the insurance sector like the reforms already under way in the other segments of the financial sector, in April, 1993 by the then Finance Minister, Dr Manmohan Singh. The main objective of the setting up of the Committee was "to examine the structure of the insurance industry as it has evolved within the existing framework and to assess its strength and weaknesses in terms of the objective of creating an efficient and viable insurance industry and providing a variety of insurance products with a high quality of service to the public and serving as an effective instrument of financial resources for development. The committee was also asked to examine various ways by which the Life Insurance Corporation of India and General Insurance Corporation of India could be made more effective. Reforms were initiated with the passage of Insurance Regulatory and Development Authority Bill in 1999.

With the IRDA Act, 1999 coming into force the insurance industry has been opened up for private players. The Act provided for the establishment of a statutory authority to protect the interests of insurance policyholders and to regulate, promote and ensure orderly growth of the insurance industry. IRDA was set up on April 19, 2000 as an independent regulatory authority, which has put in place regulations in line with global norms.

Irda Entry Regulations

1. The company has to be formed and registered under the companies Act, 1956.
2. The company's sole purpose should be to carry on life insurance business or general insurance business or reinsurance business.
3. The minimum paid-up equity capital for life or general insurance business is Rupees one hundred crores. The minimum paid-up equity

capital for carrying on reinsurance business has been prescribed as Rs. 200 crores.

4. The aggregate holding of equity shares by a foreign company, either by itself or through its subsidiary companies, should not exceed 26 per cent of the paid-up equity capital of such Indian insurance company. The Indian company, either by itself or through its subsidiary companies, should hold the balance74 per cent.
5. The insurance companies have to seek IRDA's permission for any transfer of shares beyond one per cent of its share capital. (www.irdaindia.org.)

Market Structure Following Deregulation

Following the passage of the IRDA Act, private players were allowed into the insurance business in 2000. At present, the life insurance business in India is carried on by 22 companies – one public sector company – Life Insurance Corporation of India and 21 private players as listed below:

Sl. No.	Date of Reg.	Name of the Company
1.	23.10.2000	HDFC Standard Life Insurance Company Ltd.
2.	15.11.2000	Max New York Life Insurance Co. Ltd.
3.	24.11.2000	ICICI Prudential Life Insurance Company Ltd.
4.	10.01.2001	Kotak Mahindra Old Mutual Life Insurance Limited
5.	31.01.2001	Birla Sun Life Insurance Company Ltd.
6.	12.02.2001	Tata AIG Life Insurance Company Ltd.
7.	30.03.2001	SBI Life Insurance Company Limited .
8.	02.08.2001	ING Vysya Life Insurance Company Private Limited
9.	03.08.2001	Bajaj Allianz Life Insurance Company Limited
10.	06.08.2001	Metlife India Insurance Company Ltd.
11.	03.01.2002	Reliance Life Insurance Company Limited.
12.	14.05.2002	Aviva Life Insurance Co. India Pvt. Ltd.
13.	06.02.2004	Sahara India Insurance Company Ltd.
14.	17.11.2005	Shriram Life Insurance Company Ltd.
15.	14.07.2006	Bharti AXA Life Insurance Company Ltd.
16.	04.09.2007	Future Generali India Life Insurance Company Limited
17.	25.09.2007	Star Union Dai-ichi Life Insurance
18.	19.12.2007	IDBI Fortis Life Insurance Company Ltd.
19.	08.05.2008	Canara HSBC OBC Life Insurance Company Ltd
20.	27.06.2008	Aegon Religare Life Insurance Company Ltd.
21.	27.06.2008	DLF Pramerica Life Insurance Co. Ltd.

Fig. 1.2 : Private Sector Life Insurance Companies in India

Source: www.irdaindia.org.

Prospects of Life Insurance business in India

The insurance sector is one of the most promising sectors in India. The market size went up to US$ 47.89 billion in 2007, from US$ 21.71 billion in 2000, increasing at the rate of 120 per cent. Between 2000 and 2007, overall premiums sustained an average growth rate of 11.96 per cent. This was one of the most steady growth patterns witnessed amongst emerging economies in Asian as well as global markets. Further, the country's insurance sector is likely to grow 17 per cent in the current financial year if the economy continues to expand at the pace as it did in the September quarter of 2008. India's economy grew at seven per cent in the July-September period. If GDP grows seven point six per cent, premiums would grow 17 per cent. Life insurers, which constitute the bulk of the Indian insurance market, grew their business by 23.3 per cent to US$ 18.94 billion in 2007-08, while general insurers posted growth of about 14 per cent in premium income to US$ 6.07 billion, according to IRDA data. Higher per capita income, domestic savings and availability of more instruments for parking surplus funds have facilitated growth in the activities of financial services. With the largest number of life insurance policies in force in the world, the penetration of insurance in India as a percentage of Gross Domestic Products (GDP) stood at four point eight per cent, as on February 2008, against one point two per cent in 1999–2000. Of this, life insurance accounted for four point one per cent. Also, out of 78 per cent Indian households that are aware of life insurance, only 24 per cent own a policy. (www.economywatch.com.).

McKinsey &Co report states that the premium income of India's life insurance market is said to double by 2012 on better penetration and higher incomes. The total premium income could go up to $80-100 billion by 2012 from the present $40 billion. India's ratio of life insurance premium to GDP is around four percent against six to nine per cent in the developed world. Indians rank life insurance higher than other investment options for tax benefit and protection. (Mckinsey & Co, 2007).

Statement of the Problem

Life insurance is universally acknowledged to be an institution which eliminates risk substituting certainty for uncertainty and comes as timely aid to the family in the unfortunate event of the death of the bread winner. Life insurance companies both private and public adopt different marketing practices to meet the needs of their targeted market. Customized products, pricing, multi-channel distribution system such as direct selling, banc assurance, corporate agency models serve as strategic tools for penetrating into the market. Advertisement through media and technologies help in communicating the market information to the customers as well as the company. Providing quality service through customer relationship management practices has become the need of the hour.

Life insurance is a device that provides safety, security, risk cover and adequate returns. The material consequences of accidents, illness and death, the lack of income after retirement that cannot be remedied, could be financially compensated by insurance. The important elements of the marketing mix as employed by these companies include kinds of policies(product) such as education policy, and pension policy, price (premium), promotion *i.e.,* various advertising techniques, the most powerful being through media and through agents and policy holders, mode of distribution (agents), customer-care services and physical ambience of the institutions. The role played by each one of these factors constitutes the crux of the study. The researcher wanted to look into the Unique Selling Proposition of each company that is vital for the success in their chosen fields, by both public and private sector companies. The study is made to understand the policy holders' view as regards the marketing efforts implemented by the companies.

The study on the marketing mix of the life insurance companies seeks an answer for the following questions. Do the policies offered by the insurance companies provide security?, Do they cover risk?, Is the customer content with the returns?, Is the policy holder satisfied with the need based policy taken?, Does the customer feel that he has gained by taking the policy?, Which form of advertisement is the most productive?, Do the promotional techniques induce the customers to purchase a policy?, Do the agents provide satisfactory assistance and guidance?, Are the agents well-informed?, Is customer friendly service rendered consistently?, Do the employees treat all the policy holders equally and impartially?, and are the customer care services which include speedy issue of policies, maintenance of properly updated records, prompt claim settlement and grievance redressal mechanism, satisfactory?.

Objectives of the Study

The present research has been undertaken with the general objective of analyzing the marketing mix of the select insurance companies. The specific objectives are as follows:

1. to analyse the personal and demographic and rational profile of the respondents;
2. to study the attributes of insurance products and pricing of life insurance policies;
3. to study the nature and types of promotional activities undertaken by the life insurance companies;
4. to examine the physical distribution practices undertaken by the life insurance companies;
5. to study the practices relating to the processing of life insurance products and
6. to describe the physical evidence practices of life insurance products.

Hypothesis

1. Age of the respondents has no influence in the choice of the company based on the selection criteria.
2. Sex of the respondents has no influence in the choice of the company based on the selection criteria.
3. Age of the respondents has no influence in the choice of the company.
4. Location of the respondents has no influence in the choice of the company.
5. The three companies are equally preferred in respect of product mix.
6. Each attribute of the product mix is equally preferred.
7. The three companies are equally preferred in respect of process and people mix.
8. Each attribute of the Process and People mix is equally preferred.
9. The three companies are equally preferred in respect of physical evidence mix.
10. Each attribute of the physical evidence mix is equally preferred.

Methodology

Any study, to be authentic has to be the representative of the universe and depends upon the data collected and analyzed. The characteristics of data collected and the validity of the analysis depend mainly on the methods and the methodology adopted in the study. As a result of the financial sector reforms the insurance sector was privatized in the year 2000. However, the private concerns started their business only in 2001. Therefore, the study has been undertaken for a period of five years from 2001-06. Moreover the study has been carried out in Tiruchirappalli district. The researcher consulted the officials of the three companies who assisted in the selection of policies for the purpose of the study. The pilot study also endorsed the same result.

During the year 2006, 56 policies of LIC, 16 policies of ICICI and 23 policies of Bajaj Allianz were available in the market. The researcher consulted the Branch Managers of the three companies who suggested the following policies, since 80 to 90 per cent of the volume of business of the chosen companies is procured through these policies.

Name of the company	Name of the policies
Life Insurance Corporation	* Bima Gold * Jeevan Anand * New Janraksha
ICICI Prudential life Insurance Company	* Life Time * Life Time Pension * Smart Kid
Bajaj Allianz Life Insurance Company	* Unit Gain * Unit Gain Plus * Family Gain

Pilot Study

A pilot study was conducted with the help of a draft questionnaire. The researcher randomly selected one hundred respondents from various locations. The questionnaire comprised 35 questions under the seven elements of marketing mix namely, product, pricing, promotion, physical distribution, people, process and physical evidence using Five Point Likert scale. Eight questions high-lighted the rational background of the respondents.

The following were the chief indicators:

1. The three dominant life insurance companies that emerged from the study were Life Insurance Corporation of India, the only public company, ICICI Prudential Life Insurance Company and Bajaj Allianz Life Insurance Company who were the major players in the life insurance market based on the total life insurance premium.
2. Out of the several policies available with the companies, Bima Gold, Jeevan Anand and New Janraksha of Life Insurance Corporation of India, Life Time, Life Time Pension and Smart Kid of ICICI Prudential Life Insurance Company and Unit Gain, Family Gain and Unit Gain Plus of Bajaj Allianz Life Insurance Company emerged in the study and were therefore chosen.

Table 1.1 : Market Share of Life Insurance Companies

Insurer	2001-02 (Rs. Crore)	2002-03	2003-04	2004-05	2005-06
LIC	49821.91	54628.49	63533.43	**75127.29**	**90792.22**
Aviva		13.47	81.50	253.42	600.27
Bajaj Allianz	7.14	69.17	220.80	**1001.68**	**3133.58**
Bharti Axa					
Birla Sunlife	28.26	143.92	537.54	915.47	1259.68
Future Generali					
HDFC Std	33.46	148.83	297.76	686.63	1569.91
ICICI Pru	116.38	417.62	989.28	**2363.82**	**4261.05**
IDBI Fortis					
ING Vysya	4.19	21.16	88.51	338.86	425.38
Kotak Mahindra	7.58	40.32	150.72	466.16	621.85
Met Life	0.48	7.91	28.73	81.53	205.99
Max New York	38.95	96.59	215.25	413.43	788.13
Reliance Life	0.28	6.47	31.06	106.55	224.21
Sahara				1.74	27.66
SBI Life	14.69	72.39	225.67	601.18	1075.32
Shriram					10.33
Tata AIG	**21.14**	**81.21**	**253.53**	**497.04**	**880.19**
Total (LIC+Private)	**50094.46**	**55747.55**	**66653.75**	**82854.80**	**105875.76**

Source: www.irdaindia.org.

In order to find out the reliability of the 35 items, the measure of Cronbach's Alpha was utilized.

The following table shows the factor wise reliability of the marketing mix elements.

Table 1.2 : Result of Cronbach's Alpha

	Factor	LIC	ICICI	Bajaj Allianz
Product and pricing	8	0.713	0.622	0.575
Promotion	8	0.831	0.756	0.676
Physical distribution	5	0.853	0.860	0.781
People and process	9	0.875	0.871	0.877
Physical evidence	5	0.676	0.829	0.716
Overall	35	0.946	0.935	0.917

The result of the Cronbach's Alpha suggested that the reliability co-efficient of the factors was 0.946, 0.935, and 0.917. This indicates that the marketing mix score was highly reliable (greater than recommended level of 0.6 –zero point six) and achieved internal consistency, even though the product and pricing factor of Bajaj Allianz Life Insurance Company was just 0.575 which is below the stipulated level.

Sampling Framework

The population for the study consisted of the policy holders of Life Insurance Corporation, ICICI Prudential Life Insurance Company and BAJAJ Allianz Life Insurance Company. The researcher adopted Purposive Sampling method to choose the policy holders of the three chosen companies.

The sample size of the respondents for the study was scientifically determined using the formula,

$$ni = \left[\frac{ZSi}{e}\right]^2$$

Where i = 1, 2, 3.

Where z is the standard normal variate and the value is 1.96 at 95 per cent confidence level, is the sampling error allowed at five per cent level, n is the required sample size, Si is the sample standard deviation of the marketing mix score calculated from the pilot study based on experience.

Table 1.3 : Standard Deviation of the Marketing Mix Score-Life Insurance Companies

Name of the company	Standard Deviation of the marketing mix score
LIC	0.440
ICICI	0.419
BAJAJ Allianz	0.365

The computations of n_i, i=1,2, 3 are shown below:

$$n_1 = \left[\frac{196 \times 0.440}{0.05}\right] = 298$$

$$n_2 = \left[\frac{1.96 \times 0.419}{0.05}\right]^2 = 270$$

$$n_3 = \left[\frac{1.96 \times 0.365}{0.05}\right]^2 = 205$$

Total sample size in $n_1 + n_2 + n_3 = 298 + 270 + 205 = 773$

On substituting the value of Si, z and e in the formula given, the sample size arrived at was 773 and it is the lower limit to measure the marketing mix of life insurance companies. Out of the 773 policy holders, 298 had been chosen from Life Insurance Corporation, 270 from ICICI Prudential Life Insurance Company and 205 policy holders from Bajaj Allianz Life Insurance Company.

COLLECTION OF DATA

Primary Data

Primary data have been collected through a structured questionnaire. Simple, specific and direct questions to be marked under a five point scale were included in the questionnaire to solicit information from the policy holders. Questions were designed in such a way to maintain a high degree of objectivity and consistency. The authenticity of the questionnaire was verified through informal interviews. The questionnaire comprised of three parts. The first part of the questionnaire contained eleven questions relating to demographic factors of the policy holders. The second part contained eight questions relating to rational factors and the third part contained 35 questions relating to the five factors chosen for study.

Secondary Data

Secondary data have been collected from various books, journals, magazines, IRDA Annual Reports and from company records.

Data Analysis

After data collection, data were organized and analyzed with statistical soft ware such as SPSS 13.0. It was implicitly assumed that the marketing mix followed a multivariate normal distribution. One way ANOVA and Two way ANOVA were applied to show the mean difference between the marketing mix items.

Discriminant Analysis was used to find out the predominant contributing factors with respect to each element of marketing mix. The researcher made an attempt to identify the factors that were more effective in the elements of marketing mix of the companies chosen for study. Chi-Square test has been used for testing the hypothesis.

TOOLS FOR ANALYSIS

Anova Test

Anova is a statistical technique used for determining the degree of difference or similarity between two or more groups of data. It is a statistical method used for making simultaneous comparisons between two or more means. It is a method that yields values that can be tested to determine whether a significant relation exists between variables. Analysis of variance (ANOVA) is a collection of statistical models, and their associated procedures, in which the observed variance is partitioned into components due to different explanatory variables. Analysis of variance (ANOVA) is a statistical test which compares the distribution of two or more sample groups to determine if one or more of the groups are significantly different from the others.

Duncan Post HOC Test

Post-hoc tests (or post-hoc comparison tests) are used at the second stage of the analysis of variance (ANOVA) or multiple analysis of variance (MANOVA) if the null hypothesis is rejected. The question of interest at this stage is which groups significantly differ from others in respect to the mean or, in case of MANOVA, in respect to centroid s. This post hoc test (or multiple comparison test) is used to determine the significant differences between group means in an analysis of variance setting. Duncan's test, is based on the range statistic.

Chi-square Test

The Chi-Square test is a statistical test which computes the probability that there is no significant difference between the expected frequency of an occurrence with the observed frequency of that occurrence. It tests a null hypothesis that the frequency distribution of certain events observed in a sample is consistent with a particular theoretical distribution.

Discriminant Analysis

Discriminant analysis is a technique for classifying a set of observations into predefined classes. The purpose is to determine the class of an observation based on a set of variables known as predictors or input variables. The model is built based on a set of observations for which the classes are known. These discriminant functions are used to predict the class of a new observation with unknown class.

Pareto Chart

A Pareto chart is a type of chart which contains both bars and a line graph. The bars display the values in descending order, and the line graph shows the cumulative totals of each category, left to right. The chart was named for Vilfredo Pareto. The left vertical axis is the frequency of occurrence, but it can alternatively represent cost or other important unit of measure. The right vertical axis is the cumulative percentage of the total number of occurrences, total cost, or total of the particular unit of measure. Because the reasons are in decreasing order, the cumulative function is a concave function. The purpose is to highlight the most important among a (typically large) set of factors.

Scope of the Study

Life insurance is a device that provides safety, security, risk cover and adequate returns. The material consequences of accidents, illness and death, the lack of income after retirement that cannot be remedied, could be financially compensated by insurance. The present study is confined to an analysis of the various elements of marketing mix employed by the life insurance companies and determines how far they depend up on each one of these elements to market their products. The prominent factors constituting the marketing mix are looked into and their relative importance in the total marketing strategy has been examined.

Tiruchirappalli, the fourth largest city in Tamilnadu occupies a central position in the state. It is a well-known historical and pilgrimage and tourist centre. It is an industrial centre having well known major and allied industries, run both by the Government and the private sector undertakings. It is a great educational centre having reputed educational institutions. The Life Insurance Corporation of India has 6 of its branches in Trichy constituting nearly one fourth of the total branches which come under the jurisdiction of the Tanjavur Divisional Office. The Bajaj Allianz Life Insurance Corporation has its divisional office in Trichy monitoring two satellite branches of Karur and Perambalur. The ICICI has a well established cluster office in Trichy covering nearly six to seven areas. Hence Tiruchirapalli has a potential and vibrant market for insurance, Tiruchirapalli being the home town of the researcher.

The familiarity of the research with Tiruchirappalli, her home town induced her to take this district as her study area.

The research work titled "A study on the marketing mix of life insurance companies in Tiruchirappalli District" would enable the companies to find out the status of their products. The research findings could be helpful to the actuaries to develop new policies according to the current needs of the people; to create awareness among the companies and policymakers regarding their responsibility to cater to the security and financial needs of the rural population in the event of a crisis by going beyond the minimum requirement as stipulated by the IRDA and that they should cater to the needs of both rural as well as urban masses in a more concrete and effective manner. It would be helpful to reorient their policies to suit the requirements of the prospects.

Limitations of the Study

1. The policies undertaken for study were withdrawn, renamed and reintroduced with slight modifications. The changes made are as follows:

LIC	Bima Gold	New Bima Gold
ICICI	Life Time	New Life Time
	Life Time Pension	Life time Pension Super
	Smart Kid	Smart Kid Unit Linked
BAJAJ	Unit Gain	New Unit Gain
	Unit Gain Plus	New Unit Gain Plus
	Family gain	New Family Gain

This indicates that the policies are flexible and the companies adapt themselves to suit changing market conditions.

2. As the study is mainly based on primary data collected through questionnaire, it is bestowed with certain limitations which are bound to arise in the primary data collection. Though every effort was made to elicit the correct information by systematic and careful probing, it is possible that lapse of memory and recall bias of respondents might have affected their responses.

3. The validity of the study depends upon the authenticity of the data provided by the policy holders.

Chapter Scheme

The report titled "A Study on the Marketing Mix of Life Insurance Companies in Tiruchirapalli District" is presented in five chapters, logically arranged as follows:

Chapter –I	:	Deals with the general introduction of the topic of the study undertaken and the methods employed in collection of data.
Chapter – II	:	Presents the review of literature.
Chapter – III	:	Provides a brief profile of the study area.
Chapter – IV	:	Presents the analysis and interpretation of data collected.
Chapter – V	:	Presents the findings, conclusion and suggestions.

REFERENCES

1. Sajit Ali., Riyaz Mohammad and Masharique Ahmed (2007). Insurance in India. New Delhi: Regal Publications. p. 60.
2. Neera Banzal (2004). New tool for developing life insurance marketing - Policy holders Meet and Bouquet. *The Journal of Insurance Watch*, 3(9), 23.

3. Thompson Report (2007). Urban and Rural Insurance, Accessed 18 March 2009.http://in.reuters.com/article/businessNews/idINIndia-2944262007091 0?pageNumber=2&virtualBrandChannel=0&sp=true
4. NCAER, (2006). Categories of income, Accessed 16 March 2009. http://www.indianplanning commission.com.
5. Pillai, R.S.N. and Bhagavathi, (2000). Modern Marketing Principles and Practices. New Delhi: S.Chand and Company. p. 23.
6. Varshney, R.L. and Gupta,S.L. (2004). Marketing Management, An Indian Perspective. New Delhi: Sultan Chand and Sons. p. 52.
7. Vasanthi Venugopal and Raghu, V.N. (2006). Services Marketing. Mumbai: Himalaya Publishing House. p. 8.
8. Service sector in the Indian Economy (2009). Accessed 4 April 2009. http://www.indiaonestop.com/economy-macro-view.html.
9. Marketing Decision making. (2007). Accessed 2 April 2009. http://www.londremarketing.com.
10. Motihar, M. (2004). Insurance Principles, Practices, Management and Salesmanship. Allahabad: Sharda Pustak Bhavan. p.47.
11. *Ibid.,* p.47.
12. Jha, S.M. (2003). Services Marketing. New Delhi: Himalaya Publishing House. p.164.
13. Sesha Ayyer, V. (2003). Insurance Origin Developments. *Journal of Insurance Chronicle*, 3(2), 22-24.
14. New Encyclopedia Americana. (1978), p. 295.
15. http://www.economywatch.com, Accessed 12 January 2009.
16. http://www.international insurance.org. Accessed 15 March 2006.
17. http://www.irdaindia.org. Accessed 15 June 2006.
18. http://in.reuters.com/article/business news/id/India. Accessed 18 March, 2009.
19. http://www.statistics.com. Accessed July 20, 2009.

2

Review of Literature

Chapter – II gives a comprehensive view of the various aspects and the varied critical opinion of authors and research scholars in recent times. This review helps focus on the advantages, disadvantages and the areas and scope for improvement. It also gives statistical factual data based on surveys and reports. This review is of great help to the researcher to know the pros and cons and look at the problem from a new and different perspective.

Insurance is a contract whereby, in return for the payment of premium by the insured, the insurers pay the financial losses suffered by the insured as a result of the occurrence of unforeseen events. With the help of Insurance, large number of people exposed to a similar risk makes contributions to a common fund out of which the losses suffered by the unfortunate few, due to accidental events, are made good.

Insurance is a social device, aimed at accumulation of funds to meet uncertain losses. Insurance is a co-operative device to spread the loss caused by a particular risk over a number of persons, who are exposed to it and who agree to insure themselves against the risk. (Mishra, M.N., 1979).

Dictionary of business and finance defines as follows: "Insurance is a form of contract or agreement under which, one party agrees in return for a consideration to pay an agreed amount of money to another party to make good for a loss, damage, or injury of something of value in which the insured has a pecuniary interest as a result of some uncertain event". (Motihar, 2004).

Dictionary of commerce defines as follows: "Insurance is the payment of a sum of money by one person to another on the understanding that in specified circumstances the second person will make good any loss suffered by the first." (Motihar, 2004).

In its legal aspects it is a contract, the insurer agreeing to make good any financial loss the insured may suffer within the scope of the contract and the insured agreeing to pay a consideration.

Human life is exposed to innumerable risks. Life Insurance is a contract providing for payment of a sum of money to the person assured or, failing him to the person entitled to receive the same, on the happening of certain event. Uncertainty of death is inherent in human life; it is this uncertainty that is risk, which gives rise to the necessity for some form of protection against the financial loss arising from death. Insurance substitutes this uncertainty by certainty.

Life insurance provides the necessary defence in case of financial losses arising from uncertain events, the complexity of life and changes in the social systems in India have increased the scope of life insurance.

As with most insurance policies, life insurance is a contract between the insurer and the policy owner whereby a benefit is paid to the designated beneficiaries if an insured event occurs which is covered by the policy.

"Life Insurance contract may be defined as the contract, whereby the insurer in consideration of a premium undertakes to pay a certain sum of money either on the death of the insured or on the expiry of a fixed a period". (Periyasamy, P, 2005).

Life insurance business is defined under section 2 (11) insurance act, 1938 as follows:

> Life insurance business means, the business of effecting contract of insurance upon human life, including any contract whereby the payment of money is assured on death or the happening of any contingency dependent on human life and any contract which is subject to payment of premium for a term dependent on human life and shall be deemed to include the granting of:
>
> (*a*) Disability and double or triple indemnity accident benefits, if so provided in the contract of insurance;
>
> (*b*) Annuities upon human life; and
>
> (*c*) Superannuation allowances and annuities payable out of any fund applicable solely to the relief and maintenance of persons engaged or who have been engaged in any particular profession, trade or employment or of the dependents of such person.

Fundamental Principles of Life Insurance Contracts

Life insurance contract is a contract of good faith which means that there should be no concealment of facts. Misrepresentation, non-disclosure or fraud in any document leading to acceptance of risk, automatically discharges the insurer from the liabilities under contract. It is therefore in the interest of the insured, to disclose all the material facts to the life insurance company to avoid any hardship when the claim arises.

(*a*) **Principle of insurable interest:** The life insurance contract provides for the payment of a definite sum. The loss on the death of insured cannot be quantified and therefore, the insurer is bound to pay according to the terms and conditions mentioned in the policy document. The payment is not related to the financial loss to the family upon the death of the insured. Whether the death of the insured has caused any financial loss to the beneficiary or not, is immaterial consideration for the insurer at the time of making payment on the death of the insured. Insurer cannot deny liability for the sum insured.

(*b*) **Principle of utmost good faith:** Life insurance requires that the principle of utmost good faith be preserved by both the parties to the contract that is insurer and the insured. The material facts such as age, income, health, family details, occupation and plan of insurance must be disclosed by the insured to the insurance companies. It is the duty of both the parties, to disclose all the material facts that influence the decision of the insured.

(*c*) **Principle of warranty:** In life insurance those representations which are contained by the policies and are expressly or impliedly form part of the basis of contract are known as warranties. If any statement given by the insured is false the contract shall be invalid and the insurer may forfeit the premium paid by the insured. The informative warranties are very important in life insurance contract, since the proposer is to disclose all the material facts to the insurer to the best of his knowledge and belief.

(*d*) **Indemnity is not applied to life insurance:** In life insurance the indemnity principle is not applicable because, the value of loss at death cannot be ascertained. It is not possible to ascertain the time up to which the insured would have survived and also the amount of money to be earned by him during life time. In life insurance, a fixed sum is paid, which may be the sum assured and bonus, if the policy is a participating one.

(*e*) **Life insurance is a conditional contract:** Life insurance is a conditional contract, because the insurer shall pay the assured sum only when, the contract is continuing by the payment of premium. In other words, the policy should be in force. In addition the insurers' promise to pay the sum assured is also conditional, upon the furnishing of satisfactory proof of death and other conditions mentioned in the policy. (Motihar, 2004).

Human Life Value Approach

Huebner said, "Human Life Value is the Economic Interpretation of Life Insurance". (Huebner, 1995).

Life insurance is a legal contract between the insurer and the insured based on a high degree of mutual good faith popularly known as 'Uberrima Fides' meaning the 'utmost good faith'. (Sushil Chandra Pal, 2007). In life insurance contract, each party must disclose every material fact known to him and on the basis of the facts disclosed, assessment of risk and return are made and the contract is affected.

The concept of 'human life value' can be expressed in terms of monetary value for which it should be carefully appraised and capitalized. Man through his earning power, wants to satisfy his needs – present or future. It is this earning power/productive capacity which are his human life value.

The development of Actuarial Science and Mortality tables is a landmark in the history of life insurance. (Ray, 1941). Actuarial Science and mortality rates were made reliable in the year 1755 and for the first time life insurance had been transacted on modern lines in England in 1807 (LICI, Branch Managers' Training Course, 1964) and established itself on firm footing in the wake of industrial revolution in the 19th Century.

The earliest mortality table of assured lives constructed in India related to the period 1905-25. This mortality was based on the experience of Oriental Government Security Life assurance Company. Today, the 'non-profit' premium rates in use are based on the latest mortality table constructed during the period 1975-79 and the 'inclusive of profit' premium rates based on the earlier mortality table published in 1970-73.

Role of Life Insurance

Life insurance plays a significant role, in the individual lives as well as the society. For the individuals, life insurance is a life saver since it offers protection and extends a hand of protection to those who feel depressed and are left without any support due to the sudden, unexpected demise of the breadwinner of the family. It has an element of saving for investment in future. It offers a safe and secured future, by providing financial assistance at times of need that is for meeting the educational expenses of the children or marriage and so on. It provides loan facilities which improve the credit worthiness of the policy holder. A life insurance policy may be used to avail loan facility, directly from the life insurance company or can be given as a collateral security for obtaining financial assistance from banks and other financial institutions. In case of death, life insurance provides security for the family and provides guaranteed payment when there is reduction in the earning power, due to old age, sickness, accident and so on. Life insurance is a means of savings and the relief given by the government towards the savings, promotes the habit of thrift and savings among the people.

Life insurance companies accumulate large funds which they hold as custodians. A large proportion of these funds is invested in the Government, Semi-Government and private enterprises. The money is also invested in social development projects such as housing, water supply, rural electrification and so on for the benefit of the society. It helps in providing employment opportunities, increase in the national income and standard of living of the society.

Type of investment	Per cent
Government securities	25
Government securities or other approved securities. Approved investments:	Not less than 50
Infra structure and Social sector	Not less than 15
Other to be governed by Exposure/ Prudential Norms specified in regulations	Not exceeding 20
Other than in approved investments to be governed by Exposure/ Prudential Norms specified in regulations	Not exceeding 15

Fig. 2.3 : Life insurance business-IRDA guidelines as regards investments.

Source : www.irdaindia.org, 2007

Life Insurance in the Global Scenario

Life insurance contributes significantly to the growth of any nation.

With the largest number of life insurance policies in force in the world, India's insurance sector accounted for four point one per cent of GDP in 2006-07, up from one point two per cent in 1999-2000, far ahead of China where insurance accounts for just one point seven per cent of the GDP and even the US where insurance penetration stands at four per cent of the GDP and in the year 2007, it reached four point seven per cent. (www.idil.com/insurance.html, 2009).

The two prime indicators which helped in accessing the status of an insurance market are insurance density and insurance penetration.

Insurance penetration is used as an indicator of growth potential. It expresses the relationship between insurance expenditures and economic production per household.

Country	2003-2004 Per cent	2004-2005 Per cent	2005-2006 Per cent	2006-2007 Per cent
INDIA	2.53	2.53	4.10	4.00
USA	4.22	4.14	4.00	4.20
UK	8.92	8.90	13.10	12.60
Switzerland	6.73	6.20	6.20	5.70
France	6.38	7.08	7.90	7.30
Russia	0.61	0.12	0.10	0.10
Japan	8.26	8.32	8.30	7.50
China	2.21	1.78	1.70	1.80
South Africa	11.43	10.84	13.00	12.50
World	**4.55**	**4.34**	**4.50**	**4.40**

Fig. 2.4 : International Comparison of Insurance Penetration (Premium as a percentage of GDP)

Source : www.irdaindia.org, 2008.

Insurance density is measured as the ratio between the total premium income and the population. The following table depicts the insurance density of the various nations.

Country	2003-2004	2004-2005	2005-2006	2006-2007
INDIA	15.7	18.3	33.2	40.4
USA	1692	1753	1789	1922
UK	3190	3287	5139	5730.5
Switzerland	3275	3078	3119	3159.1
France	2150	2475	2923	2928.3
Russia	—	6.3	4.0	6.1
Japan	3044	2956	2829	2583.9
China	27.03	30.5	34.1	44.2
South Africa	545	558	696	719
World	**292**	**300**	**331**	**358.1**

Fig. 2.5 : International Comparison of Insurance Density (Premium per capital in US Dollar)

Source : www.irdaindia.org, 2008.

The low level of insurance density and insurance penetration in India could be due to several factors such as low per capita income, low awareness of the benefits of insurance and the supply of insurance. But still there is a vast potential for insurance in India.

Mishra, K.C., and Sumitra Mishra (2000), have analyzed the position of insurance in USA, Japan, U.K, and Germany, which are considered to be the largest country level markets in the world. They have recalled the fact that, insurance service is one of the most important constituents of the economic development of the nations. They have emphasized the fact that, insurance plays an active role in promoting stability, facilitating trade and commerce, mobilizing savings, managing financial risks more effectively, encouraging mitigation of loss and allocating capital efficiently.

Shesha Ayyar (2000), opined that, it would take seven to 10 years for the private insurers to break-even, due to the fact that their operating cost which is high in the initial years would affect their profits.

Stuart Purdy (2003), has stated that the privatization process of the insurance industry has resulted in providing new opportunities in terms of employment, savings, new channels of insurance distribution and wider coverage to rural areas as well as the economically deprived sections of the society. The presence of the strong and unbiased regulator has contributed to the success of the industry. He has expressed hope that, the insurance industry would continue to grow by taking pensions, savings and insurance products to the door steps of more and more customers.

Tarun Kapoor (2003), identifies the major challenges ahead of the insurance industry to be: product innovations, distribution network, customer service and education .He has suggested that, in order to be successful, the insurance companies have to be innovative, select the right type of distribution channel, offer continuous training, educate the customer, provide quality service to customers and follow prudent investment pattern to increase the customer base.

The study undertaken by the Swiss Reinsurance Company (2003), has revealed that despite the growth in the premium, the penetration rate is very low and the biggest constraint on future growth has been the slow deregulation. Competition ignited by the private players, joint ventures formed by the global insurers with domestic partners and product innovations have been the achievements of deregulation. However, the untapped potential of the domestic market, high level of regulation and ensuring balance between the public and private companies have been identified as the major challenges.

Sunder Ram Korivi (2004), in his article "Insurance sector in India-challenges ahead" has stressed on the need to assess the true insurance needs of an insured and to guard against the policy lapsing .He has also emphasized the need to redirect the funds into investments that will have stable cash flows.

In his research paper, "A comparative study of the performance of life insurance players", Anil Chandok (2005), has analyzed the quantum of business procured by the private players and the total business done. The study revealed that, the public are very careful in selecting their insurers. Private players are still in the stage of extending their operations in many areas and in metropolitan cities and the market share of the private players is better when compared to the figure of India as a whole. He has concluded by saying that, with proper orientation the private insurers would be able to grow.

Rajesh .C. Jampala and Polavarapu Adilakshmi (2006), have identified the major challenges, for Indian Life Insurance Companies, to be stringent solvency norms, expense over runs, new business strain, low agent productivity, high attrition level of agents, low average premiums and high competition in the market place. They are of the opinion that, there is a great potential for insurance business as the penetration level of insurance to Gross Domestic Product is very low, and selection of the right quality of business would ensure success for the private players.

According to Geethanjali Mehlwal (2006), Life Insurance remains the primary focus of the state as well as non – state players. The government plays an active role by removing investment barriers and maintaining market checks through Insurance Regulatory Development Authority. The author has stated that, India's enormous population, abundant infrastructure facilities and globally visible corporate success add to the country's prospect for insurers looking for huge future demands and alternatives to already tapped markets.

Kishore, R.B. (2006), has highlighted the success story of Life Insurance Corporation. According to him, the Life Insurance Corporation has recorded a successful growth rate of 20.6 per cent due to the introduction of time-tested traditional products and market-savvy unit-linked plans in tune with the market demands. He identifies an upward trend in terms of number of policies sold, sum assured and the total assets held by the Life Insurance Corporation. He has expressed hope that, with the vast network of the agent force, the Life Insurance Corporation would march ahead to maintain its supremacy.

Richard Holloway and Rajagopalan Krishnamurthy (2006), are of the opinion that, the success of rural insurance business in India centers around innovative product design, increasing penetration, finding effective and lower-cost distribution channels, education, access and affordability. The risks involved and the adverse experience prevailing in rural area should be considered while intensifying efforts to tackle the rural market. The authors insisted on the introduction of suitable products at a right price and the usage of best practice actuarial technique to re-price and redesign the rural products as necessary, taking into account the actual experience that emerges.

Pillai, VNS., (2007), has analyzed the relevance of life insurance at various levels. According to the author, the best investment that offers income replacement on the occurrence of the sudden demise of the breadwinner is life insurance, for it offers security of capital. He has expressed hope that, the demand for Unit linked insurance policies would increase when compared to that of other products. According to the study conducted, the flux of new products is primarily a response to the recognition of the latent needs of the customers.

Shiv Kumar Singh, *et al.*, (2007), have made an attempt to focus on changing scenario of Indian Insurance Industry, as it has become a challenging task for the Insurance companies to sustain their competitiveness on a continuous basis along with winning the customer trust. The author has opined that, deregulation in Indian business policy has resulted in increased number of players in the market and hence, the competition; this has created a new business ambience where benchmarking can originate customer–oriented innovative policies. The study arguably states that, a competitive market should be able to ensure that quality and fairly priced products are made available. Government intervention is most needed to ensure that insurers are reliable, because the national insurance industry contributes to the overall economic development.

The report released by the Economic Times (2008), has analyzed the growth in the insurance sector after privatization. According to the report, the key driver for growth in the life insurance business was the trend towards single premium business and pension and annuity products. The industry was shifting from providing traditional products to the above mentioned sectors due to the ageing population and reduction in the social security benefits, the report has stated.

McKinsey Company (2008), in a report reveals that, with household earnings accelerating in the fast-growing economy, the life insurance income by way of premium could double from 40 billion dollars to 80 billion or even 100 billion dollars by 2012.

Marketing is a basic function of all business firms that aim at profit generation and customer satisfaction. It is the kingpin that sets the progress of the economy by providing want satisfying products and services. Marketing encompasses all activities carried on to transfer the goods from the manufacturers to the customers. It involves the exchange of goods and services for money. Determination of requirements of potential customers and supplying products to satisfy their requirements is the crux of any marketing activity.

According to American Marketing Association (1960), marketing is concerned with the people and the activities involved in the flow of goods and services from the producer to the consumer".

Kotler, P. and Armstrong, G (1996) define a service as any activity or benefit that one party can offer to another that is essentially intangible and does not result in the ownership of anything.

In the words of William J. Stanton, *et.al.*, (1994), services are identifiable, intangible activities that are the main object of a transaction designed to provide want-satisfaction to customers.

Services include core services which may be the necessary outputs of an organization that intend to provide the intangible benefits to customers and the peripheral services that are indispensable for the execution of the core service and enhance the overall quality of the service bundle.

The term insurance marketing refers to the marketing of insurance services with the motto of customer-orientation and profit-generation. The insurance marketing focuses n the formulation of an ideal mix for the insurance business so that the insurance organisations survive and thrive in a right perspective. (Jha, S.M., 2003).

Marketing Mix

Marketing mix strategy is an overall marketing approach that is used to achieve objectives of strategic marketing plans. Marketing mix is a combination of four elements - product, price structure, distribution system and promotional activities used to satisfy the needs of an organization's target markets and, at the same time achieve its marketing objectives. (Stanton, 1994).

Marketing mix serves as the linkage between a business firm and its customers. It is a system comprising subsystems of product, price, promotion and distribution. It is used as a strategy in developing marketing planning and for integrating various functions and fitting them into the total fabric of the organization. It is a dynamic concept, that keeps on changing with changes in the market conditions and the environment. As Kotler puts it "marketing mix represents the settings of the firm's marketing variables at a particular point of time." (Philip Kotler, 2005).

MARKETING MIX OF LIFE INSURANCE SERVICES

Product Mix

A life insurance product has, essentially, two basic elements :

(*i*) Risk cover, *i.e.* benefits payable in the event of death.

(*ii*) Saving, *i.e.* the benefit payable in the event of survival. (Bodla, B.S., *et.al.*, 2003).

Life insurance plans, may be classified into several categories as discussed below:

Term Life Insurance

In the case of a Term life insurance contract, the sum assured is payable only in the event of death during the term. In case of survival, the contract comes to an end at the end of term. There is no refund of premium. These policies are usually non-participating. Since only death risk is covered, the premium is low and the contract is simple. Of late however, some companies do offer participating policies under term insurance plans.

Whole Life Insurance

The risk is covered for the entire life of the policy holder. The policy money and the bonus are payable only to the nominee or the beneficiary upon the death of the policy holder. The policy holder is not entitled to any money during his or her own lifetime, i.e. there is no survival benefit.

Endowment Type Plans

Endowment policies cover the risk for a specified period, at the end of which the Sum Assured is paid back to the policyholder, along with the entire bonus accumulated during the term of the policy.

Combination of Whole Life and Endowment Type Plans

Some persons may need a lump sum amount even before the expiry of the term of the policy. If they take loans under the policies, the risk cover (amount payable on death) comes down and interest payable on the loan accumulates as a debt on the policy. To meet this need, insurers have devised plans wherein part of the sum assured is made payable periodically during the term of the policy. Notwithstanding the payments at periodic intervals, the sum assured at risk (payable at death), continues to be the same till the end of the term.

(*a*) Money Back (with profits) Scheme: These are fixed term policies. The premium is paid till the end of the term or till the death of the policyholder whichever earlier. A part of the sum assured is returned to the policyholder once in four or five years according to the plan. The risk cover continues for the full sum assured, even after payment of installments to the policyholder. The bonus is also payable for the full term.

At the end of	Per cent of Sum Assured	
	20 years	25 years
5 years	20	15
10 years	20	15
15 years	20	15
20 years	40 + bonus	15
25 years	—	40 + Bonus

Fig. 2.6 : Scheme of money back plan for a policy for 20 years and 25 years

Source : Bodla, B.S., *et.al.* (2003).

Children's Assurance Plans

Plans have been specially designed for children where the risk of the child starts much earlier, say seven years. Risk cover may not begin when the policy is issued. The date on which the risk may begin is called the "deferred date" and the period between the deferred date and the date of commencement of policy is called the "deferment period". As children cannot enter into contract, policies on the lives of children are taken out by other elders. After some time, when the child becomes major and is competent to contract, the child may assume the ownership of the policy, either by a specific action of doing so or automatically by virtue of the provisions of the policy. The policy is then said to "vest" in the child. The date on which this happens is called the "vesting date". On the vesting date, the life insured must have completed 18 years of age.

Annuities and Pension Plans

A contract providing for regular periodic payments during a specified period is an Annuity contract. If the specified period is fixed without regard to the duration of any life, it is called Annuity Certain. If it is related to life, it is called a Life Annuity. When a person purchases a life insurance contract he agrees to make a series of payments (premiums) to the insurer and in return the insurer agrees to pay a specified sum to the beneficiaries, in case of death of life assured or on maturity. (Life Insurance Guide, 2007).

Unit Linked Insurance Policies (Ulip)

An Ulip is a bundled product that combines a life cover with an investment plan (Layman's Guide to Life Insurance, 2008). Part of the premiums paid goes towards the mortality charges, that is, the cost of buying a life cover. The rest, and after deducting costs, gets invested in different plans according to the amount of risk the policy holders are willing to take. So, the policy holder can track the value of the policy holder's investments. After costs for insuring the policy holder for that amount are deducted, the rest of the funds are invested. If the policy holder survives the policy term, the policy holder gets an amount equal to the number of units the policy holders hold multiplied by its Net Asset Value. This is the fund value. In case of death of the policy holder, the beneficiary gets either, the higher of the sum assured and fund value, or, both. Unit Linked Insurance Policies give the policy holder life insurance that the policy holder can adjust to the policy holder's need, an option to save and invest and flexibility to tweak the risk profile of the policy holder's invest-ments. Unit Linked Insurance Policies offer the policy holder flexibility. The policy holder can also take additional cover against death due to accident, as well as disability or critical illness. Besides, it can offer the policy holder liquidity through partial withdrawals, although this should be among the options of last resort. In a Unit Linked Insurance Policy, the policy holder can change the amount of life cover the policy holder takes within the term of the policy without changing the premium. Naturally, the more the life cover the policy holder takes, the less will be left for investment.

Life Insurance Riders

A rider is a clause or condition that is added on, to a basic policy providing an additional benefit, at the choice of the proposer. Life insurance riders are the fringe benefits offered to the policyholders along with a life insurance policy. These riders actually are a value addition to the policies. (Life Insurance Guide, 2007).

As per the regulations made by the IRDA in April 2002 and amended in October 2002,

- The premium on all the riders related to health or critical illnesses, in the case of term or group products shall not exceed 100 per cent of the premium of the main policy.
- The premium on all the other riders put together should not exceed 30 per cent of the premium on the main policy and
- The benefits arising under each of the riders shall not exceed the sum assured under the basic product.

The Accidental Death Rider

Under this rider, the beneficiary gets an additional amount (besides the sum assured under the policy, usually an equal additional amount) if the policyholder were to die in an accident. The premium for this rider is also very reasonable and makes it doubly attractive. The term accident for this clause covers a wide range of events. However there is a maximum limit put on the amount of coverage in all the policies put together. Besides there is also an upper age limit until which the accident cover is provided (usually 70 years).

Premium Waiver Benefit Rider

The payment of further premium by the policy holder is totally waived, if the policyholder were to be afflicted with one of the covered crippling eventuality and be disabled to a live normal life. There is a condition on the extent of disability and it is covered above a certain percentage of disability.

Guaranteed Insurability rider is a rider in which the further renewal of the policy when the present term ends, is guaranteed without proving further insurability. This rider gives the flexibility of choosing shorter terms with guaranteed insurability at the end, if the policy holder so prefers.

Critical Illness rider is a rider under which, the policyholder can combine the advantage of health insurance without having to obtain a separate health insurance policy. The coverage is normally against a list of diseases mentioned under the policy which is restricted, as per the age and personal/family profile of the policy holder.

Family Income Benefit rider which ensures the regular stream of income for the family if the sole bread winner of the family dies during active, working period. This rider along with the base policy, takes care of both the cash needs as well as income needs of the family. The policyholder should be prudent in choosing the term for which the family income should be payable as it decides the rate.

Considering the exclusive risk-coverage features of the riders, IRDA has initially prescribed an upper limit on the premium paid towards the coverage of riders in a life insurance policy. This limit was set at 30 per cent of the premium to be paid on the base policy.

Pricing of Life Insurance Products

Premium is the consideration for granting insurance cover. (Sushil Chandra Paul, 2007).

On the nationalization of Life Insurance in 1956, the premium ratings of Oriental Government Security Life assurance Company were adopted by LIC with a reduction of five per cent of the tabular premium or Rupee one per thousand sum assured, whichever is less. LIC made several downward revisions in its premium rating in order to benefit the 'sub standard' lives and also substantially reduced the number of vocations that were classified as hazardous. The additional premium being charged for granting accident benefit was reduced from Rupees two to one per thousand sum assured.

The charging of extra premium in respect of policies on female lives was also discontinued.

Through an insurance contract, a life insurer undertakes an obligation to pay the amount insured on the happening of certain contingencies over a period of time on consideration of insurance premium received from the insured as specified in the contract. In order to honor its obligation it is necessary that the insurance premium is charged adequately. Pricing falls in the realm of actuarial science. It is the responsibility of an actuary to determine premium rate appropriate to an insurance contract which is viable on a long term basis.

Pricing Assumptions

Pricing Assumptions are Considerations that go into the determination of premium rates under a life insurance contract which combines both protection and savings element.

Pricing involves making assumptions in order to assess the eventual costs of liabilities (under insurance contracts) of a life insurer. The actuary draws on several principles in setting assumptions for pricing insurance contract, having regard to the management of risk and the return on capital. The assumptions themselves give rise to risks which need to be managed.

The assumptions broadly relate to demographic assumptions, investment return interest, expenses and commission, inflation of expenses, withdrawals, bonus (for Participating Policy Contracts) and profit and other contingency margins.

Mortality Rates

The average rate of mortality is one of the main considerations when designing the pricing strategy. The values assigned to these rates reflect the expected future experience of the lives who will take out the contract being priced. These rates would be derived by analyzing a life insurer's own experience for the type of contract concerned or similar contract. The rates vary according to the age and gender of the insured. Further, differentials could arise on account of occupation, geographical locations habits. Rate differentials would be significant depending on the type of contract for example, between an endowment assurance and a term assurance contract and between an assurance contract and annuity/pension contract. Standard of selection and underwriting of lives proposed for insurance is an important factor in setting the adjustment to standard table of rates of mortality(based on the above factors) to be used for pricing insurance contracts. In respect of pension and annuity contracts, future improvement in mortality rates needs to be allowed for in the pricing owing to its significant financial impact on the liabilities.

Investment Return

An insurer has to set up reserves for every contract of insurance in order to meet the liabilities. Such reserves need to be invested in a prudential manner. The expected investment rate of return is an important parameter in determining the price of the product. In deciding the investment return, aspects like investment guarantees in the product design, the intended investment mix for the assets underlying the policy reserves, current returns on the investments, reinvestment of investment proceeds are considered.

Interest

Peoples' willingness to invest in insurance policies mainly depends upon the interest rates. If the interest rate provided by the banks and other financial institutions tend to be smaller than the perceived returns from the insurance policies then the people opt for insurance products.

Expenses and Commission

The cost of processing, the kind of infrastructure costs involved and the payment made to the agents are all incorporated into the costs of installments and premium sum and forms the integral part of the pricing strategy.

Bonus

The distribution of the valuation surplus to policyholders is done through the declaration of 'Bonus'. Only policyholders who opt for 'Participating' or 'with profit' policies would be entitled to bonus. Other policyholders who have 'Non-participating' or 'Without Profit' policies would be paying a slightly lesser amount of premium for the same kind of insurance of cover because of the absence of 'bonus loading.

Bonus is declared in various ways. The most common method is the *'Simple Reversionary Bonus'*. The amount of bonus declared, is added to the sum assured. This addition is called vesting.

In a *'Compound reversionary bonus'* system, the bonus will be added to the existing Sum Assured including vested bonuses.

Profit and Other Contingency Margins

There is a risk that future experience could turn out to be adverse and this eventuality has to be allowed for in the pricing. This is done by adding margins to the various parameters. This level of margins is to be set by the actuary making his own judgment based on past experience.

A detailed analysis on the literature available on the product and price mix of insurance companies is presented below:

Shesha Ayyar (1999), has observed that, increase in the life span of the people due to the advancement in medical facilities would lead to demand for pension products. He was of the opinion that, the conduct of frequent meetings would enhance better relationship between the agents and policyholders.

Narayanan Krishnamurthy (2000), has highlighted the role of an actuary in providing a tangible solution to the selling of insurance products. He has expressed hope that the actuary would play an active role in communicating the benefits of covering risk. He has stated that people need choice and only personalized services would attract the customers.

Vijay Srinivasa, K.B. (2000), has emphasized that the insurers should link the insurance products with other benefits. Low incomes, social structure, lack of understanding among the public, lack of availability of new schemes are the main reasons for low priority of insurance in India. To avoid this, the author has insisted on return linked insurance.

Neelam Jain (2000), has expressed hope that, the private sector entry is justifiable for enhancing efficiency of operations, achieving greater density and insurance coverage in the country and for greater mobilization of the long term savings for the long infrastructure projects. There is competition not only in the issue of various ranges of products, but also in terms of customer service, channels and effective techniques of selling the products. He has suggested that, in order to survive and grow, the public sector companies have to concentrate on product innovation and adopt multi-channel distribution strategy.

Alok Mittal and Akash Kumar (2001), in their study entitled, "An Exploratory Study of Factors Affecting Selection of Life Insurance Products" have stated that, whenever there is uncertainty, there is risk which cannot be averted and it involves multi–faceted losses. The study was conducted by analyzing the factors that affect the selection of life insurance policies such as product attributes, customer delight, payment mode, product flexibility, risk coverage, grace period, professional advisor, and maturity period. It revealed that, all the factors that have been identified are important, but they have all been rated differently.

Shesha Ayyer, V. (2002), was of the opinion that, the greater scope for retirement benefits plan in Indian companies should aim at product development and better service to the clients. In order to limit the mortality risk, the level of retention of risk on individual lives should be actuarially determined and the excess risk should be reinsured. He has stressed on the need, to take extra care for the settlement of claims and for monitoring the activities of the agents.

According to Shikha Sharma (2002), the fact that the private players have captured one tenth of the market share itself is an indication of success of their efforts. The author has observed that, a wide range of products, customer focused service and professional advice have become the mainstay of the industry. Life insurance is being considered as a versatile financial planning tool and there is flexibility and sustainability in the price of the policies. There is emergence of a number of channels including bancassurance and direct marketing and there is improvement in the service attitude and delivery .The author was of the opinion that, only the credible players with long term vision and a proper business strategy would survive in the market.

Rao, R.V.S. (2003), has identified the key challenges faced by the life insurance sector due to privatization to be: product innovation, management of investments, distribution, and customer service and expense control. He has emphasized the need for providing quality service. He forecasts huge opportunities in the pension sector.

Shobhit and Sanjay (2004), have identified the following reasons for the failure of the private players to penetrate into the rural market. Perception of insurance as an additional burden rather than as a means to combat risk; differences in the objectives and expectations between urban and rural policyholders and the failure of the private players to offer products that would suit the requirements of the rural mass. According to them, in urban areas, services provided at the doorstep and efficient customer service were the two main reasons which helped in penetrating into the market.

Gupta, P.K. (2004), is of the opinion that, differential pricing is being adopted by the insurance companies for different policyholders due to the fact that, policy holders in general perceive the price in terms of what they paid for buying the risk and for the cover. According to the author, life insurance pricing is simple, since it is based on the insured's age and sex, the rigid nature of the mortality rates and the accuracy with which the mortality rates could be calculated.

Rajat Gera (2004), conceptualizes the product life insurance as a core benefit and identifies faster claim settlement, security, additional benefits, perception of risk of service provider and tax benefit as the supplementary services.

Stuart Purdy (2004), has analyzed the various issues relating to the sale of insurance products. According to him, treatment of life insurance policy only as a tax saving instrument, low level of consumer awareness about the insurance products and the manpower problem are the major factors that affect the sale of insurance products. He has stressed that, the private players need to adapt themselves to the challenging scenario and offer the customers an array of flexible and innovative products.

Jawaharlal, U. (2005), has stated that the insurance companies should revise the targets as there is a huge untapped potential market. There is a need for identification of products exclusively for the rural folk coupled with relaxation in term of the size of the products, underwriting considerations etc. He has stated that there should be a greater thrust as regards group insurance and pension related products.

According to Manchanda, S.M. (2005), the basic purpose of buying insurance should be to protect the family from loss of income due to an early death of the main income earner. The need to cover the risk of death should be predominant among all needs. Privatization has offered the customers the choice of selecting the quantum of death benefit as well as saving benefit. He has emphasized the need to educate the customers about the different products which would suit their special need.

Darling Selvi, V. (2005), has elaborately analyzed the benefits of life insurance namely protection, liquidity, aid to thrift, tax relief and so on. According to the author Life Insurance Corporation has created an invisible brand name particularly among the rural population which facilitates market extension and channelization of policies. Awareness creation making available innovative products offering right mix of flexibility, risk and return, usage of IT would enhance the demand for the Life insurance policies. It has been suggested that the welfare of the agents should be looked into.

The case study conducted by ICFAI (2005), dealt with the pricing and product development strategies being adopted by the new private players. Analysts revealed that, more than 10 per cent of Life Insurance Corporation policies reportedly lapsed or were surrendered every year. With the liberalization of the industry, not only were premiums expected to go down, but increased products, improvements in customer service and deeper insurance penetration were also expected. The involved implications of the changes in the pricing and product development strategies, have been taking place all over the insurance industry.

Krishnakumar and Kannan (2005), have discussed the position of Life Insurance Corporation after the advent of private players in the insurance sector. They have stated that the Life Insurance Corporation has been losing its market share to the private players and has to take prudent steps to expand its customer base. They have opined that if greater focus is given to generating new business and service to the existing policyholders, Life Insurance Corporation can retain its dominant position.

Anand Adhikari (2005), in his analysis of the performance of the private life insurance has stated that Unit-Linked Insurance Plan (ULIP) launched by the insurance companies has gained popularity. The author is of the opinion that life insurance policies once viewed as tax-saving instrument are now bought as a means of protection. According to him Endowment policies were once the rage; but now unit-linked policies are popular since the private players are projecting the dual benefits of protection and returns and globally Unit-Linked Insurance Plan accounts for about 80 per cent of all life insurance policies.

Shrinivas, S.S. and Anand.V (2005), have made a comparison between the conventional insurance and unit-linked products. They are of the view that investing in Unit Linked Insurance Policies would be beneficial to the investors since they can assess and take decisions on the basis of their investment at any point of time; and take decisions on the basis of the prevailing market condition. Unit-linked products offer a long term investment option where returns are expected to be far more real and are compromising the life cover protection.

Ramakrishna Rao, T.S. (2006), has stated that insurance companies have been responding well to the growing demand of the investors for unit linked instruments by offering products that suit their requirements. Unit-Linked Insurance Plan is today considered as a solution for insurance planning, financial needs, financial planning for children's future and retirement planning. The flexible nature of Unit-Linked Insurance Plans helps the customers to opt for a lower level of sum assured.

Jawaharlal, U. (2006), in this research paper has analyzed the success and failures of Insurance companies. He has stated that a significant change that has occurred in life insurance business is introduction of riders. Some of the life insurers have very few base products to show but by making different combinations with different riders, they are able to eventually come out with several products. There is inexplicable preference for savings in life insurance as against the much cheaper term or pure insurance.

Rajesham, Ch., and Rajender,K. (2006), are of the opinion that liberalization and the opening up of the insurance sector to private players have created a vast opportunity for the specific category of professionals and the demand for qualified, skilled, expertise knowledge actuaries has suddenly increased.

Rao, CS. (2007), has categorically stated that, the insurance industry has witnessed unprecedented growth in the sale of policies. The market has been enlarged and significant developments have happened in the products. Unit linked policies have attracted the attention of the insured and the availability of riders has been seen as a positive development.

Vasantha, P. (2008), in her article titled "Life Insurance – The Hot Investment" has stated that protection, aid to thrift, liquidity, tax relief and money when you need it were the motives behind taking life insurance. She has stated that life insurance will encourage the thrift among the people.

Dilip Maitra (2008), has elaborately discussed the services rendered by the life insurance policies. He is of the opinion that if planned properly, life insurance would provide for the unusual needs like higher education of children or their marriage. The add on benefits take care of the loss due to disability or pay for the medical expenses and can generate higher benefits in case of the death of the assured due to accident. It also provides regular income after retirement expenses.

Anuradha Sharma (2008), has observed that, economic factors such as prices of insurance, government tax, the general economic environment income, and inflations also have a major impact on the life insurance sector, the author has felt. Individual's social environment like culture and society also have contributed to increasing demand for the insurance products. Therefore, harnessing the enormous market potential is crucial to the success of every insurer.

RNCOS (2008), in its research report on the Indian Insurance Industry Forecast (2007-2009) points out that the Indian life insurance sector is driven by shifting consumer behaviour, changing socio-economic demography and rising insurance contribution to Gross Domestic Product. The study predicted a huge demand for life insurance products in future. A rising demand for retirement provision and pension schemes has also been predicted.

Jean Pierre Lepaud (2008), has opined that, there is a shift from the traditional saving cum protection products to pure protection; pure term products health products and so on. Today's customers are able to design the products according to their needs through rider covers, at a marginal cost. Product diversification which is considered to be a value addition, has become the order of the day. Introduction of the much sought for has brought an upward surge in the market, he has stated.

The performance of Indian Insurance companies has been impressive due to the innovations made in the product line offered by the life insurers, states Sharma, NC (2008), in his article entitled, "Performance Paradox". With the increase in the popularity of Unit Linked Life Insurance Products the size of the average policy – single premium and non- single premium has increased considerably. The moving away of the companies especially the private players from the traditional individual agent to alternate distribution channels has also been cited as a major improvement in the life insurance industry.

Jawaharlal, U (2008), stated that, add on riders have the ability to dynamically alter the coverage under a contract and eventually turn out to be customized solutions. According to the author the applicants could fulfill their needs with the help of riders, instead of looking for new policies. However, the additional cost involved in such riders,s has been cited as the main drawback of riders.

Life insurance as a product is lucrative because of diverse utility ranging from providing social and emotional security to tax advantage benefits, opines Samuel. B Sekar (2008), in his article, "Indian Insurance Industry poised for growth". The author has stated that, the insurance companies have to differentiate themselves from each other with a view to attract and keep their customers loyal. For this purpose, successful distribution strategies are to be implemented which would understand the preferences and needs of the customers, the author has opined.

Snekha Shukla (2008), has discussed in detail the norms in rural insurance, and has identified various rural insurance needs such as policy holders preferences; ability to make premium payments and so on. The author has opined that, the rural buyers view life insurance, as a reliable and essential form of saving and the insurance companies in turn offer low-cost term insurance products and small premium saving products in order to suit their requirements

PROMOTION MIX

The term 'Promotion Mix is used to refer to the combination of different kinds of promotional tools used by a firm to advertise and sell its products. The main promotional tools or activities which make-up the promotion mix are: selling, advertising, public relations and publicity and sales promotion. These are also known as elements of promotion-mix. (Chhabra, T.N. and Grover, S.K., 1999).

PROMOTIONAL MIX IN INSURANCE

The basic objectives of promotional activities in an insurance company may be to develop public relations with the clients; make a strong impression of competency and sincerity; manage to maintain a fine image by positive word of mouth and customization. The elements of the promotional mix that bring together the various promotional tools used by an organization in a coordinated way could be advertising, personal selling, public relation and sales promotion.

Personal Selling

This is a paid form of personal communication with target customers. Personal selling facilitates face-to-face contact with the target customers, which lacks in advertising. Personal selling is suitable for communicating information about expensive and premium services Personal selling can also provide more direct feedback than other methods of communication.

Advertising

The American Marketing Association (1960) has defined advertising as 'any paid form of non-personal presentation and promotion of goods, services or ideas by an identified sponsor. Life insurance is rarely bought as a response to advertisements. Advertisements are effective as reminders to intimate change of address, pay premium, make nominations; as information on bonus declaration, special revival schemes, concessions, new plans, and to build corporate image as financially strong, as responsible social citizen, etc.

The Regulations framed by the IRDA have made some stipulations about advertisements by insurers as well as by intermediaries like agents. These stipulations apply to all messages in the print and electronic media, hoardings, internet, leaflets and business cards that urge others to buy life insurance. These stipulations, inter alia, state that:

- claims made about the benefits should not be beyond the ability of the policy to deliver,

- benefits described should match policy provisions,
- words or phrases should not be used in such a way as to hide or minimize the cost of hazards,
- important exclusions, limitations and conditions of the contract should be disclosed sufficiently,
- information should not be misleading,
- illustrations about future benefits or assumptions should not be unrealistic or unrealizable in the light of current performance,
- benefits that are not guaranteed should not be referred to in ways that they are not noticed,
- there should be no implication of sponsorship, affiliation or approval that does not exist. (www.irdaindia.org.).

Unawareness	Makes ImpactFly the flag Inform aboutProduct/ serviceOvercome forgetfulness
Awareness	Convey specificityInform about whatProduct/service doesProvide assurance
Comprehension	Establish credibilityReduce hostilityEmphasize benefitsDemonstrate fitness
Conviction	Overcome apathyGet customer to take actionEncourage ownershipGenerate demand

Fig. 2.7 : Advertising and Communication

Source: Marketing Stud y course, The Chartered Insurance Institute, 2000, p.6

Publicity/Public Relation

Publicity is a non-paid form of communication, which takes the form of news reports and announcements. Public Relation tools such as publicity through the media, event sponsorship, special publications, brochures and other publicity materials enhance the relationship of the company with the public. Publicity enhances the credibility of a company's claims regarding its products or services. Public relation programmes encompass publications (press releases, annual reports, brochures, posters, articles, press conferences, and seminars), media stories (about new customers and product and service developments), exhibitions and displays, and sponsorship of charitable causes, arts or sports events.

Sales Promotion

Sales promotional tools aim at targeting at the end user or the channel members and are used by marketers to stimulate the trial of new products and maintain interest in established brands. In insurance, there is only one level in the channel i.e. agents/brokers/advisors. So insurers promote their products to agents/brokers/advisors, and they push it down to the customers.

In insurance marketing, a push or pull strategy can be used only if there is one or more independent intermediaries between the company and the customer. Generally, there are three parties in the life insurance marketing channel namely insurer, agents/brokers/advisors and customers. Agents are not the employees of the company or appointed by the insurance company, but they act as intermediaries between the consumer and the company. The agent receives a commission for every policy he sells. Insurers encourage agents to promote the products to the customers by giving certain incentives and reward.

Advertising	Sales Promotion	Public Relations	Personal Selling	Direct Marketing
Motion Pictures	Contests, games	Press kits	Sales meetings	Telemarketing
Bill boards	Exhibitions	Sponsorships	Sales	Mailings
Print & Broad-cast ads	Demonstrations	Annual reports	Presentations	Catalog
Reprints of Shopping	Coupons	Events	Incentives	Electronic ads
Posters & Leaflets	Continuity Programs	Speeches	Programs	e-mail
Displays	Rebates	Seminars	Fair & Tradeshows	
Symbols & Logos	Fair & Tradeshows	Company magazine		
Brochures & Booklets	Premiums and gifts	Publications		

Fig. 2.8 : Communication Platforms

Source: Insurance Marketing, ICFAI University, 2002, 196.

A detailed analysis on the literature available on the promotion mix of insurance companies is presented below:

Shekar Chandra Sahoo (1999), discussed the new products and emphasized the need to use technology for survival as well as for consistent growth. He expressed hope that innovative business concepts would have more impact on the future of the organization and its place in the global market.

Shikha Sharma (2002), has stated that the greatest challenge faced by the life insurance today is increasing the penetration of insurance. According to the author, conduct of seminars and workshops for the consumers, application of Information Technology– websites for transmitting information and issue of booklets containing detailed information about the products are the techniques adopted by the private players to penetrate into the market. The author concluded by saying that an innovative sales and distribution mechanism should be developed to fulfill the requirements of the people.

Hydery A Rahmanjee (2002), has stated that the insurers have to impart training to the intermediaries, provide required capital and quality service, and ensure that they are well placed. They have to make efforts to attract and retain quality people. There has been pressure on the use of information technology also. The author has stated that, the required authority should ensure that the insurers adhere to sound insurance principles and practices and maintain adequate financial resources to develop the market and to promote companies as well as innovation.

The survey on the satisfaction of the Life Insurance Corporation employees, by Madhusudana Rao, *et al.*, (2002), has revealed that, majority of the employees were satisfied with the promotional measures adopted by the Corporation, the co-operation rendered by the co-workers, grievance handling mechanism adopted by the Corporation and the housing loan facility offered. The employees have expressed satisfaction as regards the relationship maintained by the management with the employees.

Subash Lakhotia (2003), has stated that the insurance companies should analyze the positive and negative aspects of other available investment instruments in the market. The author has suggested that, in order to increase penetration, workshops should be conducted for the existing and prospective clients and the insurance advertisements should dream about selling more insurance in order to increase the market penetration.

Mony, S.V. (2003), has stated that, direct marketing would continue to play a vital role in promoting the sale of insurance products. Other channels, like alliances with banks and other bodies would help in capturing the Indian market. Sale of new products such as single premium, unit linked retirement products, money back and annuity are yet to gain momentum. He has stated that, technology plays an active role in the designing and administering of the insurance products .He has also stressed on the need to cover the non-salaried or self-employed work force by opening up the pension segment

Ramamurthy, A. (2003), has stated that the Life Insurance Corporation has revisited its objectives and has focused on vision and culture to face competition. He has stressed on the need to enhance training facilities, to introduce incentive schemes for efficient employees, to develop Customer Relationship Management plan, to raise the service standards, to simplify procedures, to speed up the settlement of claims and to introduce Information Technology. The author has suggested new strategies such as, introduction of more new and innovative products at competitive pricing and returns, alliance with the corporation bank and aggressive advertising.

Ranjan Kumar and Koushal Vaidya (2004), have discussed various strategies that are to be adopted by the insurance companies to differentiate their product and services from that of the competitors. They have stated that, possible innovations should be made in terms of products, customer service and distribution net work. The need to penetrate into the rural market, to buildup brand image and to increase the sales promotional activities also has been stressed.

Jawaharlal, U. and Kumar K.B.S. (2004), have stated that branding insurance is gaining prominence as the insurance companies have realized the inevitability of creating an impression in the minds of the consumers in order to face competition. It is suggested that, to retain and survive in the market the insurer has to be innovative.

The survey undertaken by Federation of Indian Chamber of Commerce and Industry (2004), revealed that the insurance companies have taken an aggressive approach in penetrating into the urban, semi-urban and even rural markets for greater market share. As the study revealed that the average age of people buying the policies is between 30-40 years there is a need to create awareness about insurance among youth. The survey also pointed out that, the increase in the service tax on the risk premium for life policies would have an impact on the insurance industry.

The case study conducted by ICFAI (2005), has visualized the need for an effective advertising strategy for insurers. A critical analysis of the advertisement made as a part of the study revealed that, in their relentless efforts to lead the market, insurance companies and advertising agencies were running out of ideas and symbols for advertising their products and symbols such as umbrellas, palms cupping flames and walking sticks have become obsolete.

The case study conducted by ICFAI (2005), has examined the marketing strategies, specifically the advertising and promotional measures, adopted by the new private players. According to industry observers, one of the main reasons for low insurance penetration in India was the ineffective distribution and marketing strategies adopted by Life Insurance Corporation. The advertisements of Life Insurance Corporation were limited to some print and electronic media advertisements that typically talked about Life Insurance Corporation's products being great tax saving tool for salaried individuals, who came under the income–tax bracket. Analysts commented that the private insurers seemed all set to make the industry marketing – driven, wherein technical and service excellence would be the key factors of success.

Mittal, R.K., and Anil Chandhok (2005), have stated that inter connectivity of all branches through computers and internet, launching of publicity campaigns, quick dissemination of information and training and motivation of the work force is essential for success .The authors have concluded by stating that, the awareness of the public towards insurance is growing.

Rajesh.J,Jampala,.C., and Venkateswara Rao (2005), have discussed the sales promotional activities undertaken by the Life Insurance Corporation to face competition. According to the authors the Life Insurance Corporation undertakes the sales promotional activities in three forms namely: Customer-oriented promotion that is tax benefits, payment of bonus, provision of accidental benefits and higher non-medical items ; trade promotion such as salary saving scheme and Sales force promotion given in the form of commission, gifts, advances for the purchase of cars, club membership etc.

Kaushlendra Maurya (2005), has analyzed the role of technology in implementing the business strategies in the vital business areas such as sales, distribution channel, customer service, product development and claims. The author is of the opinion that, the insurers are found committing to invest more on technology to increase their process efficiency.

According to Alagar, R. (2005), Insurance Retailing is expected to bring about radical changes in the market. Claims settlements can be made anywhere in the globe. Convergence in financial services will be enabled through dematerialized instruments of promise. E–Insurance will get prime supremacy in Insurance Retailing. Event managements, Summits, Seminars, Collaborations, Thought Leaders, and Training, Research and Development inputs and other allied host of factors will bring in new viable professional ideas for implementation. Distribution channels will proliferate in Retail Revolution and merchandising will be at the doorsteps of the policy purchasers with multiplied efficiency, the author has opined.

According to Stephen Wylie (2005), technology plays a vital role in measuring and managing productivity and increasing profitability. Interaction through the website gives the client, a more active role in selecting a policy at the best price, while reducing the amount of time spent by the agents in seeking new clients. Technology enables the agents to be better informed about new products and to provide wealth creation advice.

It has been categorically stated by Nitin Tanted (2006), that Indian Insurance companies should broaden the distribution network since distribution will be a key determinant of success for all insurance companies regardless of age or ownership. As the product moves towards the mature stages of communization, (increased awareness and popularity) they could then have a host of new channels like grocery stores, direct mails. The author has opined that, a comprehensive social security system combined with a willingness to save in India will lead to a large demand for pension products in which, current penetration is poor.

Bijal Mehta and Shubhra Anand (2007), have conducted a study on the differentiating selling strategies of different life insurance companies. The authors have stressed the importance of applying the need analyzer tool for identifying the needs of the prospective policyholders, in order to persuade them to purchase the policies.

Chinnadorai, K. M., *et.al.*, (2007), undertook a study of motivational factors and level of satisfaction of agents and development officers of Life Insurance Corporation of India. The study revealed that, team building could be enhanced by increasing the commission of agents, cooperation and coordination, innovative training and motivation through personal approach.

Commission was found to be the most motivating factor for an agent, to pursue the insurance career.

Govardhan, N.M. (2008), in his article has categorically stated that, with increase in the ageing population and governments moving from public to private pension schemes the demand for life insurance products has increased. The professional agent has been the strongest link between the life insurer and the customer. The persistency rate in bancassurance due to the continuous contact with the client is better than any other channel. The use of internet, web based sales, e- marketing, tele-calling and mobile short message service(SMS) have made great strides in the distribution task.

DISTRIBUTION STRATEGIES OF LIFE INSURANCE COMPANIES

The successful marketing of life insurance products depends upon an efficient distribution system. The intermediaries in the insurance business and the distribution channels used act as the strongest drivers of growth in the insurance sector. Distribution has been the key word for life insurance, for products to penetrate into the market and reach the customers in the most effective manner. The privatization process has significantly changed the atmosphere of the insurance industry. With the combined forces of increasing technological expertise, transformation of the industry and innovative techniques working in the market the distribution system is widening.

Traditionally, the Life Insurance Corporation has been distributing the insurance products solely through the net work of its own agents. But in the deregulated scenario, the private companies have started employing different types of distribution channels to get hold of the customers. Increasing technological expertise has provided major thrust on the new forms of distribution channels.

Mandatory Training for Insurance Intermediaries

One of the important changes made by the Insurance Regulatory and development Authority (IRDA) Act, 1999 is to insist that the new insurance agents should be trained for 100 hours and passes the prescribed test. (www.irdaindia.org, 2009). This was done, with the view to preparing the agents to market Life as well as General Insurance in the right manner and to enable them to render proper service to their customers. The new companies that have come into the industry are recruiting new agents and getting them trained. Some companies have designated them as 'Advisors', Insurance consultants and such other nick titles.

The training imparted should include both classroom and practical components. The classroom training should be consisting of:

- Code of conduct and legal liabilities, attitude;
- Product knowledge, with stress on product designing;
- Investment pattern under the IRDA Act, 1999;

- Solvency margin and share of capital;
- Market and outcome of market research vis-à-vis rules for advertising and publicity;
- Value added service before and after the sale; and
- Information technology.

The practical training, at first instance, should include:

- The office – its outlook and purpose;
- Process of working, including basis of underwriting or risks;
- Office discipline and expectations from an intermediary;
- Paper-work and use of information technology;
- The role of an intermediary and that of the office (underwriting marketing, product designing and so on) (Layman's Guide, 2008.)

A distribution channel is the route by which the product (or offer) prepared by the producer reaches the ultimate consumer (or buyer). The distribution channel bridges the distance between the producer (point of manufacture) and the consumer (point of sale). In the case of life insurance, the agent is the primary component of the distribution channel. He is the equivalent of the retailer. The supervisor of agents, by whatever name called, is an important part, because it is he who, by creating and training agents, makes the channel effective. New agents widen the channel.

Equally important would be the other intermediaries like brokers and insurance consultants. Some life insurers are trying to eliminate intermediaries to save costs by adopting direct selling. Another method being attempted is the use of the extensive network of branches of banks. The customers of both banks and life insurers are practically from the same segments of population. Through the same contact, the prospect can be helped to arrange for both bank deposits and life insurance. There would be saving in infrastructure costs and overheads. New insurers find this an easy way to access vast areas. It may be possible to develop composite products having the elements of both life insurance and banking. These trends have to develop.

Agents

Agents are the backbone of the insurance distribution system. The Insurance Act defines an insurance agent as one who is licensed under Section 42 of that Act and is paid by way of commission or otherwise, in consideration of his soliciting or procuring insurance business, including business relating to the continuance, renewal or revival of policies of insurance. He is, for all purposes, an authorized salesman for insurance and needs a license (Life Insurance Guide, 2007.).

An agent is in a position to understand the needs of the customers and can customize the products accordingly in an efficient manner. With the personal relationship he maintains with the customers, the agents can generate business. Customers also prefer this mode, since the agents provide them with a host of services such as collection of premium, processing claims and acts as an advisory to them.

FUNCTIONS OF AN AGENT

The agent's main function is to solicit and procure life insurance business for the Insurance company, which has appointed him for that purpose. At the same time, he is trusted by the prospect to advise him suitably keeping his circumstances and needs in mind. He is thus in the unique role of a person trusted by both parties to the transaction. His functions would include understand the prospect's needs and persuade him to buy a plan of life insurance that suits his interests best complete the formalities (paper work, medical examination) necessary to get the policy expeditiously, keep in touch to ensure that changing circumstances are, reflected in the arrangements relating to premium payments, nomination and other necessary alterations, facilitate quick settlement of claims, be totally honest with both the prospect and the Insurer.

Insurers	Number of agents
Aviva	2019
Bajaj Allianz Life Insurance Co. Ltd.	12756
Birla Sun Life Insurance Co. Ltd.	4893
Bharti AXA Life Insurance Co. Ltd.	997
Future Generali India Life Insurance Company Ltd.	—
HDFC Standard Life Insurance Co. Ltd.	8794
ICICI-Prudential Life Insurance Co. Ltd.	18333
IDBI Fortis Life Insurance Company Ltd.	12
ING Vysya Life Insurance Co. Ltd.	8023
Kotak Mahindra	1789
Max New York Life Insurance Co. Ltd.	1616
Metlife India Insurance Co. Ltd.	2953
Reliance Life Insurance Co. Ltd. (Earlier AMP Sanmar Life Insurance Company from 3.1.02 to 29.9.05)	18809
Sahara Life Insurance Co. Ltd.	106
SBI Life Insurance Co. Ltd.	6020
Shriram Life Insurance Co. Ltd.	1753
Tata-AIG Life Insurance Co. Ltd.	3055
Life Insurance Corporation of India	93718
Total	**185646**

Fig. 2.9 : Individual Agents – Insurer Wise for 2007-2008 in Tamilnadu

Source : www.irdaindia.org.

BROKERS

Brokers are corporate entities that act as the intermediary for more than one company. As a promotional measure, they are allowed to pass on a part of their commission to the customers. These brokers are ideally suited for group plans for corporate where they negotiate with the insurance companies on behalf of clients to tailor a product best suited to the client's requirements. Customers have the option to select a product among varieties of products offered by different companies through one broker only.

DIRECT SELLING

The intermediaries are surpassed in this mode of distribution. The company directly contacts the consumers and sells the products to them without the intervention of intermediaries. Generally group insurance products are sold to big companies through this mode. Selling activities is now entrusted mainly to development officers. Corporate customer building is entrusted to managers of branches and divisions. The managers are also entrusted with a variety of other important duties of which marketing and selling is one of them. The current primary role is managing and not marketing.

INTERNET MARKETING

The internet plays very important role for promoting sales of the insurance products and it also provides detailed information regarding the company's policy, products and future plans. The internet has proved to be one of the most potent and low-cost sale channels all over the world. The sales through this channel can be enhanced, especially when customer profiling, suitable product recommendation and finally, purchase of the policy itself. Post-sale policy servicing can also be done through the internet itself. The bank intends to significantly enhance its internet capabilities in insurance distribution business as it views a great potential in the internet for acquiring and servicing the customers. The internet can be used to offer supportive services in insurance, like the proposal forms, claims, claim intimations and E-mail correspondence.

BANCASSURANCE

Bancassurance is the simplest way of selling insurance products through a bank distribution channel. Also known as Allfinanz, Bancassurance describes a package of financial services that can fulfill both banking and insurance needs at the same time (Rachana Parihar). For banks, it acts as a diversification and additional fee income, for insurance companies it acts as a tool for increasing their market penetration and premium turnover. For the customers, it is a bonanza in terms of reduced price, high quality products delivered at their door steps.

The RBI drafted rules for the scheduled commercial banks are selected financial institutes to enter the insurance sector, are as follows:

1. Net worth should be equal or more than $5 bn.
2. Capital adequacy ratio should not be less than 10 percent.
3. The banks/financial institutes should have at least three years of continuous profits.
4. To the industry average, the level of net non-performing assets should be below one per cent.
5. The performance should be satisfactory. (Ravikumar, V.V., 2006.).

As per the Report on Currency and Finance, 2001, RBI has identified three ways through which the banks/financial institutes can participate in insurance business:

1. Without risk participation, the bank will provide fee-based insurance services.
2. The bank can invest in an insurance company to provide infrastructural and service support.
3. Initializing a joint venture with an insurance company, where risk is involved. Therefore, the bank needs to maintain an arms-length relation between its banking business and insurance outfit.

The major advantages of Bancassurance are:

1. It can boost productivity. Banks can have effective sales by the successful mining of their data base and by utilizing distribution systems.
2. It is an efficient means of market penetration as the existing customers of the bank can easily be targeted.
3. The bank personnel normally maintain personal relationship with their customers and enjoy higher trust of their clients. This would help the banks to increase the sale of the insurance products. They are in a better position to tap the small and medium entrepreneurs which leads to increase in their sales.
4. This mode of distribution is ideally suited for selling standardized products such as term assurance.

Hence this mode has been identified as the convenient channel of distribution for customers to avail standardized insurance products.

Worksite Marketing and Distribution

Worksite marketing is defined as the process of advising, selling and servicing of financial services products directly to the employees at their place of work.

Characteristics

- Products are sold on an individual basis. Thus, though the approach is to the whole group of employees at a worksite, the final sale is of an individual product.

- Voluntary benefits: the products on offer as a part of a worksite program do not form part of the employee's remuneration package, although they often complement it by filling in the gaps.

CORPORATE AGENTS

In order to spread awareness about insurance and to increase the coverage of a large section of population who have remained outside the radius of insurance coverage all these years, the IRDA introduced a variety of intermediaries as "distribution" is key to insurance penetration. The Corporate Agent is a concept introduced with a view to taking advantage of the presence of a large number of firms, corporations, banks, NGOs, cooperative societies and panchayats who are in contact with people in normal discharge of their activities and utilize their presence and services for canvassing the sale of insurance contracts.

Corporate Agents (CAs) are corporate entities (NBFCs) that source policies for the Insurance Company with whom they have a tie-up. They are authorized to source policies for one insurance company only. The difference between CA and Bancassurance arrangement is that the former trains its own employees to sell the policies while in case of Bancassurance arrangement, the employees of the insurance company (FSCs) source the business. (www.niapune.com.)

IRDA (LICENSING OF CORPORATE AGENTS) REGULATIONS 2002

IMPORTANT PROVISIONS

These Regulations are on similar lines as the IRDA (Licensing of Insurance Agents) Regulations 2000. (www.irdaindia.org.). The important provisions are as follows.

1. A corporate agent can be a firm, a company under the Companies Act, a banking company, a corresponding new bank, a regional rural bank, a cooperative society, a panchayat, a local authority, a non-government organisation, a micro lending finance organisation, a non-banking finance company, or any other organisation that may be approved by the IRDA.
2. The partnership deed or the Memorandum of Association or any other document that states the objectives of the person wanting to be the corporate agent, must state clearly that soliciting and procuring insurance business is one of its objectives.
3. The corporate agent has to nominate its partner (in the case of a firm), director (in the case of a company), or one or more of its officers or employees, as a 'corporate insurance executive'. The issue of license to the corporate agent is subject to the insurance executives satisfying the requisite educational and other qualifications, as in the case of an individual agent. He is also required to undergo the minimum training

requirements and pass the examination conducted by the Insurance Institute of India, as in the case of individual agents.

4. The corporate agent also has to nominate one or more of its partners, directors or employees as 'specified persons', who will be responsible for soliciting insurance business on behalf of the corporate agent. The specified person must have a minimum educational qualification on the same lines as individual agents, and must also not suffer from any of the disqualifications like being insane, being convicted for a criminal offence, etc. He must obtain a certification, which will be given to him after he undergoes the prescribed training and passes an examination. The fees for the certification are Rs. 500. The certification will be valid for three years and can be renewed.
5. Both corporate insurance executives and specified persons are bound by the code of conduct for agents, as applicable to individual agents. A violation of the code can result in the cancellation of the license of the corporate agent, the corporate insurance executives or certification of the specified persons. (www.irdaindia.org, 2009.).

Mishra, K.C. (2000), has viewed bancassurance as an effective distribution channel. He has stated that the bank-named insurance products capture the trust of the customers and bank brand names helped the staff to sell the products easily. He has quoted the experience of different countries in bancassurance. He has expressed hope that if , the right customer is targeted, distribution possibilities are maximized, insurance products are integrated into the bank culture, relationship managers are used for selling the product and the right products are sold, bancassurance would be successful.

Mittal, R.K. (2002), has revealed that 10 per cent of the agents procured 90 per cent of the business and the remaining 90 per cent of the agents procured the remaining 10 per cent of the business. He forecasts that private insurance companies are likely to target village population that is hitherto untapped as there is enormous potential business in this area. If awareness towards insurance is ignited vigorously, the untapped potential business can be translated into actual business.

Anand, M. (2002), in his paper titled "Indian insurance industries-Channelizing growth" has stressed on the need to handle the insurance services through a customer-friendly distribution network. He prescribes the following avenues for the insurance companies to penetrate into the insurance market: providing innovative products to the customers; building strong and effective relationships with the customers by having the right mix of distribution channels; providing professional customer service in terms of quality advice on product choice, along with policy servicing and following prudent underwriting practices and cutting down the administration and management costs.

A macro level study on the topic "Rural Insurance- Issues Challenges and Opportunities" was conducted by FORTE - Collaboration between Federation of Indian Chamber of Commerce and Industry and ING Vysya Life Insurance Company. The objectives of the study were: To understand the rural customers' knowledge, attitude and practices regarding savings, loans and insurance, to identify the factors prohibiting the purchase of insurance policies and to develop a broad cost effective distribution strategy. The findings were: Rural sector offers a huge business opportunity for insurance companies; over one third of the respondents have insurance, with life insurance having the maximum penetration i.e., 27 per cent; awareness about life insurance is near universal; 51 per cent of the respondents have expressed their intention to purchase a life policy, nearly 20 per cent of all farmers in rural India own Kissan Credit Cards, which offer a huge data base and opportunity for insurance. An extensive rural agent network for sale of Life insurance product exists and the agent plays a major role in creating awareness, motivating purchase and rendering other insurance services. Seventy eight per cent of the respondents prefer various combinations of life insurance like life and accident, life and loan, life, health and accident; Security of income and bulk returns, especially for their daughter's marriage and children's education are the persuading factors for taking life policy. The study group also stated that, while individuals are undecided about purchasing insurance from private players, members of different groups show interest in purchasing group insurance through a private player (Naren N. Joshi, 2002).

FORTE (2002), undertook another study on the topic "Developing a Rural Distribution Strategy for insurers to develop a cost effective rural distribution strategy that could be adopted by the insurers, to capitalize on the rural market business opportunities .The study revealed that, though rural market offers tremendous growth opportunities. ING Vysya Life Insurance Company is one of the few private insurance companies highly committed to the rural insurance market in India the group pointed out (Naren N. Joshi, 2002).

Jimmy John (2002), has analyzed the performance of the insurance companies after privatization. According to him, inadequate distribution channels, inadequate capital and human resources, reaching out to the rural masses and the complex nature of the government policies were the problems faced by the private insurers in widening their market. The author has recalled the strategic allowances fixed by the various insurance companies to capture the market. He has identified the bancassurance, and corporate agency models as viable distribution channels.

Rao, G.V. (2003), has analyzed the newly created intermediary structure, which consists of insurance brokers and corporate agents. He has categorically stated that the Insurance Regulation Development Authority has to play a significant role in monitoring the activities of the intermediaries so as to protect the interest of the insured public. He has stressed on the need for imparting training and making the intermediaries, professionals. It has been stated that, the insurers need to concentrate on the rich rural pockets, where there is an increased awareness of the need for insurance through networks. There is a need for the insurers to understand the rural markets better, including their current infrastructure, their credit generation, asset creation and their perception. The author has suggested that, the agency recruitment norms to work in rural areas should be liberalized and the training should be targeted for the sale of insurance products of interest, to the rural customers.

Suresh, K. (2003), has stated that the innovative distribution channels such as bancassurance, tie-ups with other service providers, short-term schemes such as insuring baggage of students going abroad for higher studies and point-of-sales channels are being employed by the players in the competitive scenario .He has also reiterated the fact that with the growth in new channels and competition opening up, the share of agent's contribution to the insurance companies' sale will progressively come down.

According to Rumeer Shah (2003), a bancassurance strategy can succeed only, if it provides a cost–effective way to build distribution capacity, especially for new market entrants; provides a shift from total dependence on tied-agency for existing insurers; helps to penetrate new market segments across a broad channel and increases the quality of business. The author has suggested that, both banks and insurance companies must have their individualities in pooling their resources. Therefore, bancassurance would be successful, only if both banks and insurers are able to identify and integrate their financial culture effectively and quickly, as soon as possible.

According to Krishnamurthy, R. (2003), bancassurance distribution in India will be prominent in pure term insurance products in the early phase of market development. Duc to the strong growth in rural regions, and the closeness of bank staff with customers in rural markets, insurance selling will be taken up more actively at bank branches in the non-metro cities and towns.

Apparao Machiraju (2003), in his article has stated that, the blurring of lines between the insurance companies, banks, and other financial service institutions as well as non-traditional distribution channels in the insurance market contributes to significant changes. Demand from customers drives the companies, on what or how to sell life insurance. The emerging embryonic shape of new business model driven by information, communication and technology is governed by the simplest of all business principles i.e. keep the promises. The author has opined that, the success in life insurance marketing depends more on professional approaches as the business depends on solicitation.

Mekala Mary Selwyn (2004), has examined different prospects of distribution channels and has opined that the scope for potential growth in life insurance market is contributed by underinsured market, changing demographic profile, low level of insurance awareness, growth of the economy and changing socio – cultural behaviour of the people. The second factor favouring bancassurance in India, according to her, would be the special features such as: the product design – a link with loan products, the special rural flavour, and information technology enabled sales approach, planned sales training to bank staff, and the special staff incentive schemes for motivating bank staff to promote bancassurance. The author has concluded that, bancassurance will become the most successful of the multi-channel distribution strategy adopted by the life insurance companies.

Pandey, K.C. (2004), has identified the changes that have taken place in the insurance market to be: direct marketing through dedicated sales force; effectively functioning bancassurance model; the major role played by the corporate agents in assisting the policy holders to select the right type of policies and telemarketing i.e., usage of databases with the aid of call centers. The author has suggested that, it is imperative for the insurance companies to reinvent themselves with the changing dynamics of the market.

Parakala, V.S. and Nagaraja Rao (2004), have stated that, individual agency system is the main channel of distribution in India. The returns provided by the policies, provision of retirement solutions, the awareness level of the customers and the ongoing demand for the health care have given way for the introduction of new channels. The author has opined that, the distribution channels should ensure that, insurance should be perceived as an additional value provided by the company and selling of products enhances the original brand value.

Survey conducted by the Life Insurance Corporation (2004), on life insurance awareness and customer perception revealed that, 93 per cent of life insurance customers would recommend Life Insurance Corporation to their children; 70 per cent of the private insurance customers would go for further insurance through Life Insurance Corporation only; 89 per cent of Life Insurance Corporation's customers felt that Life Insurance Corporation is the pride of India and 91 per cent regard Life Insurance Corporation to be the financially sound company in India. It was suggested to undertake a massive customer awareness campaign.

The outcome of the interview conducted by the Insurance World (2004), was that, 52 per cent of the people interviewed did not have any insurance policy but were willing to take policies if given proper guidance and 48 per cent had some policy. Nineteen per cent of the people did not believe in insurance, four per cent had absolutely no knowledge about insurance and 12 per cent were well aware of the benefits of insurance and believed it to be a good security.

Sumit Khana (2004), has mentioned that a life insurance policy requires servicing as well as an agent to render service and only such agents who can penetrate into rural areas and serve the poor class clients are needed. Further he stressed that, the need of the hour is to inject professionalism in the entire approach of insurance marketing, which includes continued focus on the customer, quality of performance, technological up-gradation and minimized paper work. It is obvious that, insurance salesman will require a considerable amount of imaginative power to identify these unexplored markets.

Tarun Kapoor (2004), has analyzed the various distribution channels used for marketing the insurance products and the role played by the agents in motivating the public. He recalls the role played by bancassurance, brokers and Internet in marketing the insurance products. He has also stated that, the insurance companies are opting for direct contact in certain businesses aimed at corporate, since highly specialized knowledge on risk analysis is called for.

Selling life insurance is now increasingly presenting itself as an opportunity for the life insurance companies, says Anuroop Singh (2004). Further he stressed that, the need of the hour is to inject professionalism in the entire approach of insurance marketing, which includes continued focus on the customer, quality of performance, technological up- gradation and minimized paper work. It is obvious that, insurance salesman will require a considerable amount of imaginative power to identify these unexplored markets. .He has opined that, excellent agents are required to break the barriers, to gain confidence and to convince the rural customers, in order to penetrate into the rural market.

Sharma, N.C. (2004), has stated that, the Indian life insurers need to reach out to the prospective customers and to be positive and aggressive in their marketing strategy. According to the author, the developments that have occurred in the life insurance industry after privatization are: penetration of private players in the life insurance market, increase in the awareness level about life insurance; change in the nature of products with customers showing preference for unit-linked products as against traditional or conventional products; progress in the distribution strategies; increase in the number of people associated with insurance and fierce competition among the insurance providers. He has stressed on the need for being innovative in designing the products and to apply aggressive marketing techniques.

Shikha Sharma (2004), has stated that a wide range of innovative products, customer-focused service and professional advice have become the mainstay of the life insurance industry. She has foreseen opportunities for pension products. She has stated that privatization has created many job opportunities as agents, advisors and so on.

According to Anil Chandhok (2004), only credible insurance players with a long term vision and a robust business strategy could survive in the Indian insurance market. The private companies have experimented with innovative marketing strategies, by advertising extensively on media, to inform people about their existence. He has also stated that new strategies such as alliances with the banks, direct marketing, recruiting and developing agents to enhance the company's image and applying technology to disseminate information have been employed by the insurance players to penetrate into the Indian insurance market.

Rajesh .C. Jampala (2005), has stated that, in order to reach the market private insurers concentrate on product innovation, customer service and selected distribution channel. Multi-channel distribution and marketing of insurance products have been the strategy of new players in the Indian insurance market. According to the author, direct marketing channels have been identified as a relatively inexpensive and easy launch potential distribution channel. The agency force has immense potential due to the complexity of products and the difficulty in selling them. Bancassurance that symbolizes the convergence of banking and insurance, has been viewed as bonanza in terms of reduced premium charges, a high quality product and delivery at the door step. Internet facility is considered to be a better choice for conducting research on consumer information and for getting feedback from the customers.

Chari, V.G. (2005), has stated that the insurance industries' marketing efforts have been focused on the urban middle class and affluent sections. He has recalled the IRDA's norm which states that, insurance companies should concentrate on rural and social sectors also. He has opined that, the cost-effectiveness and conversation efficiency of distribution strategies are crucial in ensuring the success of insurance business. He has suggested that, insurance should be made mandatory by the Government taking into consideration the income levels and affordability of the people.

Shankarsan Basu and Rahul Singh (2005), in their article "Bancassurance-Rest Assured" have analyzed bancassurance as an effective distribution channel for selling insurance products. They have opined that, bancassurance is gaining popularity as it gives the customers the benefit of having a universal bank. Bancassurance offering has proved to be a better capital efficiency model for organizations which, if properly planned and implemented, would be successful.

Sridevi Lakshmikutti and Sridharan Baskar (2005), in their article entitled, "Insurance distribution in India-A Perspective" have discussed the distribution channels, from the perspective of the socio-cultural ethos of the market and how these channels fit into it. They have also analyzed the areas in which insurance companies face challenges and bottlenecks. They have suggested that, the intermediaries should be empowered with the right learning, training and sales tools. They should be technology enablers and this would help the insurers to survive and flourish in the market.

Malbika Deo (2005), has stated that the bancassurance model has prompted the two major financial institutions i.e., the banks and the insurance companies to combine their strengths and create a new means for marketing their products and services with a synergetic effort. Low customer acquisition cost, quicker reach to the untapped markets, introduction of new hybrid products and economies of scale in administration have enabled the insurers to find bancassurance profitable. However, the author has identified the challenges before bancassurance to be, the cultural issues in distribution, dual regulation, channel conflict, product differentiation, customer service, image and reputation risk, technology, insufficient product promotion and poor manpower management.

Ravikumar, V.V. (2005), is of the opinion that, the private life insurance companies have gained the most from the bancassurance tie-ups, which play a vital role in selling the insurance policies in India. According to him, the corporate agency model with its peculiar features of no risk but very low investments enables banks to earn high revenues. Its simplicity of operations and potential to reduce cost enables the bank assurance model to gain momentum.

Sree Lakshmi, V. (2005), conducted a study, on behalf of HDFC Standard Life Insurance Company, with an intention of learning as to why people purchase insurance policies. The study revealed that, 30 per cent of the respondents obtained insurance for tax benefits; 30 per cent purchased insurance for economic security; 14 per cent to avail pension benefits or for old age financial security and eight per cent bought for other reasons. Out of the 250 respondents chosen from Hyderabad and Secunderabad, 48 per cent of the respondents stated that, they had an insurance policy, which showed that insurance awareness was prevalent among the people. The study revealed that, people are skeptical about private players; awareness about the insurer [HDFC Standard Life Insurance Company] was low, hence, the reach was very much limited. It was recommended that, the company should encourage potential Government and private employees with various benefit packages and the company can target more on female population, effective promotional strategies are to be undertaken; and periodic market surveys should be conducted in order to update the customers' perception about life insurance.

Krishna Kumar (2005), highlights Life Insurance Corporation's penetration in the rural market, the problems encountered and the schemes offered for the rural poor. He has stated that, there is significant growth in the total premium income collected from rural areas. He has identified the hurdles faced by the Life Insurance Corporation as: poor general awareness, lack of proper documents, inadequate market coverage, lapsing of policies and health care problems. However, he has expressed hope that, Life Insurance Corporation with its huge network would enhance its spread to cover wider areas especially the rural masses.

Rao, G.V. (2005), has stated that, it is necessary and important that the insurers should demand the implementation of the next stage of secondary reforms for them to have more elbowroom to negotiate premium prices that are reasonable, customer-specific, experience-based, and risk-assessed and what the market can truly beat.

According to Krishnamurthy, S. (2005), bancassurance increases cross selling capability of bank staff, not only for insurance products but also for other financial products. Bank customers will also buy all financial/ protection/ retirement products available from the bank which is perceived as a trust worthy financial partner. Bancassurance is also a profitable concept because it allows industrializing the selling of simple and easy to understand life insurance products to large bank customer data base. This channel saves you from the cost of building your own sales infrastructure.

The case study conducted by ICFAI (2005), has analysed the distribution strategies, specifically the bancassurance channel adopted by the new private players. Analysts commented that, the private insurers seemed all set to make the industry market–driven, wherein technical and service excellence would be the key factors of success. The private companies, to make their presence felt and expand their reach, experimented with new distribution channels.

The case study conducted by ICFAI (2005), has stated that after liberalization, a fierce battle commenced in the Indian insurance industry for garnering market share. New insurance companies used all available channels of distribution, right from individual agents and corporate agents to bancassurance. With the growing popularity of new distribution channels the private players hoped to effectively leverage the strengths of the new distribution channels. The study also examined the changes being made by LIC to remain competitive, and discussed the implications of the industry – wide changes in distribution practices on the insurance business.

The case study conducted by ICFAI (2005), revealed that, with the liberalization of the insurance sector, the insurance distribution system itself has undergone a major transition. The agency system which dominated traditional insurance distribution is facing stiff competition from the new distribution channels in insurance, such as bancassurance and brokers.

According to Ravi Kumar, V.V. (2005) Corporate Agency model has been opted by many banks and insurance companies due to the following reasons:

The bank distributes the products on a no risk basis and hence, the risk would be entirely borne by the insurer. The bank need not invest heavy sums of money except for investing in time and in licensing its identified employees termed as Specified Persons. Even the training responsibility is undertaken by the insurer. The bank gets commission as high as 35 per cent (including bonus) in the first year of procuring a new business, which no other traditional banking operations offer in the current scenario. Also, there is the distinct reality of a perennial revenue stream by means of renewal commissions on the premiums generated in the subsequent years of every policy except Single Premium policies. The author concluded saying that bancassurance being a combination of banking and insurance business is expected to tangibility increase in India due to tie-ups and post-liberalization of insurance companies.

Prasuna, DG. and Nidhi Joshi (2005), have stated that, bancassurance is gaining popularity as it gives the customers the benefits of having a Universal Bank. Bancassurance as a distribution channel facilitates insurance companies in developing networks and customer database faster than any other channel. They have foreseen that future of bancassurance is bright and the market is increasing in this sphere – this is partly fueled by the insurance companies' desire to be more accessible, banks' desire to convert to a universal bank set-up and customer desire to have one stop shop. They concluded by saying that if bancassurance is planned and implemented properly it will achieve the required success.

Sukanya Praveen (2005), has analyzed the reasons why banks are entering in to bancassurance and has described a model for banks to enter the insurance industry. According to the author, the factors that have acted as long – term drivers of bancassurance have been – culturally accepted bank transactions, fee – based services that provide better wage benefits for the employees, provision of complementary insurance products, reforming pension for private pension products and the insurance and banking regulations. The author has opined that smooth flow of information between banks' customer data base and insurance company would help in the development of bancassurance business in India.

According to the author Venkateswara Rao (2005), the basic strength of Life Insurance Corporation is its huge agency force. They are the lifeline of Life Insurance Corporation He has observed that the productivity level of the agents varies from club to club as membership in higher level clubs such as Zonal Managers' Club and Chairman's Club require exceptionally good performances on the parts of agents. He has suggested that the Life Insurance Corporation has to integrate advertising and personal selling efforts in such a way that these efforts will have a positive synergistic effect upon the performance of agents.

Tanuja, R. Kumar (2005), is of the opinion that to develop long term relationship with customers, insurance companies ought to have a stable agency organization. According to him, high inflation driven interest rates, reduction of special benefits for life insurance, opening of market for competition and making alternative services for retirement provision have pressurized the insurance companies to adopt changes in the distribution policies adopted by them. The author has suggested that, retaining the agents for a longer period of time, providing suitable training to the agents, recruiting agents with high entrepreneurship quotient would make the agents feel independent and move in the market confidently.

Rama Krishna Rao, T.S. (2006), is of the opinion that the private players have achieved a phenomenal growth in both life and non life insurance segments. He has stated that due to the new distribution channels such as bancassurance, corporate agents, brokers, direct selling through the internet, innovations and new product offerings, the insurance segment has recorded a growth of 260 per cent since privatization.

Ravi Kumar, V.V. (2006), has categorically stated that bancassurance has become a blessing in disguise for the private players. He is of the opinion that tackling the cultural issues, viewing insurance product as a competitor to the other savings products, integrating the information technology systems and balancing the requirements of the traditional agency force and the bank work force require due attention. He has also stated that from the consumers' point of view bancassurance is a value added proposition that holds good promise for the future.

According to Srinivas Subbarao, P. (2006), the bancassurance in India is at embryonic stage but has the potential to grow and take deep roots in the near future. He is of the opinion that bancassurance would play a proactive role in the prosperity of the insurance industry and would create an environment for long – term sustainable Gross Domestic Product growth due to investment in infrastructure projects.

Nalini Prava Tripathy (2006), in her article, "Bancassurance in the New Millennium" is of the opinion that in India the concept of bancassurance is just emerging and is in fact another distribution channel for insurers. The insurance sector offers ample opportunity for the banks to widen their horizon of financial intermediation. The banks can bring insurance services to the poor people at minimum cost. Training on sales of insurance products to bank staffs needs to be strengthened.

The paper on, "Role of Private Players – Opportunities and Challenges" by Rumki Banyopadhyay (2006), examines the possible strategies that can be used by insurance companies in India to differentiate their product and service offerings from their competitors. They are innovative products, customer service, large distribution network, promotion, brand building, and hedging the insurers. Market expansion can be achieved by customizing products of new segments.

Identifying the right life insurance distribution channels to harness the full potential of the market is imperative, states Mukesh Kumar Baura (2006), in his article entitled, "Bancassurance in life insurance in India". According to the author, bancassurance is an instant channel to reach out to a large number of customers and access a wide base through the network across the geographical span of the country. The challenges faced by the insurance companies in distribution, the growth potential, the benefits to the companies the critical success factors and the future of bancassurance in India, also have been dealt with in detail by the author.

Ramesh, D.V.S. (2006), has stated that involvement of an interface is essential in case of insurance products due to the intricacies involved. Availability of business potentiality, identifying the right market segments and reaching the markets are the main items in the business agenda of the insurance companies. The extension of the contours of the distribution channels to other institutions with the entry of private players has enhanced the competitive structure of distribution network in India.

Sai Kumar (2006), in his article entitled, "Life Insurance Products in India-Issues in Distribution" has stated that, the resistance to life insurance in our society casts additional burden on the distribution network, therefore, dispelling wrong notions about life insurance and convincing the customers about the need for the same is essential, The author has suggested that the life insurance companies should try to intensify the efforts of promoting the concept of insurance through all possible media and vigorous training should be provided to the sales personnel as to how to deal with the customer.

Banks have emerged as attractive distribution channels as they are being driven to increase their profitability and provide maximum value to their customers, states Stuart Purdy (2006), in his article entitled, "Challenges of insurance distribution- some Indian trends". According to the author, mass marketing is always a profitable and cost effective option for gaining market share especially in the rural sector. Likewise, the existing wide network of banks in rural areas also can be utilized for selling insurance products since penetration into rural markets becomes easier for banks than for the insurance companies, he has opined.

Anurika Vaish, and Pallavi Dixit (2007), in their article, "Insurance Companies in the Present Global Scenario", have stated that, the encouraging participation of private sector and changed priority of public sector in insurance industry was among one of the key transformations in structure change of the financial sector. In fact with the widening of the economy, the demand for new types of insurance products emerges. Insurance now extends not only to product market but also to service industries including finance. Companies competing for a greater share of consumer funds are seeking quick access to new markets, new products and new channels of distribution.

Rajendra Prasad, T. (2007), has stated that, the insurance agents act more as insurance planners and concentrate on advising the customers on the suitable plans for their current and future needs. Speedy processing of the applications presented by the customers, easy accessibility of information with the improved technology, usage of print and electronic media would help the companies in promoting the products, he has opined.

Distribution channels have a vital role to play in increasing the pace of insurance penetration, states Devarakonda, V.S. Ramesh (2008), in his article, Redefining Distribution- The changing paradigms in insurance intermediation. According to the author, so far agents have been playing a vital role in contributing to the reach of life insurance amongst the retail segments. But now there is a shift in the distribution strategy due to the complexity of products. Alternative channels such as direct marketing would perform well while complex products would be taken care of by the agency system.

Anurag (2008), concentrates on the innovations surfacing in the life insurance industry. According to him apart from the agents the insurance companies take innovative routes to spearhead their marketing plans and to capture a large pie of market share. Corporate agents have become a force in distributing the insurance products; bancassurance is poised to become a key determinant in the insurance industries; and retail assurance is gaining popularity in the insurance market. The author has expressed hope that with the aggressive marketing strategies, the innovations in the industry would be a great hit and a metamorphosis of Indian insurance industry is on its course.

Anand Pejwar (2008), writes that bancassaurance is going to be the leading distribution channel in the Indian insurance domain in the years to come, considering the vast reach and customer service potential of the bankers. In bancassurance the insurance company makes use of the vast network of the bank branches, its customer base, which is a very important 'raw material' for life insurance. According to the author, for choosing the right partner in bancassurance full commitment from both the partners in a deal, brand/franchise, large customer base, capital strength, complementary products and services and new economy distribution system, regional technology platform have been cited as the critical factors. He has suggested that products sold through bancassurance channel should be simple to sell and simple to buy.

Sithapathy, V. (2008), in his article has opined that the broker is evolving into the new role of facilitator to ensure satisfaction of the need felt by the insured. The insurance broker and the consumer are forming symbiotic relationships in which their mutual loyalties are recognized and nurtured. Hence, the broker system has to be built with high degree of professionalism and infrastructure to understand the concept of the insured.

Sethi, S.K. (2008), has observed that, brokers enjoy a place of prominence in the domain of insurance distribution since it is the only channel that comes out with a complete set of insurance solutions. The company which aims at having right coverage at right price from right insurance company opts for insurance brokerage firm. The author has also stated that, increase in the number of intermediaries has resulted in increasing penetration and the same is reflected in increase in premium collected.

Divya Gupta and Bajaj, S. (2008), have elaborately discussed the rationale behind the evolution of bancassurance. Wider coverage of markets, increase in the profit, reduction in the cost and gaining brand loyalty has been identified as the main benefits of bancassurance. According to the authors, bancassurance model assists customers in terms of diversified quality products, in time and prompt service under the same roof. The new initiative taken up by the Insurance Regulatory Development Authority to permit the banks to have multiple tie-ups with the insurance companies, has been highly appreciated by the authors, since it would provide more options to the policy holders to choose from.

Ramakrishna Rao and Samuel, .B Sekar (2008), have discussed in detail, the prospects and challenges for adopting the newly evolved distribution system Shop assurance. Size of the firm and the order, purchase complexity, purchase frequency, product life cycle stage and the degree of standardization have been cited as the major variables influencing the shop assurance model. The authors have stated that, the system would be successful if the service providers adopt the system of continuously monitoring the consumer behaviour and preference which would in turn build up long term relationship. The shop assurance model has to ensure that the retail outlets encourage affluent customers who desire face to face consultation, the authors have suggested.

Viswanathan, S. (2008), has stated that, through bancassurance initiatives, the bank branches have emerged as one stop shop by offering appropriate products to the customers covering all financial needs. Gaining new customers, retaining the existing customers and enhancing customer satisfaction have become possible with bancassurance mode of service delivery. There is an urgent need for shared vision and commitment of the top officials of the insurance company and the bank, the author has stated. Bancassurance as distribution model should be nurtured as a sustainable platform providing high degree of comfort level at all levels, thereby creating a long lasting win-win relationship for both the insurer and the bank.

Venugopal, R. (2008), has elaborately analyzed the various distribution channels adopted by the life insurance players since privatization. According to him, tied agency channel reigns supreme followed by the bancassurance model. Provision of insurance in addition to banking services, has been perceived as a value addition for the customers, and for the banks. Bancassurance channel offers cost advantage, strategic placements and immense potential, the author has opined.

PEOPLE AND PROCESS MIX (CUSTOMER CARE SERVICE)

Insurance industry involves a high level of people interaction and hence using the employees effectively is essential to satisfy customers and to have a competitive edge in the market. Training and development and building up strong relationships with the intermediaries are the two major areas that are to be taken care of by the insurance companies. Training the employees to introduce them to new products, use of information technology for efficiency both at the staff and the agents' level or the distribution organizations is the key area to be concentrated. Building strong relationship with intermediaries would enhance service quality.

Being a service industry involving a high level of people interaction, it is important to use this resource efficiently in order to satisfy customer as also to have a competitive edge in the market. The two key areas which need to be kept under consideration are training and development and strong relationships with intermediaries.

Training the employees to introduce then to new products, use of information technology for efficiency, both at staff and the agents' level or the distribution organizations is one of the key areas to look into. Also building strong relationships with intermediaries, such as agents, will help in meeting customer needs and serve them effectively.

The changing psychology, increasing expectations, rising income, the changing life styles, the increase in the number of private sector insurance companies and the changing need and requirements of customers make it as essential for the insurance companies to innovate their product mix.

The process involved in the insurance industry should be customer friendly. The speed and accuracy of payment is of vital importance. The processing methodology should be such that, it provided total ease and convenience to the customers. Installment schemes should also be streamed, to cater to growing demands of the customers and keep pace with the competition in the market. The new developments, which will smoothen the process flow, are Information Technology and data ware housing. Firstly, information technology will help in servicing large number of customers efficiently and bring down overheads. Technology can complement or supplement distribution channels cost effectively. It can also help improve customer service levels considerably. Secondly, the use of data warehousing, management and mining will help to gauge the profitability and potential of various customer and product segments. Understanding the customer better will allow insurance companies to design appropriate products, determine pricing correctly and increase profitability.

Customers are the main stake holders in business. Any business to thrive and survive competition should adopt a customer centric approach. Customer satisfaction should be the concern of every business even beyond product innovation and operational efficiency

Consumer today is unrelenting and demanding and is exposed to international quality due to the entry of Multinationals.. Therefore it has become imperative for the insurance providers to strategize its operations to deliver customer value greater than that provided by the competitors. They have to track the consumer behavior constantly and provide an optimal combination of the marketing mix factors.

The IRDA has notified *Protection of Policy holders Interest Regulation, 2001* to provide for: policy proposal documents in easily understandable language; claim procedure; setting up of grievance redressal machinery; speedy settlement of claims and policy holder's servicing..

In the competitive environment of the post-liberalization era insurance sector reforms have significantly deregulated the markets which in turn made it imperative to harness the best customer-oriented practices and perceptions and to internalize them for providing added- value to the customers.

INSURANCE OMBUDSMAN

The Grievance Redressal Cells established at various levels – (branch, divisional, zonal and central level), deal with the complaints of the customers. The Grievance Redressal Machinery has been further extended with appointment of the Insurance Ombudsman at different centers, by the Government of India

In order to bring about phenomenal value addition to the rights and privileges of the insurance consumers and to create a strong legal base to the policyholders so as to enforce their legitimate entitlement for relief or compensation in case they are affected due to deficiency in service received by them, the IRDA has appointed insurance Ombudsmen. . Complaints such as repudiation of liability under claims, delay in settlement of claims, disputes regarding premiums paid or payable in respect of policy and non issue of insurance document to customer after receipt of premium are dealt with, by the Ombudsman.

INSURANCE PROCESS

Characteristics of Insurance Process and Design Implementation

Divergence

Divergence is defined as the degree of variation from the established standards. In insurance companies, divergence is reflected in the degree of variation in the policies offered by the insurance company in its efforts to fulfill the unique choice of each customer.

Complexity

Complexity is measured in terms of the number of activities to be performed in producing and delivering a service. The activities must necessarily be those that contribute to service quality. Complexity increases with increasing divergence.

Service Location

An insurance policy can be made at a location of the customer's choice requiring the insurance agent to meet the customer at the specified location. It is also possible for the customer to take a policy at the insurer's office. In these days of online transactions, an insurance policy may also be sold over the internet in which case the. Point-of-Sale may be considered to have no physical existence.

Customer Participation

Customer participation forms the basis for process design. A customer's understanding of the process requirements makes him an active participant in the service delivery process. The quality of service is based on the customer's level of involvement. For example, the prospect has to accompany the agent for a medical examination at the doctor's place.

Contact

In the field of insurance, the level of customer contact will vary according to the mode of sale of the policy. There is a high level of customer contact in the sale of a policy by an agent, whereas there is absolutely no customer contact when the policy is offered online. The personal contact or rapport between two individuals plays a major role in contributing to service quality.

The Service

There are two types of services namely, process based service and technology or equipment based service

PROCESS-DEPENDENT SERVICE

Services that are process-dependent are more people-oriented and involve a greater level of personal contact and communication. In insurance the customer has to fill out numerous forms that subsequently go through various stages of authorization. The process-dependency of a service increases the number of contact points between the customer and the service provider. This in turn enables the service provider to deliver a quality product.

TECHNOLOGY OR EQUIPMENT BASED SERVICE

This type of service is fast to use and is marked by a low level of personal contact. The absence of personal contact hinders the delivery of personalized and customized service.

PROCESS PLANNING

Various types of resources like material, equipment and people are used in the process of insurance. There are several decisions that have to be taken by the manager of an insurance company in order to devise a process plan for delivering the insurance product.

Technology

The marketing manager has to make decisions regarding the technology that is to be used. The marketing manager also has to decide about the specific equipment that is to be for developing the insurance product and its delivery.

Process Selection

Decisions pertaining to the sequence of operations and the type of process to be used have to be made by the marketing manager before planning the insurance process.

Location and Layout Design

The insurer's office constitutes the 'place' element in the marketing mix. Layout refers to the interior arrangement within the office of the service provider. The layout of the office should be designed keeping in mind the type of process selected.

Organizational Structure

In an insurance company, decisions regarding the standardization or customization of the product (the insurance policy) have to be made while deciding the organizational structure.

In insurance company, just as in any other service company, the service quality is dependent on the performance of its employees. The marketing manager should therefore be capable of making realistic projections of the manpower requirements. He should be able to choose the right person having the right experience for the right job.

Insurance industry involves a high level of people interaction and hence using the employees effectively is essential, to satisfy customers and to have a competitive edge in the market. Training and development and building up strong relationships with the intermediaries are the two major areas that are to be taken care of, by the insurance companies. Training the employees to introduce them to new products, use of information technology for efficiency both at the staff and the agent's level or the distribution organizations, is the key area to be concentrated. Building strong relationship with intermediaries would enhance service quality.

PHYSICAL EVIDENCE IN LIFE INSURANCE MARKETING

Physical evidence is to a service what packaging is to a product. Physical evidence works as a silent salesman if it is used efficiently. It communicates service quality. Attributes and creates the service experience. It plays an important role in setting up the expectations of new customers and helping newly established insurance organizations to build a particular image. A well-planned, consistent physical evidence, that is compatible with service goals, helps in the performance and delivery of the service. It brings vitality and reinforcement to the marketing strategy. Unmanaged and inconsistent tangibles might bring a negative image to the positioning of the company, which will adversely affect the perceived value of the insurance service. In insurance marketing, both peripheral and essential evidences are significant as they tangibles the service. Peripheral evidence can be possessed as part of the service purchased since they can significantly supplement the core services sought.

It includes the physical environment, appearance of the tangible aspects such as policy papers in insurance. Customers expect that the insurance service provider, its employees, operational systems and physical resources have the requisite knowledge and skills to solve their problems in a professional way. In insurance marketing, both peripheral and essential evidences are significant as they tangibilise the service. Peripheral evidence can be possessed as part of the service purchased since they can significantly supplement the core services sought.

ELEMENTS OF PHYSICAL EVIDENCE IN INSURANCE

The major elements of physical evidence are physical environment, communications, price, personnel and corporate image and identity. The physical environment can be divided into two basic categories-Atmospherics and servicescapes. Atmospherics include ambient factors or background conditions that exist below the level of immediate awareness and typically draw customer's attention only when they are absent or unpleasant. However, they can also be used to create a positive image about the service in the customer's mind. Servicescapes is the physical environment in which the service is delivered and where the customer and the service providers interact. It has both exterior attributes (buildings, exterior design, parking, surroundings) and interior attributes (interior decor, layout, and equipment). (Insurance Marketing, 2002).

A detailed analysis on the literature available on the customer service of insurance companies is presented below:

According to Abhishek Agrawal (2002), customer relationships have to be taken care of by the life insurance companies in order to maintain the customer base on a long term basis. The insurers have to develop the infrastructure for the distribution of products, especially in the rural areas. Since the customers are becoming more net savvy and technology oriented, technology adoption should be the focus of the insurers, and they must start adopting Customer Relationship Management strategies.

Rudra Saibaba, *et.al.*, (2002), conducted a study on the perception and attitude of women towards life insurance policies. The outcome of the study was sale of life insurance policies was found to be easy in urban working class women; provision of life coverage by the policy was stated as the motivating factor for purchasing the policies followed by accidental coverage, availability of housing loan facility, safety investment and the income tax relief; Awareness about money back policy was more as compared to other policies and majority of the policyholders were satisfied with the services offered. It was suggested that, more training should be given to the agents and to introduce low premium but higher benefit policies.

Rengachary, N. (2003), has identified the challenges before the new insurance players to be: finding out the niche market, adopting the right product mix, effective branding and distribution. He has stated that, innovative marketing and distribution strategies such as work-site marketing, bancassurance should be followed by the insurers, keeping in mind the rapidly changing consumer profile. According to him, there is a huge opportunity in the rural market as well as in the pension sector.

Ravi Prakash, *et.al.,* (2003), have identified the challenges faced by the insurance sector to be: surrender of large number of policies; exit of dynamic managers to private sector; outdated products; difficulty in reaching out consumer expectations on par with the other insurance companies; provision of quality service; settlement of claims; issue of new policies; transfer and revival of policies and emerging distribution channels. It has been suggested that understanding the consumer better, selecting right type of distribution channel mix, effective Customer Relationship Management system and increase in customer base in semi-urban and rural areas would help to capture the untapped Indian market.

According to Rao, G.V. (2004), the customers of today are better educated about insurance, risk exposures, insurance pricing and claims settlement. Hence, they are more discriminating in their selection of the insurers. He has opined that, the insurers must concentrate on providing quality service to the customers .It was recommended to create customer profiles, segmented on the basis of profitability and to re-organize the structure and work procedures to build up intimacy and get closer to customers. .

According to Shikha Sharma (2004), the biggest beneficiary of the competition among the life insurers has been the customer. The privatization process has resulted in new levels of transparency and information sharing in product as well as the process. Hence, the life insurer must first analyze the needs of the customers and align his activities according to their needs. The challenge before the life insurers is to make the service a differentiating factor, through people and technology and to reconcile the business needs with the needs of the customers.

Anil Chandhok and Mittal,R.K. (2004), have conducted a research in order to find out the lapsing ratio of the various branches of Life Insurance Corporation of India, operating in the state of Haryana. They attempted to identify the reasons for the lapsing and to learn the impact of high lapsing ratio. The research revealed that, 20 per cent of the policies lapse within the first year itself. The authors are of the view that the high first year lapsing ratio highlights the fact that, more efforts are being made to procure new life insurance business, whereas adequate attention is not being paid towards the retention of the procured business. They are apprehensive that, the high first year lapsing rate would increase the overhead expenses and would affect the image of the insurer. As a concluding remark, the researchers have stated that the Life Insurance Corporation should strengthen its feedback mechanisms, identify the reasons for the high lapsing rate and adopt correct mechanisms to overcome the issue.

Shobit and Sanjay (2004), have tried to expose the reasons for failure of insurance players of private sectors in attaining a significant share in the rural market in this study. The findings of the study revealed that there is major difference in the objectives and expectations between rural and urban policyholders. In rural areas, private players have not been able to provide successfully the policies preferred by consumers having agriculture as their means of livelihood. In urban areas, consumers belonging to middle income group prefer policies of public sector players. The study also revealed that in urban areas, services provided at doorstep and efficient customer's service were the two major reasons which helped in market penetration by private players. But in rural sector there were major short comings in their products and services due to lack of popularity and mass appeal, expensive policies and high premiums, non-conformity in product differentiation and innovation. In conclusion the authors have said that, simple policies without any riders must be provided for rural consumers as they give more weightage to low premiums rather than extra benefits.

Tripathy, NP. (2004), has conducted a study called "An Application of Multidimensional Scaling Model towards Brand Positioning of Insurance Industries: A Study of Private Players" with the following objectives: to find out the perception of customers towards insurance companies through marketing variables; to analyze the preference of customers and the importance they assign to different attributes; to examine the satisfaction level of respondent customers and agents regarding customer services offered by the company; and to determine the position of different companies in the minds of the people. The finding of the study is given as follows: investors like to invest in private insurance companies because they are provided with a choice of products, servicing of policy and claims settlement. Among sources of awareness for investments majority of the investors preferred to use financial journals and business magazines for investment decisions. High reputation and good customer relationship management are the important criteria for influencing investment decisions in insurance. High degree of investors is dissatisfied due to non-availability of flexible mode of premium payment through credit cards, smart cards, internet etc. The author concludes that, to achieve greater insurance penetration, private sector insurance companies have to create a more vibrant and competitive industry, with greater efficiency, choice of products and value for customers.

Vijayakumar, A. (2004), has categorically stated that, the ever- increasing demand for the pension plans, assigning right type of policy to the policy holders after carefully assessing the profile of the customers, awareness created among the consumers about the availability of the policies, introduction of innovative policies to tap huge resources have been the emerging areas in the insurance sector. The success of the insurance companies would depend upon meeting the rising expectations of the consumers since the consumer is the real king in the liberalized market, he has suggested.

Bodla, B.S. and Sushma Rani Verma (2004), have conducted a study to examine the preference of the policy holders towards various types of policies and to probe into the reasons behind the insurance purchase in rural areas. Two hundred policy holders were taken for the study. The major findings were: risk coverage and future contingencies were the main reasons for purchasing life insurance policies; Life Insurance Corporation had the major market share among various life insurance players; money back policy was the most preferred followed by Jeevan Anand; advertisements didn't have much impact and the women segment was still untapped.

Kumar Jagendra (2005), has categorically stated that life insurance penetration is just above two per cent of Gross Domestic Product and the life insurance premium per capita is just five rupees and fifty paise only. Life Insurance Corporation has been identified as the largest player which has improved its efficiency and customer service after liberalisation. Among the private life insurance companies ICICI Prudential Life Insurance Company has been identified as the best, followed by Birla Sun Life, Bajaj Allianz and HDFC Standard Life.

Vinayagamoorthi, A. and Gopi. R. (2005), have stated that radical changes have taken place in customer profile due to the changing life style and social perception resulting in erosion of brand loyalty. Higher customer aspirations lead to new expectations and compel him to move towards the insurer who provides him the best services. To survive, the focus of the modern insurers is to be shifted from mass marketing paradigm to a customer-centric relationship. It has been suggested that the insurer has to design the products which would satisfy the emerging needs of the customers and proper awareness should be created among the rural mass, of the new and innovative life insurance products.

Rajesh, C. Jampala and Venkateswara Rao. B.H. (2005), have identified product benefits, competitive premiums, product differentiation through promotion and claim settlement to be the key success factors of the insurance sector .According to them, claim settlement is the major factor for the success of Life Insurance Corporation. They have also felt that its claim settlement operations are fair and transparent. The corporation has been prompt in settling the claims due to excellent corporate image in the insurance sector.

Prakasa Rao, B.K.S., and Venkateswara Rao (2005), have examined the opportunities for the insurers in the rural market. According to them, majority of the rural population is left uncovered, a small bundle of innovative products designed to suit the rural needs and perceptions and an efficient delivery system would help in penetrating into the vast rural markets. They have also stated that, the establishment of micro branches and the appointment of specialized insurance agents would help the insurance companies to create awareness among the people and to induce them to buy the policies.

According to Gopal, V.V. (2005), Customer Relationship Management is a vital tool used to enhance business experience and service through intermediaries. For an insurance company to survive in the competitive world, to succeed and gain, a customer centric approach is essential. The customer has to be treated as a king since he provides sustenance to the whole organization. In order to be successful, Customer Relationship Management technique should be adopted in respect of product promotion, dissemination of information and delivery of service.

According to Jawaharlal, U and Sarthak Kumar Rath (2005), building good relationship with the customers, offering efficient and excellent services leading to customer satisfaction and increased profits are the major challenges insurers face today. The author is of the opinion that, Customer Relationship Management can help to develop more profitable and long–term customer relationships by addressing various customers – centric areas, such as unified customer view; integrated multi-channel customer sales and services; targeted marketing and customer loyalty. The benefits of applying Customer Relationship Management are identified as optimizing selling strategy that helps in accurate forecasting of customer behaviour and better territory management. The author has also suggested that, insurance companies in India have to take a lead to use Customer Relationship Management technology as a decision making tool. Information technologies should support the real-time integration between various intermediaries in an insurance process including the customer.

Ravi Kumar Sharma (2005), made an empirical study on Insurance perspective in eastern Uttar Pradesh with the following objectives: to study the awareness among the rural and urban population; to study the comparative reach of different advertising and promotional medias being used by the insurance selling companies; to study the relative brand awareness or top of mind recall by the respondents; to study the insurance product awareness and the insurance agents' performance in different areas; to analyze the relative faith of the private and public insurance players in the rural mass and in the urban populations and to probe into the reasons or the casual factors behind the insurance product purchase. Eight hundred and ninety four respondents were taken for the study and the major findings were: majority of the policy holders were aware of life insurance; Life Insurance Corporation was the most preferred followed by ICICI Prudential Life Insurance Company; Television and newspaper were identified to be the major sources of information; Life Insurance Corporation agents were more active followed by ICICI Prudential Life Insurance Company's agents; future security and uncertainty of life were the most prominent reasons for purchasing the policy. The author has suggested that the private players have to inculcate a private culture and faith among the public in order to reach the rural market.

Nalini Prava Tripathy (2006), conducted a study on the topic "An Application of factor analysis approach towards designing insurance products in India." The objectives of the study have been to examine the customers' preference and priorities towards various insurance products, to identify the key features of insurance products and services attributes that are essential in the purchase decision of the customers and to suggest some measures to design the products that will satisfy the personal needs of the customers. It was revealed that, factors such as awareness of the product, service behaviour, advertisement, product feature and safety of the scheme played a major role in influencing the behaviour of the customers. The researcher has suggested that, the insurance companies should concentrate on the personnel procedure and the process in order to lure customers towards them.

Namasivayam, N. *et.al.*, (2006), conducted a study on the topic "Socio-economic Factors Influencing the Decision in Taking Life Insurance Policies", with the objective of analyzing the socioeconomic factors that are responsible for taking life insurance policies, examining the preferences of the policyholders towards various types of policies of Life Insurance Corporation and to offer suggestions for popularizing life insurance policies among the public. The major findings of the study stated that socioeconomic factors such as age, education, income, sex and family size of the policyholders played a major role making the purchase decision of life insurance policies of Life Insurance Corporation.

Kishore, R.B. (2006), has stated in his article that it is essential that a sizeable cake of premium is garnished from affluent segments. This segment is soaked in prosperity and hence any sensible marketer would ensure prospecting such rich harvests well before competitor agent or advisor arrives. The whole topography of insurance prospecting is changing with so many indicators, lifestyles, migration, financial instruments leading to a shift in various parameters. A few private insurance companies are also embarking on an aggressive rural thrust now, as they see good dividends to be reaped in the years to come, instead of merely sticking to Insurance Regulatory and Development Authority (IRDA) stipulations in terms of rural coverage.

Rajesh, C. Jampala (2006), has stated that life and non-life insurance premiums in emerging markets have grown annually, due to strong economic growth, increased stability, good regulatory mechanisms, adaptation of international best practices, innovative product offerings and new distribution channels in emerging markets by insurers. The author has identified the trends of the emerging markets to be: high economic growth; increase in competition; higher penetration of foreign players, and consolidation in some fragmented markets. He has stated that, improving economic fundamentals, rising income levels, more competition, introduction of new products and distribution systems are helping insurers to ride to the boom. He has suggested that in order to get higher growth and sustain this momentum, insurers will have to understand market dynamics.

Vinayagamurthy, A. (2006), is of the opinion that, in order to achieve a competitive edge over the other life insurance players, the company should standardize the process and bring about quality improvement and get feedback from the customers regarding the quality of service rendered .According to the author, the modern approach adopted by the insurance players comprises, market research, segmenting, targeting and positioning, focusing on the marketing mix, implementation and control. The service standards vary, based on the intermediary involved in the process. Therefore, providing quality service would help in the customer acquisition and customer satisfaction, he has stated.

According to Subrahamanya Sarma, M. and Kalyani, .V (2006), Customer Relationship Management is a comprehensive approach for creating, maintaining and expanding customer relationship. Life Insurance Corporation has a focused, committed strategy in providing quality service to policy holders. A well developed system with latest technologies such as internet, touch screen, kiosks, green channel and e-mail has been adopted to enhance corporation's ability to serve the policy holders. The authors have suggested that segmenting the available costumer information would help in targeting new customer prospects.

According to Samuel, B. Sekar (2006), the involvement of the customers in the conception phase makes an innovation demand driven, which focuses more on customers social and economic relationship. According to him, a company can enhance its innovation by building strong relationship with the insurer; expanding the business relationship to reach competitor's customers, through competitive services and innovative solutions and looking for opportunities to reach the unmet needs of the uninsured population. He has categorically stated that, the companies would be able to recoup the time and money they have spent on learning about customers, if the innovations are patented.

Rajesham, Ch. and Rajender, K. (2006), have stated that, quality based timely customer services, focus on health insurance, services through innovative products, smart marketing and aggressive distribution with internet facility, transparency and flexibility to increase the quality and volume of insurance business would bring success, to the insurance companies.

Knowing the customer enables the insurer to understand the exact needs of the customer in promoting and delivering the products says Samuel, .B. Sekar, (2007), in his article "Know your policy holder". He also says that it helps in developing a deeper understanding of customer's intention to avail insurance service. Networking through computers has made it possible for the insurers to access information about the claims of the customers and to exchange information about the customers. He further states that monitoring and surveillance of customers has become easy with arrival of information technology.

Paromita Goswami (2007), in the paper titled "Customer satisfaction with service quality in the Life Insurance Industry in India" has stressed on the implementation of Customer Relationship Management as it would help to acquire new customers as well as to retain the old customer. It is said that improved customer satisfaction would also result in positive word-of-mouth and consequently better customer acquisition and retention. It was found that the responsiveness dimension of service quality provides maximum customer satisfaction in the life insurance industry.

The research done by Capgemini and European Financial Management and Marketing Association (2007), reveals the key themes that, customers insist on competitive pricing and see product specifications and quality advice as differentiators. Insurers and distributors can benefit from knowing their customers better – a step that will improve their ability to more effectively meet their needs and to attain profitable growth. To drive profitable growth, the study prescribes that; insurers need to be more effective in aligning their pricing and product strategies with the needs of their target customers, while enabling their distribution network's capabilities accordingly. Insurers can optimize distributor strategy by proactively seeking to retain and attract quality distributors, enable distributors to function more effectively, integrate distributors more deeply in to the enterprise, and build an enterprise view of the customer.

Shilpi Malaiya and Jain, V.K. (2007), in their article entitled, "A study of policy purchasing behaviour and situations for settlement of claims – A customer's perspective" have stated that, the settlement of claims constitutes one of the important functions in an insurance organization. Indeed the payment of claims may be regarded as the primary service of insurance to the public. The proper settlement of claim requires the sound knowledge of the terms and condition of the standard policies and various extensions and modifications under them. The study concluded that there is no significant difference between the various insurance policies. Almost everyone prefers to have insurance cover and also suggest to others to have it. Finally, it was concluded that, all insurance policy buyers have the same buying pattern and they prefer buying insurance policies because it is useful and reduces uncertainty by providing risk sharing.

Nalini Prava Tripathy (2007), in her article, "Brand Positioning of Insurance Industries – A study on Private Players" has categorically stated that, insurance industry in India has undergone a sea change in terms of delivering value-added services to the rising consumerism in India. A wide range of products customer – focused service and professional advice has become the mainstay of the industry. Thus in this context, priorities, preferences and brand positioning of insurance products have become essential for customers and insurance companies as well. The study has been undertaken with the object of identifying the perception of customers towards insurance company, to examine the satisfaction level of customers and agents regarding customer service offered by company and to determine the position that different insurance companies gained in the minds of people. It is observed from the study that, majority of investors like to invest in private sector companies, and the two factors such as high reputation and good customer relationship were the important criteria for investing in insurance companies. As the market moves from an emerging to an emerged, a change in approach is necessary. To achieve greater insurance penetration, private sector insurance companies are to create a more vibrant and competitive industry, with greater efficiency, choice of products and value to customers.

Amita Fatterpeker (2007), has categorically stated that, personal relationships, product quality, customer service, price and other brand values enable insures to retain their customers. Relationship with the customers can be enhanced, by prioritizing the company's strategies and operational goals, focusing on the issues most important to customer satisfaction and fine-tuning the sales messaging to reflect customer issues. So also being aware of the current level of customer satisfaction and discovering areas of concern. The author has suggested that, in order to further their own goals that would have a distinct advantage over the other companies, the insurance companies should pro-actively measure the success of its relationship with the customers.

Sheela. P. and Arti, G. (2007), conducted a study to know the awareness level of the customers regarding life insurance policies; the relative preference of products offered by life insurance companies and to know why customers purchased life insurance policies and from which company they purchased the policies. The study revealed that, though majority of the respondents were of life insurance policies and it's significance; only 41.7 per cent of them had purchased their policies; majority of the policy holders had purchased the policies only because of the saving element associated with the policies; in spite of the drastic changes that have taken place in the distribution channels, the sales agents continued to be the primary means of selling the policies and there was tremendous scope for life insurance companies to create awareness among the public. It has been suggested that the insurance companies must try more to identify the needs and wants of the customers.

Ramkumar, D (2007), has stated that Relationship Marketing plays a vital role in providing easy-to- apply solutions and strategies for establishing meaningful bonds with customers and turning them into reliable life-long partners. According to the author, the important objectives of relationship marketing have been, to acquire new customers, maintain and enhance relationship with existing customers reactivation of ex-customers and handling of customer terminations. Developing a clear and holistic vision of all stakeholder relationships, coordinating the relationship marketing strategy and customizing it, providing a consistent customer experience through multiple contact points building better relationships through data base and initiating effective change management processes that involve all employees in an internal partnership have been cited as the best relationship marketing practices.

The issue of consumer awareness has a deeper significance in emerging markets as economic growth outweighs the social growth due to absence of awareness levels on the financial tools like life insurance, states Prabhakara, G (2007), in his article entitled, "Creating consumer awareness- Life insurance". The author has opined that, the life insurance market is gradually transforming itself by attaching priority to capital market- linked products over the traditional endowment products. Hence, creating awareness of the various products has become essential. The role of intermediaries in creating awareness is paramount, as these advisors identify and meet the prospects at their doorsteps and render invaluable services, the author has stated.

Rajendra Prasad, T. (2007), in his article entitled, "Emergence of new players in Indian insurance sector" has stated that, the higher standards set by the private players in the customer service, quick dissemination of information through web sites, speedy processing of applications, making the premium payment easier, provision of quality training to the agents, introduction of innovative customer friendly products, usage of print and electronic media have enhanced the private players and help them to increase their business.

Hasanbanu, S and Nagajothi, R.S. (2007), have conducted a study on the insurance perspective in Uthamapalayam Taluk with the following objectives: to study the insurance perspective of the people of Uthamapalayam Taluk on the Life Insurance Corporation; to study the socio-economic profile of the policy holders who take insurance policies and their level of investment with the Life Insurance Corporation; to study the attitude of policy holders towards the Life Insurance Corporation and to offer suggestions and recommendations to improve the life insurance business. One hundred respondents were taken for the study and with regard to the attitude of the policy holders towards Life Insurance Corporation. It was found that faith in the company was ranked first followed by increasing investment habit, risk coverage, consideration of future security and uncertainty of life, fewer formalities, easy to take loan, easy payment of premium, tax savings, familiarity, attractive bonus, good customer service and compulsion by agent. The authors have suggested that transparency of product terms and conditions, simple for public to understand, arrangement of meetings to popularize their schemes among public; easy disposal of claims; to provide more training for agents; to build consumer awareness and confidence among public; to advertise through various mass media and implement Customer Relationship Management, would yield better results.

Reddy, C.R. and Vidyasagar Reddy (2008), have examined the reforms adopted in the insurance market with particular reference to Life Insurance Corporation of India. According to the authors, life insurance business should focus on Customer Relationship Management, diversification and globalization with new technologies so that the schemes of Life Insurance Corporation of India become more marketable for the development of the human asset. Hence, re-engineering human resource development for growth and services of life insurance business is an ingredient. Finally, it is said that, competence should not be associated with competition but for outcome of social welfare, nation-building and human resource development.

Gopala Krishna, G (2008), categorically states that the insurance companies must radically change their business patterns and revamp their organizational structure to meet and suit the present-day demands and expectations of the customers. The customer composite should be the cornerstone of an overall company strategy designed to gain a competitive market advantage. According to the author, Customer Relationship Management could be used as a building block to develop strategies based on four important areas such as value propositions, customer segmentation, service delivery models and marketing at a one to one level. Customer Relationship Management has been viewed by the author as a practical solution to the clamoring demands by the customers for a higher grade of insurance service. The study conducted with a view to find out the success of bancassurance revealed that nearly 90 per cent of the respondents expected an increase in new business income to the extent of at least 75 per cent, from the bancassurance channel. The survey further revealed that the quality of customer data was to be improved and the absence of simple Customer Relationship Management techniques made it difficult to launch special initiatives to cross sell insurance products.

According to Bala Krishnamohan, R. and Muralidhar,K. (2008), the key factor distinguishing the multinational companies from others is the sophisticated customer service standards and practices. Life insurance is a service business that requires customer centric processes such as online linking of the various distribution channels; online help desks and communication assistance to respond to the demanding customer and his information requirements; net working of various offices and transmission of information and controlling costs. It has been remarked that Customer Relationship Management revolutionizes the business and the customer service approach and leads to the success of the business. Life insurance is highly data dependent and hence, the low penetration of insurance, increase in the number of products, complexity of pre and post sales operations such as generating product awareness, policy management, claims management etc., have necessitated the application of Customer Relationship Management. The authors have opined that, Customer Relationship Management is essential to have a competitive edge over the competitors on-line linking of various alternative channels to respond to the queries of the customers, to network the various offices and to control cost.

Rao, G.V. (2008), has stated that today's customers are more demanding, seeking lower prices, wider coverage and quicker settlement of claims. Buying insurance is seen as one big option to seek financial protection against uncertain events. Innovations both in marketing management and strategic leadership to guide it need fresh thinking on retail consumers' needs. New marketing strategies and introduction of new products to suit the particular needs of broader sections of the retail customers are essential to broaden the customer base. The insurers have to review their current business plans and strategies as to how closer they could come to the retail customers through the agency force, he has suggested.

Sri Jyothi, T. (2008), has analyzed the Customer Relationship Management strategies adopted by the insurance companies. The author has stated that, identification of potential customers, understanding their needs and preferences are the requirements of Customer Relationship Management. The following suggestions have been made by the author for the successful implementation of Customer Relationship Management strategies: providing training to the agents in order to improve their competencies; offering varied policies to suit the varying demands of customers; providing web portals for easy facilitation of online payments, settlement of claims, account details and so on.

Amit Shrivastava, *et al.*, (2008), have examined the effect of demographical element in consumer behaviour in the life insurance industry. Factors such as age, gender, marital status and income level play a significant role in the purchase pattern of the policy holders. The findings were: 75 per cent of the male respondents and 66 per cent of the female respondents preferred to buy their policies from Life Insurance Corporation than from any other company; business men had 75 per cent preference for Life Insurance Corporation while policy holders employed in the service sector had 80 per cent preference since they believed that, Life Insurance Corporation was more secure than any other company. It was recommended that companies dealing in life insurance should give emphasis on demographic elements to grab the opportunity available in the life insurance sector.

Gregory A. Kuhlemeyer and Garth, H. Allen (2008), have categorically stated that, trust, competence and product appropriateness play an integral part in customer satisfaction. Customer satisfaction with the life insurance purchase is primarily a function of the trust the consumer has, in the agent or the insurance company, the consumer's perception about the agents' competence, the product selected by the consumer, the consumer analysis or feeling regarding the financial safety and consumer goals. The survey conducted by them revealed the following facts: Two predominant forms of life insurance products owned by the customers were term and whole life insurance; consumers who owned term insurance policies were more satisfied than the whole life policy holders; satisfaction of their life insurance company differed somewhat with consumers who purchased products directly from the company; those consumers who purchased their policies directly and through an agent owned a greater variety of products.

The paper entitled "A study on the consumer preference and comparative analysis of life insurance companies" by Devasenathipathi, *et al.*, (2008), point out that with the entry of private players in life insurance the industry has become competitive. Both the public and private companies offer a wider choice in terms of products and services, and the awareness created among the public about the benefits and significance of insurance. It has been suggested that the private companies should reduce their premiums and increase the returns in the process of building their brand image.

Mckinsey and Company (2008), report has identified factors such as strong growth potential for the market, an unmet need for long term savings products, popularity of life insurance due to the perception of that it is a low risk and high return investment, rapid growth in household income leading to higher penetration of financial services, new distinct customer segments and emergence of rural India as an attractive opportunity, to be the factors contributing to the growth of the life insurance industry. The report has suggested that making available tailored products to suit the requirements of the customers and the distribution mode that would serve the low income urban segments and the agency channel more professional, targeting self-directed customers through a direct channel and applying potential innovative models for life insurers would help the players to survive in the ever competing insurance market.

According to Ghodeswar, B.M. (2008), the key success factors in insurance market in India have been: understanding the customer in a better way, designing appropriate products, determining the right price for the products, offering better quality service, and customer satisfaction exert a strong influence on purchase intentions. Therefore, identifying the attributes that influence the customers' perception of service quality is essential. Expected returns of the policy, fringe benefits offered by the service provider, quality of service rendered and the company's reputation play a major role in influencing customers' purchase decisions. Excellent service enables the company to increase customer satisfaction and retention and hence, companies should build capabilities, skills and resources that offer superior value to the customers in order to delight the customers, the author has suggested.

As stated in article in Asia Insurance post (2008), innovations have come not only in the form of benefits attached to the products but also in the delivery mechanisms which have emanated from various marketing tie-ups. Unit-linked insurance products provide liquidity, flexibility and transparency. Life insurance companies have been quick to recognize the huge need for structured retirement plans.

Customer satisfaction is the agent's continuing challenge since retention of customers is vital for long term growth states Ramamurthy, P., (2008), in his article, "Selling life insurance art or science?." The author is of the opinion that, apart from the regular prospecting of customers the agent has to take up tasks such as, developing and presenting an appropriate plan for the prospects, implementing the plan and rendering after sales services. Thorough knowledge of the plans and identifying the needs and convincing the prospect are essential. Hence, life insurance selling is an art as well as science, he has concluded.

Giresh Kumar, G.S. and Eldhose, KV. (2008), have undertaken a case study on the topic, "Customer perceptions on Life Insurance services- A Comparative study", with a view to compare the knowledge level of customers about the insurance products, service quality and to know the problems confronted by the customers across public and private sectors. The Life Insurance Corporation and the ICICI Prudential Life Insurance Company were selected for the purpose of the study. The major findings were: The awareness level of the customers on various aspects of insurance products in the public sector is far better than the private sector; Public sector organization provides better quality services to the customers than the private players; hidden charges, delay in the settlement of claims misleading information from the agents were the problems with the private sector; dissatisfaction over the grievance redressal mechanism adopted by the public sector organization. However, it has been pointed out that the rationale behind investments in life insurance policies is the same in both the sectors. The author has suggested that fostering a true service culture, empowerment of customers and adopting a fundamental outside-in approach would enhance the qualitative development of the business.

REFERENCES

1. Mishra, M.N. (1979), Insurance – Principles and Practices. New Delhi : S.Chand & Company Ltd. p.5.
2. Motihar, M. (2004), Insurance Principles, Practices, Management and Salesmanship. Allahabad: Sharda Pustak Bhawan. p. 7.
3. *Ibid.*, p.7
4. Periyasamy, P. (2005), Principles and Practice of Insurance. Mumbai: Himalaya Publishing House. p.27
5. Motihar, M. (2004), Insurance Principles, Practices, Management and Salesmanship. Allahabad: Sharda Pustak Bhawan. p. 52.
6. Huebner (1995). Quoted in Insurance Industry in New Millennium (A Case of LIC: Challenges and Response) by Sushil Chandra Pal, (2007). New Delhi: Rajat Publications. p. 6
7. Sushil Chandra Pal (2007). Insurance Industry in New Millennium (A Case of LIC: Challenges and Response). New Delhi : Rajat Publications. p. 7
8. Ray, R.M. (1941). Quoted in Insurance Industry in New Millennium (A Case of LIC: Challenges and Response) by Sushil Chandra Pal, (2007). New Delhi: Rajat Publications. p. 9
9. LICI, Branch Managers' Training Course (1964). Quoted in Insurance Industry in New Millennium (A Case of LIC : Challenges and Response) by Sushil Chandra Pal, (2007). New Delhi : Rajat Publications. p.9.
10. www.irdaindia.org, accessed December 20, 2007
11. www.idil.com/insurance.html, accessed March 27, 2009
12. www.irdaindia.org, accessed March 27, 2008
13. Mishra, K.C. and Simita Mishra (2000). Global Insurance Market structure. *The Journal of the Management accountant*, 35(3), 23.
14. Shesha Ayyar (2000), Insurance Reforms – What are the implications. *The Journal of Insurance Institute of India*, 15, 63.
15. Stuart Purdy (2003), Huge opportunity. *IRDA Journal,* 2(1),30.
16. Tarun Kapoor (2003), Issues and challenges facing the insurance industry. *The journal of Insurance watch*, 2(5), 25.
17. Swiss Reinsurance Company (2003), *The journal of Insurance Chronicle,* 3(12), 25.
18. Sunder Ram Korivi (2004), Insurance sector in India. Challenges ahead. *The journal of Insurance chronicle*, 4(1), 39.
19. Anil Chandok (2005), A comparative study of the performance of life insurance players. *The journal of Insurance Chronicle*, 5(4), 75-77.
20. Rajesh, C. Jampala. and Polavarapu Adilakshmi (2006), Scale up for Success-The Mantra for Private Insurance in India. *The journal of Insurance Chronicle*, 6(11), 26-31.
21. Geethanjali Mehlwal (2006), The face of the Insurance Industry in India. *The journal of Insurance chronicle*, 6(1), 59-64.
22. Kishore, R.B. (2006), A Holistic view of the Insurance Reforms and a Blue print for strengthening LIC. *The Journal of Insurance Institute of India*, 38, 35.
23. Richard Holloway and Rajagopalan Krishnamurthy (2006), Insuring rural India. *The journal of Insurance Chronicle*, 6(12), 47-51.

24. Pillai, VNS. (2007), Simple Approach to Life Insurance and Pension- When I am not there – While I'm there. *The journal of Insurance Chronicle*, 7(2), 23-28.

25. Siva Kumar Singh, Kushendra Mishra and Sanjay, M. Bhale (2007), Insurance Industry: A Changing Scenario. *The journal of Insurance Chronicle*, 7(3), 19.

26. India's share of world insurance rises. *The Economic Times*, June 2008.

27. Mckinsey and Co. (2008), Report on Indian Life Insurance. *The journal of Yogashema,* 52(1), 9-11.

28. American Marketing Association (1960), Report of the definitions committee of the American Marketing Association. Chicago, p.13.

29. Kotler, P. and Armstrong, G (1996). Quoted in Marketing Management – Concepts and Practice by Chhabra, T.N. and Grover, S.K. (1999). New Delhi : Dhanpat Rai & Co. p.7.5

30. William J. Stanton, Michael J. Etzel and Bruce J. Welker, (1994). Quoted in Marketing Management – Concepts and Practice by Chhabra, T.N. and Grover, S.K. (1999). New Delhi : Dhanpat Rai & Co. p.7.5

31. Jha, S.M., (2003). Services Marketing, Mumbai : Himalaya Publishing House, p. 164.

32. Stanton, (1994), Fundamentals of Marketing. New York: Mc Graw Hill Road, Company, p.662.

33. Philip Kotler (2005). Marketing Management, Analysis, Planning and control. New Delhi: Prentice-Hall of India. p.59.

34. Bodla, B.S., Garg, M.C. and Singh, K.P. (2003), Insurance – Fundamentals, Environment and Procedures, New Delhi : Deep & Deep Publications Pvt. Ltd., p.123,124

35. Life Insurance Guide, 2007, Mumbai: Insurance Institute of India. pp.66-71.

36. Layman's Guide to Life Insurance, 2008, New Delhi : Outlook Publishing (India) Private Limited, pp.104-109.

37. Life Insurance Guide, 2007, Mumbai: Insurance Institute of India. p.69

38. Sushil Chandra Pal (2007), Insurance Industry in New Millennium (A Case of LIC: Challenges and Response). New Delhi : Rajat Publications.

39. Sesha Ayyar (1999), New Insurance products in the next century. *The Journal of Insurance Institute of India*, 21(1), 47-50.

40. Narayanan Krishnamurthy (2000), From the Sidelines. *Advertising and Marketing Journal*, 18(5), 110.

41. Vijay Srinivasa, K.B. (2000), How returns linked insurance products can be popularize. *The Journal of Insurance Institute of India*, 12, 67.

42. Neelam Jain (2000), Liberalisation of Insurance in India: Opportunities and Challenges. *The journal of Southern Economist*, 39(3), 7-11.

43. Alok Mittal and Akash Kumar (2001), An Exploratory Study of Factors Affecting Selection of Life Insurance Products. *The journal of Insurance Chronicle*, 1(4), 23.

44. Shesha Ayyer, V. (2002), Life Insurance in India: Opportunities, challenges and pitfall. *The journal of Insurance Chronicle*, 2(11), 57-61.

45. Shikha Sharma (2002), Changing face of Life Insurance in India. *The journal of Insurance chronicle*, 2(12), 41-43.

46. Rao, R.V.S. (2003), Life Insurance Private Players' initiatives. *The Hindu Survey of Indian Industry,* 78.

47. Shobhit and Sanjay (2004), An Empirical study and analysis of failure of private players rural areas. *The journal of Insurance chronicle*, 4(5), 30-32.
48. Gupta, P.K. (2004), Pricing of insurance products- actuarial to managerial. *The Management Accountan,* 39(2), 96-101.
49. Rajat Gera (2004), Life Insurance Marketing in India – The missing product. *The journal of Insurance watch,* 2(6), 25.
50. Stuart Purdy (2004), Selling Insurance Products – A challenge for players. *The Hindu Survey of Indian Industry*, 73.
51. Jawaharlal, U. (2005), Indian Life Insurance Industry – A retrospect. *The journal of Insurance chronicle*, 5 (9), 15-17.
52. Manchanda, S.M. (2005), Importance of the Need to Cover the Death Risk. *The journal of Insurance Chronicle*, 5(9), 23-28.
53. Darling Selvi, V. (2005), Insurance Industry – A source for investment and employment. *Kissan World*, 32(12), 15-16.
54. Life Insurance Marketing in India. The Changing Product & Pricing Norms. (2005), Case Studies in Insurance. Hyderabad : ICFAI Centre for management Research, 109-121.
55. Krishna Kumar and Kannan, R. (2005), LIC – Countering threat from private players. *The journal of Insurance Chronicle*, 5(2), 24-26.
56. Anand Adhikari (2005), Five Years After Privatisation. *The journal of Business Today*, 25(8), 110-112.
57. Srinivas, S.S. and Anand, V. (2005), Unit Linked Investor Guidance Note. *The journal of Insurance chronicle*, 5(12), 42-51.
58. Ramakrishna Rao, T.S. (2006), Unit Linked Insurance Product – The Big Leap. *The journal of Insurance Chronicle,* 6(3), 15-18.
59. Jawaharlal, U. (2006), Indian Insurance Industry – A comprehensive Analysis. *The journal of Insurance Chronicle, 6(5),* 61-65.
60. Rajesham, Ch. and Rajender, K. (2006), Changing Scenario of Indian Insurance Sector. *Indian Journal of Marketing*, 36(7), 9-15.
61. Rao, C.S. (2007), Indian Insurance Industry- A Remarkable journey. *The journal of Insurance Chronicle,* 7(8), 32.
62. Vasantha, P. (2008), Life Insurance – The Hot Investment. *HRD Times*, 20-21.
63. Dilip Maitra (2008), Life insurance is essential for everyone. *The journal of Banking and Finance, 5(3), 22.*
64. Anuradha Sharma (2008), Life insurance evaluation and current perspectives. *The journal of Asia Insurance Post*, 8(9), 22-25
65. RNCOS (2008), *Indian Insurance Industry Forecast 2007-2009*. Accessed 18 September 2008. http://www.mcos.com/2008.
66. Jean Pierre Lepaud (2008), Unit linked business.product development. *IRDA journal*, 5(2), 12-13.
67. Sharma, NC. (2008), Performance Paradox. *The journal of Asia Insurance Post*, 8(6), 21-23.
68. Jawaharlal, U. (2008), Providing product flexibility. Riders in insurance. *IRDA journal*, 6(11), 6.

69. Samuel, B Sekar (2008), Indian Insurance Industry poised for growth. *The journal of Insurance Chronicle*, 8(6), 39-45.

70. Snekha Shukla (2008), Insuring the bottom of the pyramid. *The journal of Insurance Chronicle*, 8(9), 27-29.

71. Chhabra, T.N. and Grover, S.K. (1999). Marketing Management – concepts and Practice. New Delhi : Dhanpat Rai & Co. p.5.11

72. American Marketing Association (1960), Report of the definitions committee of the American Marketing Association. Chicago, p.13.

73. Marketing Study course, The Chartered Insurance Institute, 2000,

74. Insurance Marketing (2002). Hyderabad: ICFAI Centre for Management Research. 196.

75. Shekar Chandra Sahoo (1999), Future Marketing strategies for Life Insurance. *The Journal of Insurance Industry of India*, 13, 81-84.

76. Shikha Sharma (2002), Life insurance – The challenges ahead – Paper presented at the 7th Insurance Summit 2002 – "Deepening Penetration from 1.5 per cent to 5 per cent" conducted by Confederation of Indian Industry.

77. Hydrey, A. Rehmanjee (2002), The challenges before insurers today. *The journal of Insurance chronicle*. 2(12), 64-65.

78. Madhusudana Rao., et al., (2002), Job satisfaction of employees- A survey of LIC employees. *Indian Journal of Marketing*, 32(10), 28-34.

79. Subhash Lakhotia (2003), How to sell more life insurance products. The *journal of Insurance watch.*, 3(5), 26.

80. Mony, S.V. (2003), Life insurance private players Initiatives. *The Hindu Survey of Indian Industry*, 78-80.

81. Ramamurthy, A. (2003), LIC Advantage of strong base. *The Hindu Survey of Indian Industry*, 81.

82. Ranjan Kumar and Koushal Vaidhya (2004), Differentiation strategies of Insurance companies. *The journal of Insurance Chronicle*, 4(3), 27.

83. Jawaharlal, U. and Kumar, K.B.S. (2004), Branding Insurance: An Indian Perspective. *The journal of Insurance Chronicle*, 4(12), 23.

84. Federation of Indian Chambers of Commerce. 2004.

85. Effectiveness of Symbols and Ideas in Advertising Insurance Products (2005). Case Studies in Insurance. Hyderabad : ICFAI Centre for Management Research. 187.

86. Life Insurance Marketing in India (A) The Changing Advertising and Promotion Norms (2005), A private insurance advisor in 2001. Case Studies in Insurance, Hyderabad : ICFAI Centre for Management Research, p. 81.

87. Mittal, R.K. and Anil Chandhok (2005), Privatisation of Life Insurance Services in India – Impact and Perspective. *The journal of Insurance chronicle*, 5(3), 24.

88. Rajesh, J. Jampala and Venkateswara Rao, C. (2005), Sales promotion in the insurance sector. A Study of L.I.C . *The journal of Insurance chronicle*, 5(4), 48-50.

89. Kaushlendra Maurya (2005), Business Strategies and I.T. solutions. *The journal of Insurance Chronicle*, 5(3), 62-68.

90. Alagar, R. (2005), Retailing with Supply Chain Management. *The journal of Insurance Watch*, 3(4), 50.51.

91. Stephen Wylie (2005), Agency Management Trends. *Insurance Watch*, 3(7)), 42-43.
92. Nitin Tanted (2006), Growth and survival strategy for Indian Insurance companies in the era of emerging global competition. Accessed 20 March 2008. http://www.indianmba.com/Faculty - Column/FC349/fc349.html
93. Bijal Mehta. and Shubhra Anand (2007), Study of the Need Analyser Tools used by LIC for the insurance markets. *The journal of Insurance Chronicle*, 7(4), 66-74.
94. Chinnadorai, K.M., Kalpana, B. and Sadana, B. (2007), A study of motivational factors and level of satisfaction of agents and development officers of LIC of India. *The ICFAI Journal of services Marketing,* 5(1), 45-53
95. Govardhan, N.M. (2008), Relevance of distribution channels. Emerging Insurance markets. *IRDA journal,* 6(11), 7-10.
96. www.irdaindia.org, accessed March 27, 2009.
97. Life Insurance Guide, 2007 Mumbai: Insurance Institute of India, p. 205-207.
98. www.niapune.com, accessed April 28, 2009.
99. Ravikumar, V.V. (2006). Bancassurance – Trends and Opportunities. Hyderabad; The ICFAI University Press, p.144.
100. www.irdaindia.org, 2009, accessed March 28, 2009.
101. Mishra, K.C. (2000), The game is changing. Bancassurance .*The journal of The Management Accountant*, 35(6), 374.
102. Mittal, R.K. (2002), Privatization of Life Insurance sector in India. *Indian Journal of Marketing*, 22(6), 5.
103. Anand, M. (2002), Indian Insurance Industry – Channelising growth. *The journal of Insurance Chronicle*, 2(12), 66.67.
104. Naren, N. Joshi (2002), Rural Insurance Issues Challenges and opportunities. paper presented at National Workshop on Insurance – Growth Prospects of Emerging Insurance Market: Challenges and Opportunities'
105. Naren, N. Joshi (2002), Developing a Rural Distribution Strategy for Insurers paper presented at National Workshop on Insurance – Growth Prospects of Emerging Insurance Market: Challenges and Opportunities.
106. Jimmy John (2002), Private companies still upbeat. *The journal of Asia Insurance review,* 2(2), 30-32.
107. Rajesh, C. Jampala and Venkateswara Rao, B.H. (2005), Impact of Liberalization on LIC .*The journal of Insurance Chronicle*, 5(2), 37.
108. Rao, G.V. (2003), What Brokers are. *IRDA Journal*, 1(10), 19.
109. Suresh, K. (2003), Innovations in Indian Insurance Distribution *The journal of Insurance chronicle,* 3(12), 41-44.
110. Rumeer Shah (2003), What Makes Bancassurance Happen. *IRDA Journal*, 1(11), 18-19.
111. Krishnamurthy, R. (2003), Blueprint for Success – Bringing Bancassurance to India. *IRDA Journal*, 20-23.
112. Apparao Machiraju (2003), A Distribution Odyssey. *IRDA Journal*, 1(10), 25-27.
113. Mekala Mary Selwyn (2004), An Evaluation of Distribution Channels in Life Insurance: Agents Vs Bancassurance. *The journal of Insurance Chronicle*, 4(3), 46-48.

114. Pandey, K.C. (2004), Insurance sector changing with time. *The Management Accountant*, 39(2), 102-104.

115. Parakala, V.S. and Nagaraja Rao (2004), Alternative channels of India Sixth Global Conference of Actuaries.18-19 .

116. Life Insurance Corporation Survey (2004), *Magarantham - Life Insurance Journal*, 22.

117. Insurance World Interview, (2004), *Journal of Insurance World,* 3(2), 16.

118. Sumit Khana (2004), *The journal of Insurance Chronicle*, 4(12), 26.

119. Tarun Kapoor (2004), Marketing of Insurance product. *The journal of Insurance watch,* 3(6), 27.

120. Anuroop Singh (2004), Challenging opportunity. *The journal of Asia Insurance Post*, 5(1), 28-29.

121. Sharma,.N.C. (2004), Top Gear. *The journal of Asia Insurance Post*, 4(6), 35-38.

122. Shikha Sharma (2004), Growing with customers. *IRDA Journal,* 2(5), 21.

123. Anil Chandhok (2004), Emerging issues in the distribution of life insurance products. *The journal of Insurance Chronicle,* 4(12), 28-32.

124. Rajesh, C. Jampala (2005), Insurance Sector: Emerging Distribution Channel. *Indian Journal of Marketing,* 35(7), 24-27.

125. Chari, V.G. (2005), Insurance – A Relook at the distribution strategy. *The journal of Insurance Chronicle,* 5(3), 28-36.

126. Shankarsan Basu and Rahul Singh (2005). Bancassurance- Rest Assured. *The journal of Insurance Chronicle,* 5(4), 23-25.

127. Sridevi Lakshmikutti and Sridharan Baskar (2005), Insurance Distribution in India – A Perspective. *The journal of Insurance Chronicle,* 5(6), 17-22.

128. Malabika Deo (2005), Bancassurance: A win-win solution for banks and insurers. *The journal of Facts for you*, 31(6), 39-42.

129. Ravikumar, V.V. (2005), Emerging structure of Bank assurance in India. *The journal of Insurance chronicle*, 5(12), 35-41.

130. Sree Lakshmi, V. (2005), How Indian Insurance Industry should go. *The economic Challenger*, 7(1), 67.

131. Krishna Kumar (2005), L.I.C making inroads to rural India. *The journal of Insurance Chronicle*, 5(7), 42-45.

132. Rao, GV. (2005), Emerging Trends in the Asian Insurance Scene – Impact of Global Trends. *The journal of Insurance Chronicle*, 5(6), 13-19.

133. Krishnamurthy, S. (2005), Bancassurance is the most cost effective channel to make insurance products available to masses. *The journal of Asia Insurance Post*, 6(1), 28.29.

134. Life Insurance Marketing in India. The Changing Distribution Norms (2005), Case Studies in Insurance. Hyderabad : ICFAI Centre for Management. 97-102

135. The Art of Selling Insurance Products (2005), Case Studies in Insurance. Hyderabad: ICFAI Centre for Management, 204.

136. Bancassurance. A Business Option (2005), Case Studies in Insurance. Hyderabad: ICFAI Centre for Management, 206-20.

137. Ravi Kumar, V.V. (2005), The Emerging Structure of Bancassurance in India. *The journal of Insurance Chronicle*, 5(9), 35.

138. Prasuna, DG. and Nidhi Joshi (2005), Rest Assured. *The journal of Charted Financial Analyst*, 23(4), 14-16.

139. Sukanya Praveen (2005), Bancassurance in India. *The journal of Insurance Chronicle,* 5(7), 75-78.

140. Venkateswara Rao, BH. (2005), LIC Agents – Are they all Productive? *The journal of Insurance Chronicle*, 5(9), 39-42.

141. Tanuja, R. Kumar (2005), Insightful intermediary. *Asia Insurance Post*, 5(5), 38-39.

142. Rama Krishna Rao, T.S. (2006), Private insurers come of age. *The journal of Insurance chronicle*, 6(4), 13-16

143. Ravi Kumar, V.V. (2006), Bancassurance in India. An emerging concept. *The journal of Insurance chronicle*, 6(4), 35-37.

144. Srinivas Subbarao, P. (2006), Bancassurance – Challenges and Strategies. *The journal of Insurance Chronicle*, 6(8), 27.

145. Nalini Prava Tripathy (2006), Bancassurance in the New Millennium. *The journal of Insurance Chronicle*, 6(9), 18.

146. Rumki Banyopadhyay (2006), Role of Private Players – Opportunities and Challenges. *The journal of Business Toda y, 40(3), 20.*

147. Mukesh KumarBaura (2006), Bancassurance in life insurance in India: The brick and mortar model. *The ICFAI Journal of Risk and Insurance*, 6, 42-52.

148. Ramesh, D.V.S. (2006), Retaining a life policy. Distributor's ethics. *IRDA journal*, 5(1). 18-19.

149. Sai Kumar (2006), Life Insurance Products in India. Issues in Distribution. *IRDA Journal,* 5(1), 22-23.

150. Stuart Purdy (2006), Challenges of insurance distribution- some Indian trends. *IRDA Journal,* 5(3), 26-27.

151. Anurika Vaish and Pallavi Dixit (2007), Insurance Companies in the Present Global Scenario. *The journal of .Insurance Chronicle*, 7(1), 32.

152. Rajendra Prasad. T. (2007), Emergence of new players in Indian Insurance sector. *Southern Economist*, 46(7), 31-33.

153. Devarakonda, VS Ramesh (2008), Redefining Distribution. The changing paradigms in insurance intermediation. *The journal of Insurance Chronicle*, 8(1), 28.

154. Anurag (2008), *Innovative channel strategies on life insurance*, Accessed 15 March 2008. http://www.123 ENG.com.

155. Anand Pejwar (2008), Bancassurance in India. Potential Unlimited. *IRDA journal,* 6(10), 23-28.

156. Sithapathy, V. (2008), What has been and what will be? Role of an insurance broker. *IRDA journal*, 6(11), 42.

157. Sethi, S.K. (2008), Role of intermediaries in Insurance. Importance of brokers. *IRDA journal,* 6(11), 45.

158. Divya Gupta and Bajaj, S. Polygamous (2008), Bancassurance. A boon or bane. *The journal of Insurance Chronicle*, 8(6), 20-25.

159. Ramakrishnarao, TS. and Samuel, B. Sekar (2008), Shopassurance. New kid on the block. *The journal of Insurance Chronicle*, 8(8), 17-20.

160. Viswanathan, S. (2008), Bancassurance The modern fable of hare and tortoise. *The journal of Yogashema,* 52(9), 22-24.

161. Venugopal, R. (2008), Bancassurance in India.Problems and potential. *The journal of Yogashema.* 52(3), 9-11.

162. Insurance Marketing (2002), Hyderabad : ICFAI Centre for Management Research. p. 196.

163. Abhishek Agarwal (2002), Distribution of Life Insurance products in India. *The journal of Insurance Chronicle,* 2(8), 53-55.

164. Rudra Saibaba., *et.al.*, (2002), Perception and attitude of women towards life insurance policies. *Indian Journal of Marketing,* 32(12), 10-12.

165. Rengachary, N. (2003), Life Insurance –Vision for the future. *The Hindu Survey of Indian Industry,* 39-41.

166. Ravi Prakash, S., Satyanarayana, T. and Shyam Sundar, C. (2003), Globalisation – It's impact on insurance industry. *Indian Journal of Marketing,* 33(10), 5.6.9.

167. Rao, G.V. (2004), Liberalized Customers: A Challenge for insurers. *IRDA Journal,* 2(5), 24.

168. Shikha Sharma (2004), Benefits of competition. *The Hindu Survey of Indian Industry,* 59.

169. Anil Chandhok and Mittal, R.K. (2004), Critical study of the first year lapsation ratio of Life Insurance business. *The journal of Insurance Chronicle,* 4(9), 76-79.

170. Shobit and Sanjay (2004), An Empirical Study & Analysis of Failure of Private Insurance players in Rural Areas. *The journal of Insurance chronicle,* 4(5), 56-62

171. Tripathy, NP. (2004), An Application of Multidimensional Scaling Model Towards Brand Positioning of Insurance Industries: A Study of Private Players. *The journal of Insurance Chronicl, 4(7), 25-28.*

172. Vijayakumar, A. (2004), Globalization of Indian Insurance sector- Issues and challenges. *The Management Accountant,* 39(3), 195-198.

173. Bodla, B.S. and Sushma Rani Verma (2004), Life Insurance Policies in Rural area. Understanding buyer behaviuor. *Indian Journal of Marketing,* 34(5), 6-8.

174. Kumar Jagendra (2005), Innovative environment in renovated insurance industry. *Insurance Times,* 25(4), 20.

175. Vinayagamoorthi, A. and Gopi, R. (2005), Life Insuranace in rural India. *Kisan World,* 32(11), 14-15.

176. Rajesh, J. Champala and Venkateswara Rao, C. (2005), Claim settlement, the key success factor of LIC. *The journal of Insurance Chronicle,* 5(7), 20-22.

177. Prakasa Rao and Venkateshwara Rao, B.L. (2005), Buoyant Rural Markets Immense potential for Insurance. *The journal of Insurance chronicle,* 5(8), 47-49.

178. Gopal, V.V. (2005), Indian Insurance Industry. Embracing the CRM Philosophy. *The journal of Insurance chronicle,* 5(9), 35-39.

179. Jawaharlal, U. and Sarthak Kumar Rath. (2005), Customer – centricity in the Insurance Industry. *The journal of Insurance Chronicle,* 5(6), 20-24.

180. Ravi Kumar Sharma (2005), Insurance Perspective in Eastern Up – An Empirical Study. *Indian Journal of Marketing*, 35(6), 14-20.

181. Nalini Prava Tripathy (2006), An Application of factor analysis approach towards designing Insurance Products in India. *The journal of Insurance Chronicle,* 6(2), 84-90.

182. Namasivayam, N., Ganesan, S. and Rajendran, S. (2006), Socioeconomic Factors Influencing the Decision in Taking Life Insurance Policies. *The journal of Insurance Chronicle*, 6(8), 65-67.

183. Kishore, R.B. (2006), Life Insurance and Affluent Segments of Market. *The journal of Insurance Chronicle*, 6(10), 40-45.

184. Rajesh, C. Jampala and Polavarapu Adi Lakshmi. (2006), Emerging Markets. Changing the Landscape of the Insurance Sector. *The journal of Insurance Chronicle*, 6(3), 39-43.

185. Vinayagamurthy (2006), Indian Insurance: Modern Marketing Approach. *Southern Economist,* 45(12), 17-19.

186. Subrahamanya Sarma, M. and Kalyani, V. (2006), C.R.M. in LIC – Some Reflections. *The Journal of Management Accountant,* 41(9), 707-713.

187. Samuel, B. Sekar (2006), Know your policy holder. *The journal of Insurance Chronicle,* 7(5), 35-38.

188. Rajesham, Ch. and Rajender, K. (2006), Changing Scenario of Indian Insurance Sector. *Indian Journal of Marketing*, 36(7), 9-15.

189. Samuel, B. Sekar (2007), Know your policy holder. *The journal of Insurance Chronicle,* 7(5), 35-38.

190. Paromita Goswami (2007), Customer satisfaction with service quality in the Life Insurance Industry in India. *The ICFAI Journal of services Marketing*, 5(1). 25-30.

191. Capgemini and European (2007), Financial Management and Marketing Association. Market Training Centre of LIC India.

192. Shilpi Malaiya and Jain, V.K. (2007), A study of policy purchasing behaviour and situations for settlement of claims – A customer's perspective. *The journal of Insurance watch,* .5(2).

193. Nalini Prava Tripathy (2007), *Brand Positioning of Insurance Industries – A study on Private Players,*Accessed 25 March 2008. www.bimaonline.com.

194. Amita Fatterpekar (2007), Measuring customer loyalty: A New Marketing Research tool. *The journal of Yogakshema*, 40.42.

195. Sheela, P. and Arti, G. (2007). A study on the awareness of Life insurance policies in VIshakhapatnam. *The journal of Insurance Chronicle*, 7(9), 25.

196. Ramkumar, D. (2007), *Relationship Marketing. The new mantra for Life insurance sector.*Accessed 18 April 2008, www.indiabschools.com/marketing.

197. Prabhakara, G. (2007), Creating consumer awareness-Life Insurance. *IRDA journal*, 5(12), 36.

198. Rajendra Prasad, T. (2007), Emergence of new players in Indian insurance sector. *The journal of Southern Economist*, 46(7), 31-34.

199. Hasanbanu, S. and Nagajothi, R. S. (2007), A study of the insurance perspective in Uthamapalayam taluk. *Indian Journal of Marketing*, 37(5), 10-15.

200. Reddy, C.R. and Vidyasagar Reddy, G. (2008), Reforms of Insurance Service Sector: Startegic approach. *Southern Economist*, 47(14), 19-22.

201. Gopala Krishna, G. (2008), Customer relationship management in Insurance. *The journal of Insurance Chronicle*, 8(1), 23.

202. Bala Krishnamohan, R. and Muralidhar, K., CRM Mantra for life insurance industry. Accessed 18 April 2008. http.www.oecd.org.dataoecd/40/10/ 18578.pdf.

203. Rao, GV. (2008), Retail shift. *The journal of Asia Insurance Post*, 6(3), 37-39.

204. Sri Jyothi, T. (2008). CRM Practices in Indian Insurance sector. *The journal of Insurance Chronicle*, 8(3), 16.

205. Amit Shrivastava., et al., (2008), *Effect of demographic factors in consumer buyer behaviour: A study with specific reference to Indian Life Insurance Industry*. Accessed March 24 2008, http://www.indiamba.com/Faculty. column/FC604.html.

206. Gregory, A. Kuhlemeyer and Garth, H. Allen. (2008), *Consumer satisfaction with Life insurance .A Bench mark survey*. Accessed 25 March 2008. http://www.afcpe.org/doc/vol1024.pdf

207. Devasenathipathi., et al., (2008), *A study on the consumer preference and comparative analysis of life insurance companies*. Accessed 25 March 2008, http://www.iupindia.org/1207/IJCB.Focus.asp 26

208. Mckinsey and Co., (2008), Report on Indian Life Insurance. *The journal of Yogashema,* 52(1), 9-11.

209. Ghodeswar, B.M. (2008), Customer connections: A key advantage in life insurance sector. *The journal of Yogashema*, 52(9), 22-24.

210. Customers' Choice. *Asia Insurance Post*, 6(4), 20-22.

211. Ramamurthy, P. (2008), Selling life insurance art or science? *The journal of Yogakshema*, 52(5), 7-8.

212. Giresh Kumar, GS. and Eldhose, KV.(2008), Customer perceptions on Life Insurance services. A Comparative study. *The journal of Insurance Chronicle*, 8(8), 65-74.

3

Profile of the Study Area

Tiruchirappalli, situated on the banks of the river Cauvery is the fourth largest city in Tamil Nadu after Chennai, Madurai and Coimbatore with an estimated population of 1,067,915 (as of 2008). It was a citadel of the early Cholas which later fell to the Pallavas. Tiruchirappalli is a fine blend of tradition and modernity built around the Rock Fort. Apart from the Fort, there are several churches, colleges and missions dating back to the 1760s. The town and its fort, now in Tiruchirappalli were built by the Nayaks of Madurai. This city has given great Tamil scholars whose contributions to the Tamil literature have been very significant. Tiruchirappalli is also a preferred healthcare destination to the population from nearby towns and districts.

The most famous land mark of this bustling town is the Rockfort Temple, a spectacular monument perched on a massive rocky out crop which rises abruptly from the plain to tower over the old city. It is reached by the flight of steep steps cut into the rock and from its summit you get a fantastic view of the town plus its other main landmark, Sri Ranganatha Swami Temple (Srirangam). Shrouded in a haze of coconut palms away to the north, Sri Ranganatha Swami temple is one of the largest and most interesting temple complexes in India, built on an island in the middle of Cauvery river and covering a staggering two and a half square kilometers. There is also another huge temple complex nearby, the Jambukeshwara Temple. It was one of the main centers around which the wars of the Carnatic were fought in the 18th century during the British-French struggle for supremacy in India.

The city is a thriving commercial centre in Tamil Nadu and is famous for artificial diamonds, cigars, handloom cloth, glass bangles and wooden and clay toys, itself is an industrial town, where a number of industries flourish.

Tiruchirappalli is a major engineering hub and energy equipment and fabrication center of India. A number of small scale industries have also sprung up in Tiruchirappalli, mostly around Thuvakudi and Mathur. Leather tanneries are located on the way to Pudukottai. Viralimalai, considered an industrial suburb on Madurai road has the factories. Manachanallur has numerous rice mills supplying polished rice all over Tamil Nadu and outside is located about 7 km from Main Guard gate. The economy of the city is driven to a certain extent by IT/ITES companies encouraged by the support from state government. A dedicated stretch of land has been identified and developed to increase the state's share in national IT/ITES exports. The important industries are BHEL, OFT, HAPP and Golden Rock Railway Work Shop. Monuments aside, the city offers a good range of hotels and an excellent local bus system.

Tiruchirappalli is famous for the number of Christian churches it contains — it is said to have the greatest number of chapels in India. The most famous are Holy Redeemer's Church (Sagayamatha Koil), St.Lourdes Church, and The Cathedral. Tiruchirappalli also is famous for Arcot Nawab masjid (one of the oldest), with its large water storage tank (Ahil).

Geography and Climate

The topology of Tiruchirappalli is flat. It lies at an altitude of 78 m above sea level. The river Kaveri (also called Cauvery) and the river Coleroon (also called Kollidam) flows here, the latter forms the northern boundary of the city.

Thiruverumbur is a zone in the city of Tiruchirappalli in the Indian States and territories of India of Tamil Nadu....

There are few reserve forests along the river Cauvery, located at the west or the north-west of the city. The southern and the south-western part of the district is dotted by several hills which are thought to be an offset of the Western Ghat Mountain range - the soil here is considered to be very fertile. As two rivers flow through the city, the northern part of the city is greener than other areas of the city.

Tiruchirappalli has a moderate and pleasant climate, with humidity slightly above normal. The city experiences mild winters and humid summers. The timing of the monsoon in this part of the country, has lately become unpredictable, with the rainy season starting from mid-October until early-November and the rains then extending until early or mid-January.

Demographics

As of the 2001 national census, Tiruchirappalli had a population of 752,066. Males constitute 49.97 per cent of the population and females 50.03 per cent. Tiruchirappalli has an average literacy rate of 91.45 per cent. Male literacy is 94.17 per cent and female literacy is 88.73 per cent. In Tiruchirappalli nearly 10 per cent of the population is below six years of age.

Kongu Nadu is an administrative region in the north west of the Southern Indian state of Tamil Nadu where it borders on Kerala. Its main town is the industrial city of Coimbatore....Tiruchirapalli served as the headquarters of the South-Indian Railways (which was renamed later 'Southern Railways', with Madras/Chennai as the headquarters) during the pre-independence era, for a few years. Anglo-Indians, many of whom worked in the 'South-Indian Railways', started settling in 'Golden Rock-Township' and 'Crawford' located within the city, during that time.

Culture

The city has a multi-cultural society with a sizeable presence of Tamil, English, Telugu, Hindi, and Malayalam-speaking population. Sikhs and Jains also are present in smaller numbers. In addition to Pongal, the 'Thamizhar Thirunaal', Ugadi, Holi and Onam are festivals celebrated by their respective communities retaining their cultural roots.

People living in Tiruchirapalli district have rich cultural heritage. The city served as the centre of fine arts since sangam literature. Uraiyur, the old name of Tiruchirapalli city, was the capital of early Cholas. Here lived a number of Tamil Scholars and contributed to the Tamil literature.

Administration

The city is a Municipal Corporation. It also serves as the headquarters of the district with the same name. The city has one Member of Parliament representing the Tiruchirappalli constituency, but the southern part of the district including the Manapparai town has been merged with Pudukkottai parliamentary constituency for administrative reasons. Both -I and -II are assembly constituencies.

Tiruchirappalli is a Lok Sabha constituency in Tamil Nadu....

The city is headed by a Mayor, under whom are the Deputy Mayor and several councilors elected by people representing administrative wards; as well as a corporation Commissioner of the rank of IAS to administer the city. The district is headed by the District Collector of the rank of IAS. The District court is the highest court of appeal in Tiruchirappalli/. The city has seen moderate to high development in spite of funds constraint. The city police force is headed by the City Police Commissioner of the rank of IPS. One of the five Central prisons of the state is located here.

Education

Considered an educational city, Tiruchirapalli has schools and colleges that are hundreds of years old. College Road in Chatram has three colleges and five schools.

Health-care

The city has numerous hospitals. Apart from the Government hospital, several multi-facility hospitals function in the city. The district's health department is one of the best in terms of implementing government-initiated healthcare schemes. Rare surgical procedures have taken place in some of the hospitals in the city. The polio eradication programme is heavily assisted by various NGOs and clubs in the city. It also has many sidhdha/unani/ayurveda/ homeopathic clinics.

Roadways

Tiruchirappalli is well connected to various parts of Tamil Nadu, by private and public bus services. The Chathram (Main Guard Gate) bus stand, near Rock Fort temple, runs local and [[mofussil (City-to-Town) bus services which connect people to nearby towns and villages. Bus services are frequent, once every two to five minutes. One can get buses from Tiruchirappalli to almost any part of the state, due to its geographical location in the center of Tamil Nadu.

On the road infrastructure front, with the completion of highway projects in Tamil Nadu state, Tiruchirappalli will have four track highways from the city branching to destination Chennai, Madurai, Nagappattinam and Coimbatore. Tamil Nadu Government introduced the Share -Auto scheme in the year 2001.The city has a very wide network of city buses and mini buses.

Railways

Tiruchirappalli is the hub of Southern Railway's operation to connect this central part of Tamil Nadu to various parts of India, notably regions in Kerala, Andhra Pradesh, Bengal, Maharashtra, Karnataka, Delhi, and Madhya Pradesh. Tiruchirappalli Railway Junction has five branches leading to Madurai, Rameswaram, Erode, Tanjore and Chennai.

Airways

Tiruchirappalli has an international airport about five kilometres from the city, which operates flights to Indian cities, territories, and neighbouring countries including Malaysia, Singapore, Sri Lanka and the Gulf by Air Asia, Indian Airlines, Air India Express, Srilankan Airlines, Mihin Lanka,Kingfisher Airlines,Paramount Airways. Tiruchirappalli airport is the second largert airport in Tamil Nadu next to Chennai to get international connectivity to Colombo (Srilanka) in 1981. Nowadays, flights are operated to Gulf countries such as the United Arab Emirates and Kuwait.

Plans are being made to upgrade it to a full fledged international airport in the next three years.

Tourism

A number of temples of historic importance stands here in Tiruchirappalli include Sri Rangam, Rock Fort, Samayapuram, Thiruvanaikkaval, Vekkaliyamman, Iyappan Temple, Vayalur Murugan Kovil, Somarasam Pettai Mariyamman Kovil, Uyyakondan Thirumalai, Erumbeeshwar Temple, Rettai Malai Sami Kovil, etc.

Planetarium/Science Centre

The Anna Science Centre-Planetarium is located 5 km from Tiruchirappalli-Central bus terminus on Pudukkottai road, close to Tiruchirappalli Airport. Grand Anicut at Kallanai (24 km) is an ancient dam built (according to legends) by Karikala Chola across the river Cauvery. It still is in use as part of the district's irrigation system. Mukkombu or Upper Anicut (18 km) is a wonderful picnic spot where the river Kollidam or Coleroon branches off from the Cauvery.

Tiruchirappalli - A Low-cost High-quality Healthcare Destination

Fast pace of economic development with the increase in the health awareness has led to the growth of the healthcare industry in the city. The city stands next to Chennai in Tamilnadu for affordable and quality healthcare deliveries of high-standards.

Area	146.90 sq.kms
Population	1,067,915 (as of 2008).
Altitude	78 metres
Temperature	Summer : Max. 37.1°C , Min. 26.4°CWinter : Max. 31.3°C, Min. 20.6°C
Rainfall	83.5 cms.

Fig. 3.1 : Profile of Tiruchirappallli City Corporation

Source : http://www.trichycitycorporation.com

Life Insurance Corporation of India

The LIC of India has 100 Divisional offices working under the Head office at Mumbai. Tanjavur is one among such divisional offices, under the jurisdiction of which the branches are operated.

In Tiruchirappalli District there are six branches namely

Unit I Branch – Junction Branch

Unit II Branch – Cantonment Branch

Unit III Branch – Career Agents Branch

Unit IV Branch – Rock Fort Branch

Unit V Branch – Thiruverumbur Branch

Unit VI Branch – Srirangam Branch

The Satellite Branch at Lalgudi comes under the jurisdiction of the Srirangam Branch.

The personnel employed in each branch are grouped into three categories namely:

- Class I Officers and
- Class II Officers.
- Class III Category

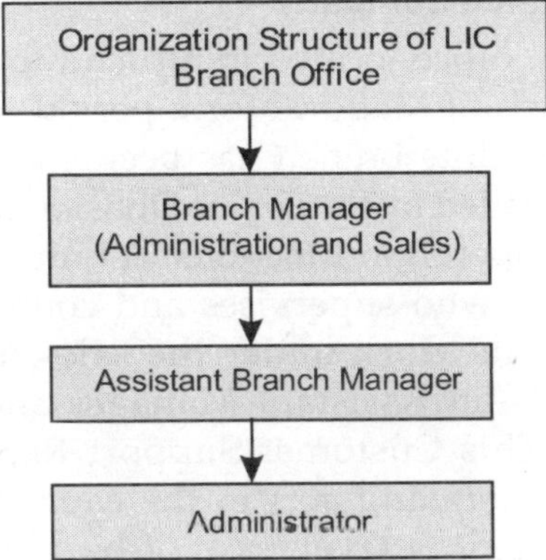

Fig. 3.2 : Organization structure of LIC Branch Office

Officers at Class I category are comprised of

- Branch Manager,
- Assistant Branch Manager (Sales)
- Administrative Officer and
- Assistant Administrative Officer.

However, Branch manager and Administrative Officer are employed at an equal rank and the same is the case of Assistant Administrative Officers and Assistant Branch Managers. Class II category consists of the Development officers and Class III category has Higher Grade Assistants.

The development officers employed under II category are vested with the power to recruit, train, motivate agents and procure business through them. The agents who are appointed by the development officers are not the employees of the corporation. However, depending on the volume and the consistency maintained in the procurement of business they can become members in the following clubs:

1. Branch Manager Club
2. Divisional Manager Club
3. Zonal Manager Club
4. Chairman Club

For undertaking Bancassurance business, the LIC is appointing Financial Service Executives who are not permanent employees of the corporation. They are employed on contract basis with a stipend of Rs. 10,500/-. The LIC has Bank Assurance tie-ups with Indian Overseas Bank (IOB), Uco Bank, Corporation Bank, Central Bank of India and Repco Bank, to mention a few. Corporate agents are also employed by the corporation but they procure minimum business only.

Bajaj Allianz Life Insurance Company

The Bajaj Life Insurance office located in Tiruchirappalli was operating as a satellite under the branch of Madurai for a period of two years. Now, with effect from 2006, this satellite branch has been converted into a Divisional Office. This division is headed by the Senior Divisional Manager who manages the sales as well as the operation functions. A branch manager is employed under the sales manager who supervises and controls the sales managers. The insurance consultants work under the sales manager. In case of the operative wing, there is an Assistant Manager and a Customer Support Representative (CSR). This Customer Support Representative establishes contacts with the customers and acts in the capacity of a public relations officer. Finance department is taken care of by the Branch Accountant. A trainer, who is employed in the training department of the office, imparts training to the Insurance consultants, which has been made mandatory under the IRDA provisions.

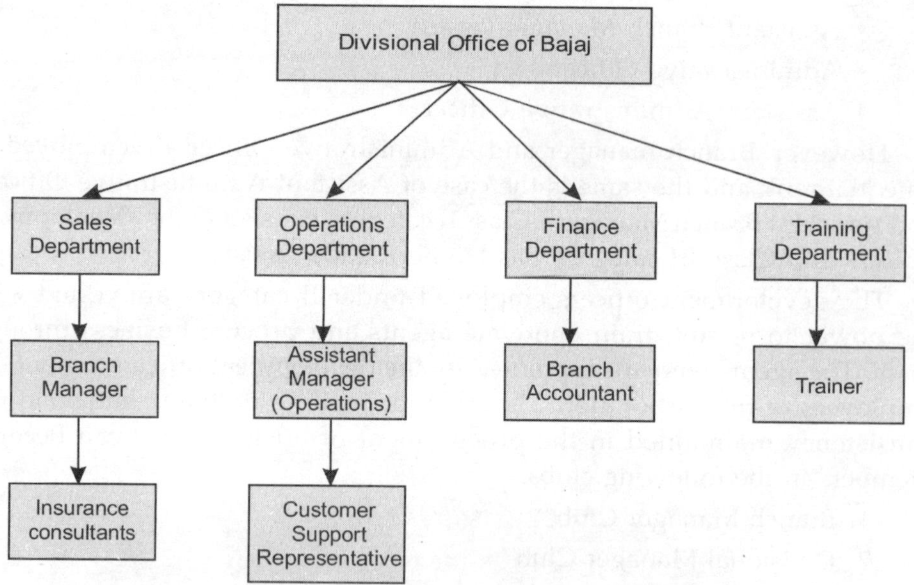

Fig. 3.3 : Organisation Structure of Bajaj – Tiruchirappalli

A branch office comes under the jurisdiction of the divisional office. Karur and Perambalur branches function under the divisional office located at Trichy.

ICICI Prudential Life Insurance Company

The ICICI Prudential Life Insurance Office located at Tiruchirappalli is a Cluster Branch, which is managed by a Cluster Manager. The Cluster Manager supervises and controls the entire office. The cluster office at Tiruchirappalli has two separate divisions namely sales and distribution and administration.

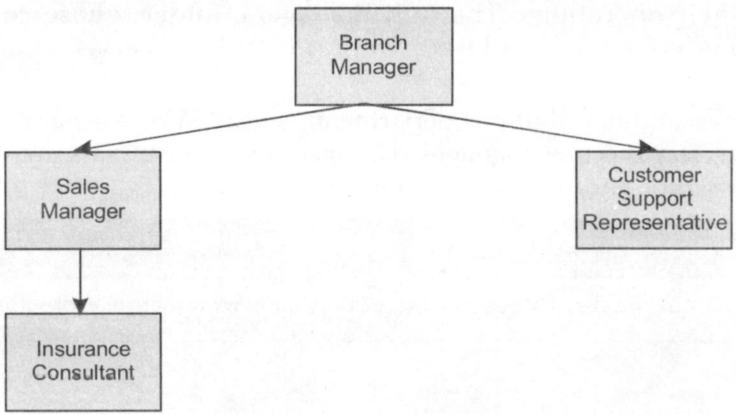

Fig. 3.4 : Organisation Structure of a Branch Office of Bajaj

DEPARTMENTS IN THE CLUSTER OFFICE OF ICICI

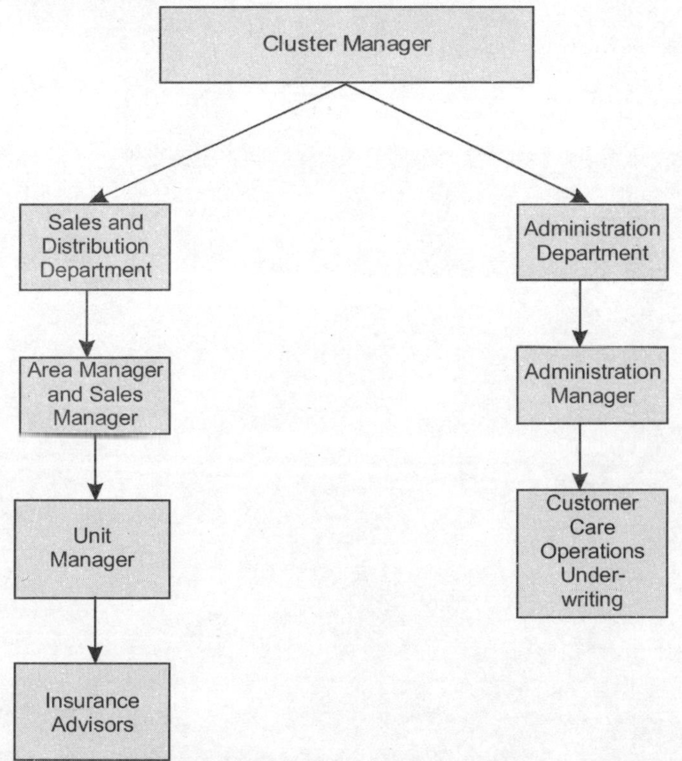

Fig. 3.5 : Departments in the Cluster Office of ICICI

There is a separate operations manager to whom the personnel working under the customer care and underwriting wing are to report. Likewise, administrations department is headed by a manager and the sub-manager renders their operations. The unit managers, under whose control the insurance advisors are employed, work under the supervision of the area managers.

The sales and distributions department is headed by a separate manager who supervises the unit manager. The insurance consultants are employed under the senior and divisional managers.

REFERENCES

1. Trichy District Profile, Accessed 10 May 2009, http://www.trichycitycorporation.com

4

Analysis and Interpretation of Data

The study on the marketing mix of select life insurance companies is based on the response of people to the questionnaire administered. This is the data base used to explain and prove the hypotheses. The analysis of the data collected is based on some important factors that influence/determine the decision making regarding purchase of life insurance policy. These deciding factors are highlighted through the first part of the questionnaire concerning the personal and socio-economic profile of the respondents.

The four major factors identified as the determinants of the insurance policy taking are age, income, family profile and location.

The data collected and the inference drawn are indicated in the following pages.

Table 4.1 : Classification of the Respondents Based on Age

Age Group	Frequency	Per cent
21-40	351	45.4
41-60	371	48.0
Above 60	51	6.6
Total	**773**	**100.0**

Source: Primary data

Table 4.1 indicates the age-wise composition of respondents. Out of 773 respondents, the maximum number, 48 per cent of the respondents belonged to the age group of 41-60, followed by 45.4 per cent respondents within the age group of 21-40. The respondents who were in the age group above 60 years, constituted 6.6 per cent of the total respondents.

Hence, it can be concluded that, majority of the respondents belong to the age group of 40-60. It may be due to greater awareness in this age group and also due to greater family responsibilities.

Table 4.2 : Classification of the Respondents Based on Gender

Gender	Frequency	Per cent
Male	503	65.1
Female	270	34.9
Total	**773**	**100.0**

Source: Primary data

It is clear from Table 4.2 that, among the 773 respondents chosen for the study, 65.07 per cent of the respondents were male and the remaining 34.9 per cent were female respondents. It is observed that, majority of the respondents were male. This may be because, in majority of the families residing in both urban and rural areas, men are the breadwinners of the family.

Table 4.3 : Classification of the Respondents Based on Religion

Religion	Frequency	Per cent
Hindu	537	69.5
Christian	175	22.6
Muslims	57	7.4
Others	4	0.5
Total	**773**	**100.0**

Source: Primary data

Table 4.3 discloses the religion of the respondents. It is clear that, out of 773 respondents, maximum number of the respondents (69.5 per cent) followed Hinduism and 22.6 per cent respondents followed Christianity. The followers of Islam were 7.37 per cent. Hence, majority of the respondents were Hindus.

Table 4.4 : Classification of the Respondents Basd on Education

Education	Frequency	Per cent
Schooling	188	24.3
Under graduate	273	35.3
Post graduate	154	19.9
Professional	118	15.3
Diploma	40	5.2
Total	**773**	**100.0**

Source: Primary data

Table 4.4 exhibits the educational qualification of respondents. Out of 773 respondents, 24.3 per cent of the respondents studied up to higher secondary school, 35.5 per cent of the respondents were graduates, 19.9 per cent respondents were post graduates and 15.3 per cent had professional qualification. However, the diploma holders were the minimum.

Based on the table it is inferred that, the graduates, which includes under graduates and post graduates (55.2 per cent) have shown preference for purchasing life insurance policies. This may be, because of their income potential and expectation of a higher standard of life in future.

Table 4.5 : Classification of the Respondents Based on Location

Location	Frequency	Per cent
Rural	235	30.4
Urban	538	69.6
Total	**773**	**100.0**

Source: Primary data

It is clear from Table 4.5 that, out of the 773 respondents, 69.6 per cent lived in urban areas and the remaining 30.4 per cent of respondents lived in rural areas. Hence, majority of the respondents lived in urban areas, where the business potential was high.

Table 4.6 : Classification of the Respondents Based on Occupation

Occupation	Frequency	Per cent
Government Employee	131	16.9
Entrepreneur	196	25.4
Professional	105	13.6
Private sector	250	32.3
Rural sector	77	10.0
Others	14	1.8
Total	**773**	**100.0**

Source: Primary data

Table 4.6 reveals that, out of 773 respondents, 32.3 per cent of the respondents were employed in private sector, 25.4 per cent of the respondents being engaged in business. Sixteen point nine per cent of the respondents were employed in Government organizations and professionals constituted, 13.6 per cent of the total respondents. However, 10 per cent of the respondents were employed in rural sector and those belonged to other categories were minimum. Hence, it can be inferred from the table that, the respondents from the private sector followed by the business men showed great interest in purchasing life insurance policies as one of their choices of financial planning, for reasons of safety and security.

Table 4.7 : Classification of the Respondents Based on Monthly Income

Monthly Income	Frequency	Per cent
Less than 5000	68	8.8
5001-10000	219	28.3
10001-15000	223	28.9
15001-20000	126	16.3
20001-25001	69	8.9
Above 25000	68	8.8
Total	**773**	**100.0**

Source: Primary data

Table 4.7, depicts the monthly income of the respondents. It is clear from the table that, 28.86 per cent of the respondents earned monthly income of Rupees 10,001-15,000; 28.3 per cent of the respondents earned Rupees. 5,001-10,000 per month. An equal number of respondents, that is, eight point eight per cent of the respondents earned a monthly income of either Rs. 5,000 or above Rs. 25,000.

It is inferred that, the maximum number of respondents, fell within the monthly income ranging between Rs. 5,001 to 15,000 for, it would supplement their limited monthly income which is inadequate, to meet all family needs such as education, marriage, illness, housing and so on.

Table 4.8 : Classification of the Respondents Based on Nature of the Family

Nature of the Family	Frequency	Per cent
Nuclear	480	62.1
Joint	293	37.9
Total	**773**	**100.0**

Source: Primary data

Table 4.8 discloses the nature of family of respondents. It is evident that, out of 773 respondents, nearly two third, 62.1 per cent of the respondents who purchased the policies belonged to nuclear families while the rest lived in joint families.

It is inferred that, the life insurance policy purchasing is more among the nuclear families. Their preference indicates, the dire need to save for the future because of the limited income and also to assert their self confidence and potential for saving.

It is clear from Table 4.9 that, out of the 773 respondents, 45.7 per cent of the respondents had four to six members in the families and 43.7 per cent have less than four members. The number of respondents who had above six members, was just 10.6 per cent.

Table 4.9 : Classification of the Respondents Based on Size of the Family

Family Size	Frequency	Per cent
1-3	338	43.7
4-6	353	45.7
Above 6	82	10.6
Total	**773**	**100.0**

Source: Primary data

It could be concluded that, majority of the respondents had families consisting of four to six members.

Table 4.10 : Classification of the Respondents Based on Decision Maker

Decision Maker	Frequency	Per cent
Husband	163	21.1
Wife	196	25.3
Both	354	45.8
Self	60	7.8
Total	**773**	**100.0**

Source: Primary data

Table 4.10 indicates the decision maker of the family as regards the purchase of the policy. It is evident that, a majority of the respondents,(45.8 per cent), have stated that, purchasing the policy was the joint decision of husband and wife. Seven point eight per cent decided on their own to purchase the policy, followed by 21.08 per cent by husband individually and 25.32 per cent by wife.

Table 4.11 : Classification of the Respondents Based on LIC Policy Holding

Name of the Policy	Frequency	Per cent
Bima Gold	112	37.6
Jeevan Anand	125	41.9
New Janraksha	61	20.5
Total	**298**	**100.0**

Source: Primary data

Table 4.11 indicates the preference of the policy holders of LIC. It is clear, that majority of the respondents, (41.9) had purchased the Jeevan Anand policy, an exclusive policy which was to give life protection for an additional 70 years than the normal policy term. Bima Gold the Golden Year special policy was owned by, 37.6 per cent of the respondents. New Janraksha, the policy specially designed for the rural mass was owned by, 20.5 per cent of the respondents.

Table 4.12 : Classification of the Respondents Based on Bajaj Policy Holding

Name of the Policy	Frequency	Per cent
Unit Gain	77	37.6
Unit Gain Plus	73	35.6
Family Gain	55	26.8
Total	**205**	**100.0**

Source: Primary data

From Table 4.12 it is inferred that majority (37.6 per cent) of the policy holders of Bajaj had a preference for the Unit Gain policy, which was expected to get good returns in future. Their second priority was for the Unit Gain Plus policy (35.6 per cent) which was aimed wealth creation. However, the holders of Family Gain policy, which was meant exclusively for the rural mass, were less.

Table 4.13 : Classification of the Respondents Based on ICICI Policy Holding

Name of the Policy	Frequency	Per cent
Life Time	136	50.4
Life Time Pension	91	33.7
Smart Kid	43	15.9
Total	**270**	**100.0**

Source: Primary data

Table 4.13 indicates the preference of the policy holders of ICICI for its policies. It is obvious that, the Life Time Policy which was expected to give greater yield in the future was the choice of majority (50.4 per cent) of the policy holders. Life time Pension policy, which was meant to give retirement benefits for the policy holders, was the second choice of the policy holders. Smart Kid policy, designed to meet the children's needs was preferred by 15.9 per cent of the respondents.

Table 4.14 : Criteria for the Selection of the Life Insurance Company

Factor	Frequency	Per cent
Brand Image	471	60.9
Prompt Service	41	5.30
Reputation	68	8.8
Security	193	25.0
Total	**773**	**100.0**

Source: Primary data

Table 4.14 indicates the reasons for choosing the life insurance company. Out of 773 respondents, a majority of respondents, that is 60.93 per cent, had chosen the select life insurance companies, for the brand image they have created. Security was the second reason for their choice. However, reputation had been cited as the reason by eight point eight per cent of the respondents and prompt service has been indicated as the reason only by five point three per cent of the respondents.

Table 4.15 : Classification of the Respondents Based on the Additional Benefits Availed

Additional Benefits	Frequency	Per cent
Accidental Death Benefit	476	61.6
Disability Benefit	72	9.3
Critical Illness Benefit	72	9.3
Hospital Cash Benefit	58	7.5
Others	95	12.3
Total	**773**	**100.0**

Source: Primary data

Add-on riders provide additional cover to the respondents along with the main policies. It is evident from Table 4.15 that out of the several additional benefits available to the policyholders, Accidental Death benefit was the most sought rider with 61.58 per cent of the respondents opting for it. Disability benefit and critical illness benefit were equally preferred by nine point three one per cent of respondents each. Hospital cash benefit was opted by only seven point five per cent of the respondents. Hence, it could be concluded that, majority of the policy holders preferred the add-on rider – Accidental Death benefit.

Table 4.16 : Classification of the Respondents Based on the Source of Information

Source	Frequency	Per cent
Agent	556	71.9
Bank	66	8.5
Corporate Agents	84	10.9
Franchisee	36	4.7
Advertisements	31	4.0
Total	**773**	**100.0**

Source: Primary data

Table 4.16 discloses the various sources of information about the policies to the respondents. It is worth noting that, the agents were the main source of information, with 71.93 per cent of the respondents citing them. Corporate agents marked by 10.87 per cent of the respondents and banks eight point five four per cent of the respondents. However, Franchisees and advertisements were the source of information, for a minimum number of respondents only.

It can be inferred that, the important source of information for majority of the policy holders was agents.

Table 4.17 : Classification of the Respondents Based on the Intermediaries Involved in the Purchase of Policies

Intermediaries	Frequency	Per cent
Agent	605	78.3
Bank	55	7.1
Corporate Agents	82	10.6
Franchisee	31	4.0
Total	**773**	**100.0**

Source: Primary data

Table 4.17 gives the role of intermediaries in the sale of life insurance policies. Agents play a predominant role, in selling the policies. It is evident from the fact that, 78.27 per cent of the respondents have purchased the policies through the agents. Respondents, who purchased the policies through corporate agents, were 10.61 per cent and the number of respondents who had purchased the policies through franchisees has been the minimum.

It is observed that, agents play a leading role in stimulating and motivating the respondents in purchase of policies.

Table 4.18 : Classification of the Respondents Based on their Preference Towards Various Categories of Policies

Various Policies	Frequency	Per cent
Endowment	195	25.2
Money Back	205	26.5
Unit Linked	180	23.3
Pension	58	7.5
Children	135	17.5
Total	**773**	**100.0**

Source: Primary data

The preference of the policyholders towards the various types of policies has been depicted in Table 4.18. A majority of respondents, that is 26.52 per cent, had favoured the money-back policies for the returns they get. The number of respondents favouring endowment policies was 25.23 per cent of the respondents. The Unit-linked policies were preferred by 23.29 per cent of the respondents and children's policies by 17.46 per cent of the respondents. However, only seven point five per cent of the respondents preferred the pension schemes.

It is observed that, the traditional policies namely Endowment and money back policies were the much sought policies. The preference for unit-linked policies was also good. However with the privatization process, it is expected that the demand for pension products would go up.

Chi-Square Test – Cross tabulation of the Age and the Reason for the selection of the company.

Null Hypothesis H_0 : Age of the respondents has no influence in the choice of the company based on the selection criteria.

Alternate Hypothesis H_1 : Age of the respondents has influence in the choice of the company based on the selection criteria.

Level of Significance (α) = 0.05

Chi-square test statistic : $\chi^2 = \sum_{i=1}^{N} \frac{(O_i - E_i)^2}{E_i}$

Table 4.19

Age	Selection Criteria				Total
	Brand Image	Prompt Service	Reputation	Security	
21-40	214	25	30	82	351
41-60	227	12	33	99	371
Above 60	30	4	5	12	51
Total	**471**	**41**	**68**	**193**	**773**

Source: Primary data
Chi-Square p value = .342

Calculated p value (0.342) > 0.05 (level of significance). It indicates the acceptance of H_0 at five per cent level. Hence it is inferred that, age of the respondents has no influence in choosing a company, based on the selection criteria namely brand image, prompt service, reputation and security.

Chi-Square Test – Cross tabulation of the Sex and the Reason for the selection of the company.

Null Hypothesis H_0 : Sex of the respondents has no influence in the choice of the company based on the selection criteria.

Alternate Hypothesis H_1 : Sex of the respondents has influence in the choice of the company based on the selection criteria.

Level of Significance (α) = 0.05

Chi-square test statistic: $\chi^2 = \sum_{i=1}^{N} \frac{(O_i - E_i)^2}{E_i}$

Table 4.20

Sex	Selection Criteria				Total
	Brand Image	Prompt Service	Reputation	Security	
Male	303	22	48	130	503
Female	168	19	20	63	270
Total	**471**	**41**	**68**	**193**	**773**

Source: Primary data
Chi-Square *p* value = .282

Calculated *p* value (0.282) > 0.05 (level of significance). It indicates the acceptance of H_o at five per cent level. Hence it is inferred that, sex of the respondents has no influence in choosing a company based on the selection criteria namely brand image, prompt service, reputation and security.

Chi-Square Test – Cross tabulation of the Age and the Choice of the life insurance company.

Null Hypothesis H_o : Age of the respondents has no influence in the choice of the company.

Alternate Hypothesis H_1 : Age of the respondents has influence in the choice of the company.

Level of Significance (α) = 0.05

Chi-square test statistic: $\chi^2 = \sum_{i=1}^{N} \frac{(O_i - E_i)^2}{E_i}$

Table 4.21

Age	Name of the company			
	LIC	Bajaj	ICICI	Total
21-40	125	112	114	351
41-60	158	78	135	371
Above 60	15	15	21	51
Total	**298**	**205**	**270**	**773**

Source: Primary data
Chi-Square p value = .011

Policy holders falling under the age-group of 21-40 years and above 60 years have given almost equal preference to the policies of all the three companies. But policyholders, falling under the age group of 41-60 years of age, showed preferences for LIC followed by ICICI. They showed less preference for Bajaj.

Calculated p value (0.011) < 0.05 (level of significance). Hence, H_o is rejected and H_1 is accepted. It is concluded that, age of the respondents has influence in the choice of the company.

Chi-Square Test – Cross tabulation of the Location and the choice of the life insurance company.

Null Hypothesis H_o : Location of the respondents has no influence in the choice of the company.

Alternate Hypothesis H_1 : Location of the respondents has influence in the choice of the company.

Level of Significance (α) = 0.05

Chi-square test statistic: $\chi^2 = \sum_{i=1}^{N} \frac{(O_i - E_i)^2}{E_i}$

Table 4.22

Location	Name of the company			
	LIC	Bajaj	ICICI	Total
Rural	97	52	86	235
Urban	201	153	184	538
Total	**298**	**205**	**270**	**773**

Source: Primary data
Chi-Square *p* value = .185

Calculated *p* value (0.185) > 0.05 (level of significance). Hence, H_o is accepted and H_1 is rejected. It is concluded that, location of the respondents has no influence in the choice of the company.

The analysis of the personal and demographic profile of the respondents of LIC revealed that out of the 298 respondents,

- Majority of the respondents, (68.1%), were male and the maximum number of the respondents, (52.7%) were in the age group between 41-60 years.
- Majority of the respondents, (61.4%) followed Hinduism and 29.9 per cent of respondents followed Christianity.
- Thirty point nine per cent respondents had completed school education, followed by, 27.5 per cent of respondents who were undergraduates.
- Majority of the respondents, (67.4%) resided in urban areas.

Table 4.23 : Personal and Demographic Profile of the Respondents

Factors		Name of Insurance Company					
		LIC		BAJAJ		ICICI	
		N = 298	Per cent	N = 205	Per cent	N = 270	Per cent
Age	21-40	125	41.9	112	54.6	114	42.22
	41-60	158	52.7	78	38.0	135	50
	Above 60	15	5.0	15	7.3	21	7.78
Sex	Male	203	68.1	133	64.9	167	61.9
	Female	95	31.9	72	35.1	103	38.1
Religion	Hindu	183	61.4	157	76.6	197	73.0
	Christian	89	29.9	36	17.6	50	18.5
	Muslims	22	7.4	12	5.9	23	8.5
	Others	4	1.3	0	0	0	0
Educational Qualification	Schooling	92	30.9	39	19.0	57	21.1
	Undergraduate	82	27.5	93	45.4	98	36.3
	Postgraduate	61	20.5	42	20.5	51	18.9
	Professional	58	19.5	19	9.3	41	15.2
	Diploma	5	1.7	12	5.9	23	8.5
Location	Rural	97	32.6	52	25.4	85	31.5
	Urban	201	67.4	153	74.6	185	68.5
Occupation	Govt. official	52	17.4	36	17.6	43	15.9
	Businessman	88	29.5	59	28.8	49	18.1
	Professional	54	18.1	20	9.8	31	11.5
	Private sector	71	23.8	71	34.6	108	40.0
	Rural sector	28	9.4	15	7.3	34	12.6
	Others	5	1.7	4	2.0	5	1.9
Monthly Income	Less than 5000	32	10.7	23	11.2	13	4.8
	5001-10000	89	29.9	54	26.3	76	28.1
	10001-15000	76	25.5	62	30.2	85	31.5
	15001-20000	50	16.8	32	15.6	44	16.3
	20001-25000	26	8.7	18	8.8	25	9.3
	Above 25000	25	8.4	16	7.8	27	10.0
Nature of family	Nuclear	177	59.4	132	64.4	171	63.3
	Joint	121	40.6	73	35.6	99	36.7
No. of family members	1-3	97	32.6	93	45.4	146	54.1
	4-6	169	56.7	86	42.0	100	37.0
	7 and Above	32	10.7	26	12.7	24	8.9

Source: Primary data

- Majority of the respondents, (29.5%) were engaged in business and 23.8 per cent of the respondents were employed in private concerns.
- The income earned by 30 per cent of the respondents was between Rs. 5,001-Rs.10, 000 per month. Twenty five point five per cent of the respondents were earning a monthly income of Rs. 10,001-Rs.15, 000.
- Majority of the respondents, (59.4%), lived in nuclear families and majority of the respondents (56.7%) had 4 to 6 members in the family.

The analysis of the personal and demographic profile of the respondents of Bajaj Allianz Life Insurance Company revealed that out of the 205 respondents:

Majority of the respondents (64.9%) were male and the maximum number of the total respondents (54.6%) was in the age group between 21-40 years.

- Majority of the respondents, (76.6%) were Hindus followed by Christians being 17.6 per cent of the respondents.
- Majority of the respondents, (45.4%), were undergraduates of and 20.5 per cent of the respondents were post graduates.
- The highest proportion of 74.6 per cent of the respondents resided in urban areas.
- Out of 205 respondents, 34.6 per cent were employed in private sector and 28.8 per cent were business men.
- Majority of the respondents, (56.5%), were earning a monthly income ranging from Rs. 5,001-Rs.15.000.
- Majority of the respondents, (64.4%) lived in nuclear families and majority of the respondents (45.4%) had one to three members in the family.

The analysis of the personal and demographic profile of the respondents of ICICI Prudential Life Insurance Company revealed that, out of the 270 respondents:

- Majority of the respondents, (61.9%) were male and 38.1 per cent of the respondents were in the age group between 36-50 years.
- Majority of the respondents (73%) were Hindus.
- Majority of the respondents (36.3%) were undergraduates followed by 21.1 per cent of the respondents who had completed their Higher Secondary course.
- Majority of the respondents (68.5%), resided in urban areas.
- The respondents employed in private sector constituted 40 per cent of the total respondents, followed by 18.1 per cent of respondents who were businessmen.
- The monthly income of majority of the respondents was Rs.10,000 to Rs.15.000 (31.5%) and Rs.5,001-Rs.10,000 (28.1%).

Table 4.24 : Rational Profile of the Respondents

Factors		Name of Insurance Company					
		LIC		BAJAJ		ICICI	
		N = 298	Per cent	N = 205	Per cent	N = 270	Per cent
Decision to take insurance	Husband	67	22.5	52	25.37	45	16.67
	Wife	33	11.1	26	12.68	28	10.37
	Both	175	58.7	106	51.7	158	58.5
	Self (Unmarried)	23	7.7	21	10.25	39	14.46
Reasons for choosing the company	Brand Image	161	54.02	115	56.1	195	72.22
	Prompt service	10	3.4	18	8.8	13	4.8
	Reputation	14	4.7	28	13.7	26	9.6
	Security	113	37.9	44	21.5	36	13.3
Additional benefits	Accidental death benefit	242	81.2	85	41.5	149	52.2
	Disability benefit	17	5.7	21	10.2	34	12.6
	Critical illness benefit	10	3.4	38	18.5	24	8.9
	Hospital cash benefit	1	.3	33	16.1	24	8.9
	Others	28	9.4	28	13.7	39	14.4
Sources of Information	Agent	265	88.9	106	51.7	185	68.5
	Bank	17	5.7	9	4.4	40	14.8
	Corporate Agents	4	1.3	57	27.8	23	8.5
	Franchisee	2	.7	23	11.2	11	4.1
	Advertisements	10	3.4	10	4.9	11	4.1
Intermediaries	Agent	296	99.3	117	57.1	192	71.1
	Bank	1	.3	10	4.9	43	15.9
	Corporate Agents	1	.3	63	30.7	19	7.0
	Franchisee	0	0	15	7.3	16	5.9
Life Insurance policy	Endowment	130	43.6	35	17.1	30	11.1
	Money Back	104	34.9	36	17.6	65	24.1
	Unit-linked	26	8.7	79	38.5	75	27.8
	Pension	14	4.7	13	6.3	31	11.5
	Children	24	8.1	42	20.5	69	25.6

Source: Primary data

- The number of respondents living in nuclear families was more, (63.3 per cent), when compared with the number of respondents living in joint families (36.7 per cent). Majority of the respondents (54.1 per cent) had 1-3 members in the family.

An analysis of the rational profile of the respondents revealed that, in respect of Life Insurance Corporation of India (LIC),

- Majority of the respondents (58.7%) stated that purchasing the life insurance was decided by both husband and wife jointly, whereas for 22.5 per cent of respondents it was the individual decision of the husband.
- Brand image was the vital factor that motivated the respondents of Life Insurance Corporation. However, security offered by the company was considered to be, the next important reason for choosing the company.
- For 81.2 per cent of the respondents of Life Insurance Corporation, Accidental Death benefit was the much sought add-on-rider.
- Agents were the prime source of information for majority (88.9 per cent) of the respondents of Life Insurance Corporation.
- Agents play a vital role in selling the policies of Life Insurance Corporation. It is evident from the fact that, 99.3 per cent of the respondents have purchased the policy through the agents. Other intermediaries played an insignificant role in selling the policy.
- Endowment policy was the policy most preferred policy, by 43.6 per cent of the respondents followed by, Money Back policies which were preferred by 34.9 per cent of the respondents.

An analysis of the rational profile of the respondents revealed that, in respect of Bajaj Allianz Life Insurance Company,

- Majority of the respondents, (51.7%) revealed that, the decision to purchase the policy was taken jointly by husband and wife and for 25.37 per cent of the respondents, it was the decision taken by the husband.
- Brand image was the prime factor that motivated the policy holders to purchase its policy. It is evident from the fact that, 56.1 per cent of the respondents chose the Bajaj Allianz Life Insurance Company for the brand image it had created.
- Of the various add-on-riders made available to the policy holders, Accidental Death benefit was the much sought rider, for majority (41.5%) of the respondents.
- Majority of the respondents (51.7%) had received information about the policy only through the agents, followed by 27.8 per cent of respondents who had received information through the corporate agents.
- Agency system of selling the life insurance products was the dominating intermediary of Bajaj Company. However, corporate agents also have been the source of purchase for 30.7 per cent of the respondents.

- Of the various categories of policies available, unit-linked policies were favoured by 38.5 per cent respondents of Bajaj, followed by the policies meant exclusively for children's education, marriage and so on.

An analysis of the rational profile of the respondents revealed that, in respect of ICICI Prudential Life Insurance Company,

- The decision to take life insurance policy was made jointly by husband and wife (58.5%).
- For the policy holders of ICICI Prudential Life Insurance Company, Brand image was the first reason that motivated them to purchase the policy followed by the security factor.
- Majority of the respondents, (52.2%), preferred the Accidental Death Benefit compared to the other benefits.
- Majority of the respondents (68.5%) of ICICI Prudential Life Insurance Company, had knowledge about the policy only through the agents and 14.8 per cent of the respondents through banks.
- Agents were the prime source of purchase for 71.1 per cent of the respondents of ICICI Prudential Life Insurance Company. Banks had sold the Life Insurance policy to 15.9 per cent of the respondents.
- The policy holders of ICICI had a preference for the unit-linked policies followed by the policies designed exclusively for children.

ANALYSIS OF MARKETING MIX

In order to gauge the opinion of the policyholders in respect of the dimensions of the marketing mix of the chosen companies, a study has been undertaken by the researcher. The views of the policyholders regarding their opinion have been qualified on the basis of five point Likert scale. The five point and their respective score values in the scale are shown below.

Points of Scale	Assigned Score
Strongly agree	5
Agree	4
No opinion	3
Disagree	2
Strongly disagree	1

A high score in the corresponding dimension indicates a very high positive response of the customers. Scores in the low range indicates conversely a low/negative response of the policyholders. The dimensions selected for the study have been as follows.

1. Product Mix
2. Price Mix

3. Promotion Mix
4. Distribution Mix
5. People and Process Mix (Customer Care Services)
6. Physical Evidence Mix

Each dimension is supplemented by various variables. The data have been analysed with statistical tools such as One way anova, Two way anova, Chi-square Test and Discriminant analysis to deduce conclusion.

Product Mix

The first dimension of the marketing mix is the product mix. Product in the present context means the various life insurance policies offered by the three chosen life insurance companies namely Bajaj Allianz Life Insurance Company, Life Insurance Corporation and ICICI Prudential Life Insurance Company. The product mix has been analysed with reference to the features of life insurance policies namely provision of security for the future, risk cover, adequate returns, fulfillment of specific requirements such as children's education, marriage, provision of tax relief and the provision of additional benefits to cover risk.

The response of the policyholders towards the enquiries made determines the effectiveness of the variable product mix. The opinion has been exhibited in the following tables :

Table 4.25 : Product Mix-LIC

Variables	Strongly agree	Agree	Neutral	Disagree	Strongly disagree
Company's policies provide security for the future	105 (35.2)	183 (61.4)	6 (2.0)	3 (1.0)	1 (0.3)
Company's policies provide Risk cover	116 (38.9)	169 (56.7)	11 (3.7)	2 (0.7)	—
Company's policies provide Adequate returns	71 (23.8)	203 (68.1)	19 (6.4)	5 (1.7)	—
Company's policies provide fulfill specific requirements	70 (23.5)	174 (58.4)	49 (16.4)	5 (1.7)	—
Company's policies provide Tax relief	92 (30.9)	140 (47.0)	59 (19.8)	5 (1.7)	2 (0.7)
Additional Benefits offer adequate risk cover	86 (28.9)	171 (57.4)	39 (13.1)	2 (0.7)	—

Source: Primary data
Figures in ( ) represent percentage.

Table 4.25 discloses the opinions of the policyholders of LIC as regards the product mix of the company. It can be inferred that, a majority, 96.6 per cent (strongly agree and agree responses) of respondents revealed that the company's policies provided security for the future. Only one point three per cent of the respondents felt that the company's policies did not provide security for the future. Remaining two per cent were undecided to give a clear answer. Thus, policyholders appeared to have strong belief towards the fact that the company's policies provide security for the future.

As regards the statement that, the company's policies provide risk cover, a majority (strongly agree and agree responses) of the respondents, (95.6 per cent) felt that, the statement was true. A negligible percentage (zero point seven per cent) felt that it was not true. Three point seven per cent was undecided to give a clear answer.

In respect of the statement that, the company's policies provide adequate returns a majority, 91.9 per cent (strongly agree and agree responses) of the respondents felt that adequate returns were provided by the policies of the company. Only one point seven percent (disagree and strongly disagree responses) felt that, it was not true. Six point four per cent was indecisive to give a clear answer.

As regards the statement that the additional benefits offer adequate risk cover, a majority, 86.3 per cent (strongly agree and agree responses) of the respondents felt the statement to be true. A negligible percentage (zero point seven per cent) felt that it was not true. Thirteen point one per cent was reluctant to give a clear answer.

With reference to the statement that the company's policies fulfill specific requirements, a majority, 81.9 per cent (strongly agree and agree responses) of respondents revealed that the company's policies fulfill their specific requirements. Only one point seven per cent of the respondents felt that the company's policies did not fulfill specific requirements. Remaining 16.4 per cent were undecided to give a clear answer.

As regards the statement that the company's policies provide tax relief, a majority, 77.9 per cent (strongly agree and agree responses) of respondents responded in the affirmative. Only three two point three per cent of the respondents expressed a negative opinion. Remaining 19.8 per cent were neutral in their opinion.

Hence it could be concluded that provision of security, risk cover and provision of adequate returns have been the most influencing factors for the policyholders of LIC.

Table 4.26 reveals the opinions of the policyholders of Bajaj as regards the product mix of the company. It is clear that as regards the statement that the company's policies provide security for the future, a majority, 94.1 per cent (strongly agree and agree responses) of the respondents felt that the

Table 4.26 : Product Mix-Bajaj

Variables	Strongly agree	Agree	Neutral	Disagree	Strongly disagree
Company's policies provide security for the future	79 (38.5)	114 (55.6)	12 (5.9)	—	—
Company's policies provide Risk cover	83 (40.5)	105 (51.2)	16 (7.8)	1 (0.5)	—
Company's policies provide Adequate returns	57 (27.8)	120 (58.5)	28 (13.7)	—	—
Company's policies provide fulfill specific requirements	70 (34.1)	115 (56.1)	11 (5.4)	9 (4.4)	—
Company's policies provide Tax relief	79 (38.5)	104 (50.7)	19 (9.3)	3 (1.5)	—
Additional Benefits offer adequate risk cover	74 (36.1)	107 (52.2)	22 (10.7)	1 (0.5)	1 (0.5)

Source: Primary data
Figures in ( ) represent percentage.

statement was true. No respondent felt that it was not true. Five point nine per cent of the respondents were undecided to give a clear answer. Thus, policyholders appeared to have strong belief towards the fact that the company's policies provide security for the future.

A majority, 91.7 per cent (strongly agree and agree responses) of respondents revealed that the company's policies provide risk cover. Zero point five per cent of the respondents felt that the company's policies did not provide risk cover. Remaining seven point eight per cent were indecisive to give a clear answer.

With reference to the statement that the company's policies fulfill specific requirements, a majority, 90.2 per cent (strongly agree and agree responses) of respondents revealed that the company's policies fulfill their specific requirements. Only four point four per cent of the respondents felt that the company's policies did not fulfill specific requirements. Remaining five point four per cent per cent were undecided to give a clear answer.

As regards the statement that the company's policies provide tax relief, a majority, 89.2 per cent (strongly agree and agree responses) of respondents responded in the affirmative. Only one point five per cent of the respondents expressed a negative opinion. Remaining nine point three per cent were neutral in their opinion.

As regards the statement that the additional benefits offer adequate risk cover, a majority, 88.3 per cent (strongly agree and agree responses) of respondents revealed that the additional benefits offer adequate risk cover. Only one per cent of the respondents felt that the additional benefits did not offer adequate risk cover. Remaining 10.7 per cent were indecisive to give a clear answer.

In respect of the statement that, the company's policies provide adequate returns a majority, 86.3 per cent (strongly agree and agree responses) of the respondents felt that adequate returns were provided by the policies of the company. No respondent felt that it was not true. Remaining 13.7 per cent was undecided to give a clear answer.

It is concluded that, Bajaj Allianz Life Insurance products are favoured mainly for their security aspect followed by risk cover, fulfillment of specific requirements such as children education and daughter's marriage.

Table 4.27 : Product Mix-ICICI

Variables	Strongly agree	Agree	Neutral	Disagree	Strongly disagree
Company's policies provide security for the future	87 (32.2)	137 (50.7)	32 (11.9)	10 (3.7)	4 (1.5)
Company's policies provide Risk cover	79 (29.3)	143 (53.0)	35 (13.0)	11 (4.1)	2 (0.7)
Company's policies provide Adequate returns	67 (24.8)	162 (60.0)	36 (13.3)	2 (0.7)	3 (1.1)
Company's policies provide fulfill specific requirements	79 (29.3)	123 (45.6)	46 (17.0)	18 (6.7)	4 (1.5)
Company's policies provide Tax relief	79 (29.3)	134 (49.6)	34 (12.6)	14 (5.2)	9 (3.3)
Additional Benefits offer adequate risk cover	66 (24.4)	130 (48.1)	48 (17.8)	18 (6.7)	8 (3.0)

Source: Primary data
Figures in ( ) represent percentage.

Table 4.27 depicts the opinions of the policyholders of ICICI as regards the product mix of the company. In respect of the statement that, the company's policies provide adequate returns a majority, 84.8 per cent (strongly agree and agree responses) of the respondents felt that adequate returns were provided by the policies of the company. Only one point eight per cent (disagree and strongly disagree responses) of the respondents felt that, it was not true. Thirteen point three per cent was indecisive to give a clear answer.

It can be inferred that, a majority, 82.9 per cent (strongly agree and agree responses) of respondents revealed that the company's policies provided security for the future. Only five point two per cent of the respondents felt that the company's policies did not provide security for the future. Remaining 11.9 per cent were undecided to give a clear answer.

As regards the statement that, the company's policies provide risk cover, a majority (strongly agree and agree responses) of the respondents, (82.3 per cent) felt that, the statement was true. Four point eight per cent felt that it was not true. Remaining 13 per cent was undecided to give a clear answer.

As regards the statement that the company's policies provide tax relief, a majority, 78.9 per cent (strongly agree and agree responses) of respondents responded in the affirmative. Only eight point five per cent of the respondents expressed a negative opinion. Remaining 12.6 per cent were neutral in their opinion.

With reference to the statement that the company's policies fulfill specific requirements, a majority, 74.9 per cent (strongly agree and agree responses) of respondents revealed that the company's policies fulfill their specific requirements. Only eight point two per cent of the respondents felt that the company's policies did not fulfill specific requirements. Remaining 17 were undecided to give a clear answer.

As regards the statement that the additional benefits offer adequate risk cover, a majority, 72.5 per cent (strongly agree and agree responses) of the respondents felt the statement to be true. Nine point seven per cent of the respondents felt that it was not true. Remaining seventeen point eight per cent was reluctant to give a clear answer.

Therefore it could be concluded that, ICICI Prudential Life Insurance products were favoured since they provided security, adequate returns, and risk cover.

Table 4.28 : Mean Score of Product Mix of the Life Insurance Companies

Variables	LIC	Bajaj	ICICI
Company's policies provide security for the future	4.30	4.33	4.09
Company's policies provide Risk cover	4.34	4.32	4.06
Company's policies provide Adequate returns	4.14	4.14	4.07
Company's policies provide fulfill specific requirements	4.04	4.20	3.94
Company's policies provide Tax relief	4.06	4.26	3.96
Additional Benefits offer adequate risk cover	4.14	4.23	3.84
Grand Average	**4.17**	**4.25**	**3.99**

Table 4.28 depicts the mean score of the variable product, calculated on the basis of the response of the policy holders of the companies selected for study.

It is striking to note that the policy holders of Bajaj have given higher ranking for the statement that the company's policies provide security for the future. It is revealed by the high mean score (4.33) obtained by the company. The policy holders of LIC also appreciated that statement by giving a mean score of (4.30). However, ICICI has been ranked third in this aspect.

With regard to the statement that company's policies provide risk cover, LIC has been ranked first by getting the highest mean score of (4.34) Bajaj policy holders have ranked the company second in this aspect and the third rank has been awarded to ICICI.

The LIC and Bajaj have been ranked on the same footing in respect of the fact that company's policies provide adequate returns ICICI has obtained the least mean score.

In respect of the statement company's policies fulfill specific requirements the highest mean score (4.20) has been given to Bajaj. LIC has been ranked second (4.04) in this aspect followed by ICICI that has been ranked third with 3.94 as the mean score.

Bajaj has been the highest scorer in respect of the statement that company's policies provide tax relief followed by LIC which has scored 4.06 ICICI has obtained the least mean score 3.96.

The statement that the additional Benefits offer adequate risk cover has been ranked high (4.23) by the policy holders of Bajaj. LIC has been given 4.14 as mean score ranking second, followed by ICICI which was ranked third with 3.84 as the mean score.

The grand average of the mean scores calculated reveals that Bajaj has been ranked first with four point two five as its score followed by LIC which has scored four point one seven.

Life Insurance Companies and the Product Mix

Null Hypothesis H_{o1} : The three companies are equally preferred in respect of product mix.

Null Hypothesis H_{o2} : Each attribute of the product mix is equally preferred.

Alternate Hypothesis H_{11} : Atleast one company is different from the other two companies.

Alternate Hypothesis H_{12} : Atleast one attribute is different from the other attributes.

Level of Significance (α) = 0.05

Calculated p value = .003.

Table 4.29 : Anova Table

Source	Type III Sum of Squares	df	Mean Square	F	Sig.
Corrected Model	.304a	7	.043	9.022	.001
Intercept	308.016	1	308.016	63903.776	.000
Insurance Company	.203	2	.101	21.010	.000
Factors	.102	5	.020	4.227	.025
Error	.048	10	.005		
Total	308.369	18			
Corrected Total	.353	17			

R squared = 0.863 (Adjusted R Squared = .7680

Inference H_{o1} : Calculated p value (0.000) < 0.05 (level of significance). Hence H_{o1} is rejected and H_{11} is accepted. It is concluded that the product mix of at least one company is different from the other companies.

It has also been proved with the help of Duncan's Test which showed the following result.

Table 4.30 : Result of Duncan Post HOC Test—Life Insurance Companies

Company	Subset Value	
	1	2
ICICI	3.9933	—
LIC		4.1700
Bajaj		4.2467

In respect of product mix LIC and Bajaj were equally preferred while ICICI was less preferred.

Inference H_{o2}: Calculated p value (0.025) < 0.05 (level of significance). Hence H_{o2} is rejected and H_{12} is accepted. It is concluded that atleast one attribute is different from the other attributes.

It has also been proved with the help of Duncan's Test which showed the following result.

It is inferred from the Duncan Test that attributes such as security and risk cover are viewed differently when compared to other attributes which are viewed together.

Price Mix

The second dimension of the marketing mix is the price mix. In this context, price mix has been analysed from two angles namely the premium charged by the company and the bonus declared by the three chosen life insurance companies – Bajaj Allianz Life Insurance Company, Life Insurance Corporation and ICICI Prudential Life Insurance Company.

Table 4.31 : Result of Duncan Post HOC Test—Attributes of Product Mix

Company	Subset Value	
	1	2
Company's policies provide fulfill specific requirements	4.0600	
Additional Benefits offer adequate risk cover	4.0700	
Company's policies provide Tax relief	4.0933	
Company's policies provide Adequate returns	4.1167	
Company's policies provide security for the future		4.2400
Company's policies provide Risk cover		4.2400

The response of the policyholders towards the enquiries made determines the effectiveness of the variable price mix. The opinion has been exhibited in the following tables:

Table 4.32 : Price Mix-LIC

Variables	Very high	High	Moderate	Low	Very Low
Premium	18(6.0)	50(16.8)	159(53.4)	67(22.5)	4(1.3)
Bonus	15(5.4)	84(28.2)	150(50.3)	43(14.4)	5(1.7)

Source: Primary data

Figures in ( ) represent percentage.

It is inferred from Table 4.32 that, majority (53.4 per cent) of the respondents have felt that the premium charged by the LIC has been moderate and for 23.8 per cent of the respondents the premium charged was low/ very low. However, the percentage of respondents, who felt that the premium was very high / high was 22.8 per cent.

As regards the bonus declared by the company, 50.3 per cent of the respondents have felt that, it was moderate. Thirty three point six per cent of the respondents felt that, the bonus was high. However, the percentage of respondents who felt that the bonus was very low or low was 16.1 per cent.

Table 4.33 : Price Mix - Bajaj

Variables	Very high	High	Moderate	Low	Very Low
Premium	24(11.7)	50(24.4)	86(42.0)	38(18.5)	7(3.4)
Bonus	37(18.0)	76(37.1)	82(40.0)	7(3.4)	3(1.5)

Source: Primary data

Figures in ( ) represent percentage.

It is clear from Table 4.33 that, majority (42 per cent) of the respondents have felt that the premium charged by Bajaj has been moderate. According to 36.1 per cent of the respondents the premium charged was very high / high. However, the respondents, who felt that the premium was low/ very low constituted 22.8 per cent of the total respondents.

As regards the bonus declared by the company, the percentage of respondents who felt that, the bonus was very high/high was 55.1 per cent and 40 per cent of the respondents have felt that, it was moderate. However, the percentage of respondents who felt that, the bonus was very low or low was just four point nine per cent.

It is concluded that, the premium charged by the company has been considered as reasonable whereas the bonus declared has been considered as high.

Table 4.34 : Price Mix–ICICI

Variables	Very high	High	Moderate	Low	Very Low
Premium	43(15.9)	108(40.0)	70(25.9)	33(12.2)	16(5.9)
Bonus	29(10.7)	101(37.4)	93(34.4)	34(13.7)	10(3.7)

Source: Primary data
Figures in ( ) represent percentage.

It is inferred from Table 4.34 that, the premium charged by the company was considered to be very high/high by majority (55.9 per cent) of the respondents. However the premium charged was considered to be moderate by 25.9 per cent of the respondents and 18.1 per cent of the respondents have felt that, the premium was low/very low.

Interestingly it has been observed that, the bonus offered by the company was considered to be high by 48.1 per cent of the respondents. According to 34.4 per cent of the respondents, the bonus declared by the company was moderate while for 17.4 per cent of the respondents it was very low or low.

Hence it is concluded that, for majority of the respondents the premium charged was high and the bonus declared also was high.

Table 4.35 : Mean Score of Price Mix of the Life Insurance Companies

Variables	LIC	Bajaj	ICICI
Premium	2.96	2.78	2.52
Bonus	2.79	2.37	2.62

Table 4.35 depicts the mean score of the variable price calculated on the basis of the response of the policy holders of the companies selected for study.

From the mean score based on the response, it is inferred that LIC has been given the first preference in spite of the fact that the premium paid is higher than that of the other two companies due to the fact that the bonus given by the company is also higher than that of the other two.

It is inferred that, the policyholders had an opinion that the LIC policy premium was moderate and bonus also was moderate.

PROMOTION MIX

The third dimension of the marketing mix is the promotion mix. Promotion mix in the present context means the various promotional tools used by the three chosen life insurance companies namely Bajaj Allianz Life Insurance Company, Life Insurance Corporation and ICICI Prudential Life Insurance Company. The promotion mix has been analysed with reference to the advertisement, technology, website, posters exhibited by the company, pamphlets issued and the interactions held with the policyholders.

The response of the policyholders towards the enquiries made determines the effectiveness of the variable promotion mix. The opinion has been exhibited in the following tables:

Table 4.36 : Promotion Mix-LIC

Variables	Strongly agree	Agree	Neutral	Disagree	Strongly disagree
Visual appeal of Advertisement is Good	46(15.4)	194(65.1)	53(17.8)	3(1.0)	2(0.7)
Advertisements are informative	55(18.5)	192(64.4)	39(13.1)	10(3.4)	2(0.7)
Technology is useful	58(19.5)	172(57.7)	59(19.8)	7(2.3)	2(0.7)
Website is informative	60(20.1)	116(38.9)	113(37.9)	8(2.7)	1(0.3)
Advertisement is motivating	58(19.5)	185(62.1)	43(14.4)	11(3.7)	1(0.3)
Posters are impressive	48(16.1)	192(64.4)	41(13.8)	16(5.4)	1(0.3)
Pamphlets are informative	45(15.1)	172(57.7)	67(22.5)	12(4.0)	2(0.7)
The company interacts with the policyholders regularly	37(12.4)	126(42.3)	115(38.6)	17(5.7)	3(1.0)

Source: Primary data
Figures in ( ) represent percentage.

Table 4.36 discloses the opinions of the policyholders of LIC as regards the promotion mix of the company. It can be inferred that, majority of the respondents that is 82.9 per cent (strongly agree and agree responses) revealed that the advertisements were informative. Only four point one per cent of the respondents felt that the advertisements were not informative. Remaining 13.1 per cent were undecided to give a clear answer.

As regards the statement that the advertisement is motivating, majority of the respondents that is 81.6 per cent (strongly agree and agree responses) felt that the statement was true. Only four percent of the respondents felt that it was not true. Fourteen point four per cent were indecisive to give a clear answer.

In respect of the statement that the visual appeal of advertisement is good, majority of the respondents that is 80.5 per cent (strongly agree and agree responses) agreed that the statement was true. Only one point seven per cent (disagree and strongly disagree responses) disagreed with the statement. Seventeen point eight per cent was reluctant to give a clear answer.

As regards the statement that the posters are impressive, majority of the respondents that is 80.5 per cent (strongly agree and agree responses) answered in the affirmative. Only five point seven per cent of the respondents answered negatively. Thirteen point eight per cent were neutral in this regard.

With reference to the statement that the technology is useful, majority of the respondents that is 77.2 per cent (strongly agree and agree responses) revealed that the technology was useful. Only three point seven per cent of the respondents felt that the technology was not useful. Remaining 16.4 per cent of the respondents neither agreed nor disagreed.

In respect of the statement that the pamphlets are informative, majority of the respondents that is 72.8 per cent (strongly agree and agree responses) felt that adequate information was provided by the pamphlets. Only four point seven percent of the respondents (disagree and strongly disagree responses) differed in their opinion. Twenty two point five per cent was undecided to give a clear answer.

As regards the statement that the website is informative, majority of the respondents that is 59 per cent (strongly agree and agree responses) felt the statement was correct. Only three point seven per cent of the respondents felt that it was incorrect. Thirty seven point nine per cent of the respondents neither agreed nor disagreed to the statement.

Majority of the respondents that is 54.7 per cent (strongly agree and agree responses) revealed that the company interacted with the policyholders regularly. Six point seven per cent of the respondents felt that the company did not interact with the policyholders regularly. Remaining 38.6 per cent were undecided to give a clear answer.

Hence it is concluded that, for the customers of Life Insurance Corporation the advertisements played an effective role as a promotional tool, since majority of the respondents felt that the advertisements were informative (82.9 per cent), advertisements were highly motivating (81.6 per cent) and had good visual appeal and the posters were also highly impressive.

Table 4.37 : Promotion Mix-Bajaj

Variables	Strongly agree	Agree	Neutral	Disagree	Strongly disagree
Visual appeal of Advertisement is Good	50(24.4)	100(48.8)	48(23.4)	7(3.4)	—
Advertisements are informative	54(26.3)	97(47.3)	53(25.9)	1(0.5)	—
Technology is useful	59(28.8)	95(46.3)	47(22.9)	4(2.0)	—
Website is informative	67(32.7)	111(54.1)	25(12.2)	2(1.0)	—
Advertisement is motivating	61(29.8)	84(41.0)	55(26.8)	5(2.4)	—
Posters are impressive	43(21.0)	96(46.8)	63(30.7)	3(1.5)	—
Pamphlets are informative	83(40.5)	98(47.8)	21(10.2)	3(1.5)	—
The company interacts with the policyholders regularly	57(27.8)	116(56.6)	31(15.1)	1(0.5)	—

Source: Primary data
Figures in ( ) represent percentage.

Table 4.37 reveals the opinions of the policyholders of Bajaj as regards the promotion mix of the company. In respect of the statement that the pamphlets are informative, majority of the respondents that is 88.3 per cent (strongly agree and agree responses) felt that adequate information was provided by the pamphlets. Only one point five per cent of the respondents (disagree and strongly disagree responses) differed in their opinion. Ten point two per cent was undecided to give a clear answer.

As regards the statement that the website is informative, majority of the respondents that is 86.8 per cent (strongly agree and agree responses) felt the statement was correct. Only one per cent of the respondents felt that it was incorrect. Twelve point two per cent of the respondents neither agreed nor disagreed to the statement.

Majority of the respondents that is 84.4 per cent (strongly agree and agree responses) revealed that the company interacted with the policyholders regularly. A negligible per cent of the respondents felt that the company did not interact with the policyholders regularly. Remaining 16.1 per cent were undecided to give a clear answer.

With reference to the statement that the technology is useful, majority of the respondents that is 75.1 per cent (strongly agree and agree responses) revealed that the technology was useful. Only two per cent of the respondents felt that the technology was not useful. Remaining 22.9 per cent of the respondents neither agreed nor disagreed.

It can be inferred that, majority of the respondents 73.6 per cent (strongly agree and agree responses) revealed that the advertisements were informative. A negligible per cent of the respondents felt that the advertisements were not informative. Remaining 25.9 per cent were undecided to give a clear answer.

In respect of the statement that the visual appeal of advertisement is good, majority of the respondents that is 73.2 per cent (strongly agree and agree responses) agreed that the statement was true. Only three point four per cent (disagree and strongly disagree responses) disagreed with the statement. Remaining 23.4 per cent was reluctant to give a clear answer.

As regards the statement that the advertisement is motivating, majority of the respondents that is 70.8 per cent (strongly agree and agree responses) felt that the statement was true. Only two point four per cent of the respondents felt that it was not true. Remaining 26.8 per cent were indecisive to give a clear answer.

As regards the statement that the posters are impressive, majority of the respondents that is 67.8 per cent (strongly agree and agree responses) answered in the affirmative. Only one point five per cent of the respondents answered negatively. Remaining 30.7 per cent were neutral in this regard.

Therefore it could be concluded that, the sales promotional activities of Bajaj Allianz Life Insurance Company have been appreciated due to the issue of informative pamphlets, provision of information through website and the interactions the intermediaries had with the policy holders. However, advertisement made through the posters and hoarding have been less attractive.

Table 4.38 : Promotion Mix-ICICI

Variables	Strongly agree	Agree	Neutral	Disagree	Strongly disagree
Visual appeal of Advertisement is Good	57(21.1)	151(55.9)	48(17.8)	7(2.0)	7(2.6)
Advertisements are informative	49(18.1)	166(61.5)	43(15.9)	9(3.3)	3(1.1)
Technology is useful	68(25.2)	121(44.8)	68(25.2)	8(3.0)	5(1.8)
Website is informative	58(21.5)	135(50.0)	61(22.6)	15(5.6)	1(0.4)
Advertisement is motivating	66(24.4)	148(54.8)	42(15.6)	11(4.1)	3(1.1)
Posters are impressive	53(19.6)	136(50.4)	66(24.4)	6(2.2)	9(3.3)
Pamphlets are informative	74(27.4)	144(53.3)	37(13.7)	12(4.4)	3(1.1)
The company interacts with the policyholders regularly	74(27.4)	117(43.4)	64(23.7)	9(3.3)	6(2.2)

Source: Primary data
Figures in ( ) represent percentage.

Table 4.38 depicts the opinions of the policyholders of ICICI as regards the promotion mix of the company. In respect of the statement that the pamphlets are informative, majority of the respondents that is 80.7 per cent (strongly agree and agree responses) felt that adequate information was provided by the pamphlets. Only five point five per cent of the respondents (disagree and strongly disagree responses) differed in their opinion. Remaining 13.7 per cent of the respondents were undecided to give a clear answer.

It can be inferred that, a majority, 79.6 per cent (strongly agree and agree responses) of respondents revealed that the advertisements were informative. Four point four per cent of the respondents felt that the advertisements were not informative. Remaining 15.9 per cent were undecided to give a clear answer.

As regards the statement that the advertisement is motivating, majority of the respondents that is 79.2 per cent (strongly agree and agree responses) felt that the statement was true. Only five point two per cent of the respondents felt that it was not true. Remaining 26.8 per cent were indecisive to give a clear answer.

In respect of the statement that the visual appeal of advertisement is good, majority of the respondents that is 77 per cent (strongly agree and agree responses) agreed that the statement was true. Only five point two per cent of the respondents (disagree and strongly disagree responses) disagreed with the statement. Remaining 17.8 per cent was reluctant to give a clear answer.

As regards the statement that the website is informative, majority of the respondents that is 71.5 per cent (strongly agree and agree responses) of the respondents felt the statement was correct. Only six per cent of the respondents felt that it was incorrect. Remaining five point six per cent of the respondents neither agreed nor disagreed to the statement.

Majority of the respondents that is 70.8 per cent (strongly agree and agree responses) of respondents revealed that the company interacted with the policyholders regularly. Five point five per cent of the respondents felt that the company did not interact with the policyholders regularly. Remaining 23.7 per cent were undecided to give a clear answer.

With reference to the statement that the technology is useful, majority of the respondents that is 70 per cent (strongly agree and agree responses) revealed that the technology was useful. Only four point eight per cent of the respondents felt that the technology was not useful. Remaining 25.2 per cent of the respondents neither agreed nor disagreed.

As regards the statement that the posters are impressive, majority of the respondents that is 70 per cent (strongly agree and agree responses) answered in the affirmative. Only five point five per cent of the respondents answered negatively. Remaining 24.5 per cent were neutral in this regard.

Hence, it could be concluded that ICICI Prudential Life Insurance company has been appreciated by the policy holders for its informative pamphlets, informative advertisements and motivation of customers through advertisements.

Table 4.39 : Mean Score of Promotion Mix of the Life Insurance Companies

Variables	LIC	Bajaj	ICICI
Visual appeal of Advertisement is Good	3.94	3.94	3.90
Advertisements are informative	3.97	4.00	3.92
Technology is useful	3.93	4.02	3.89
Website is informative	3.76	4.19	3.87
Advertisement is motivating	3.97	3.98	3.97
Posters are impressive	3.91	3.87	3.81
Pamphlets are informative	3.83	4.27	4.01
The company interacts with the policyholders regularly	3.59	4.12	3.90
Grand Average	**3.86**	**4.05**	**3.91**

Table 4.39 depicts the mean score of the variable promotion calculated on the basis of the response of the policy holders of the companies selected for study.

The LIC and Bajaj have been ranked on the same footing (3.94) in respect of the fact that Visual appeal of Advertisement is Good. ICICI has obtained the least mean score (3.90).

With regard to the statement that advertisements are informative, LIC has been ranked first by getting the highest mean score of (4.34) Bajaj policy holders have ranked the company second in this aspect and the third rank has been awarded to ICICI.

In respect of the statement that technology is useful the highest mean score (4.20) has been given to Bajaj. LIC has been ranked second (4.04) in this aspect followed by ICICI that has been ranked third with 3.94 as the mean score.

In respect of the statement website is informative the highest mean score (4.09) has been given to Bajaj. LIC has been ranked second (4.07) in this aspect followed by ICICI that has been ranked third with 3.69 as the mean score.

As regards the statement that advertisement is motivating Bajaj has been the high scorer (4.14) followed by ICICI which has obtained a mean score 4.03 the LIC has been awarded the third place with 3.82 as the mean score.

With regard to the statement that posters are impressive, LIC has been ranked first by getting the highest mean score of (4.34) Bajaj policy holders have ranked the company second in this aspect and the third rank has been awarded to ICICI.

With respect to the statement that the pamphlets are informative Bajaj has scored the highest mean score of 4.27 followed by ICICI which secured 4.13 as mean score. The mean score of LIC was the least (3.84) among all the companies.

In respect of the statement that the company interacts with the policyholders regularly, Bajaj has been the top scorer with 4.15 as mean score. ICICI has bagged the second rank with 4.11 as its mean score followed by LIC which has obtained the least mean score of 3.62.

The grand average of the mean scores calculated reveals that, Bajaj has been ranked first with four point zero five as its score followed by ICICI which has scored three point nine one.

DISTRIBUTION MIX

The fourth dimension of the marketing mix is the distribution mix. Distribution mix analyses the role played by the intermediaries of the three chosen life insurance companies namely Bajaj Allianz Life Insurance Company, Life Insurance Corporation and ICICI Prudential Life Insurance Company. The distribution mix has been analysed with reference to the assistance rendered by the intermediaries to the policyholders in the purchase of the policy, claim settlement, grievance settlement and information provided at the introduction of policies. The policyholders' opinion as regards the knowledge of the agents has also been analysed.

Table 4.40 : Distribution Mix-Lic

Variables	Strongly agree	Agree	Neutral	Disagree	Strongly disagree
Intermediaries provide information at the introduction of new policy	75(25.2)	211(70.8)	9(3.0)	3(1.0)	—
Intermediaries assist in purchase of new policy	105(35.2)	189(63.4)	2(0.7)	1(0.3)	1(0.3)
Intermediaries assist in claim settlement	100(33.6)	140(47.0)	48(16.1)	9(3.0)	1(0.3)
Intermediaries assist in grievance settlement	80(26.8)	165(55.4)	42(14.1)	10(3.4)	1(0.3)
Intermediaries have thorough knowledge of the products	126(42.3)	145(48.7)	26(8.7)	1(0.3)	—

Source: Primary data
Figures in ( ) represent percentage.

The response of the policyholders towards the enquiries made determines the effectiveness of the variable distribution mix. The opinion has been exhibited in the following tables.

Table 4.40 discloses the opinions of the policyholders of LIC as regards the distribution mix of the company. It can be inferred that, a majority, 96 per cent (strongly agree and agree responses) of respondents revealed that the intermediaries provided information to the policyholders about the introduction of new policies. Only one per cent of the respondents felt that the intermediaries did not provide information. Remaining three per cent were undecided to give a clear answer.

As regards the statement that the intermediaries render valuable assistance for the purchase of policy, a majority, 98.6 per cent (strongly agree and agree responses) of the respondents felt the statement to be true. A negligible percentage (zero point six per cent) felt that it was not true. Zero point seven per cent were indecisive to give a clear answer.

In respect of the statement that, intermediaries possessed thorough knowledge about the company's policies, majority of the respondents, 91 per cent (strongly agree and agree responses) of the respondents felt the statement to be true. A negligible percentage (zero point three per cent) felt that it was not true. Eight point seven per cent were undecided to give a clear answer.

With reference to the statement that the intermediaries assist in settlement of grievances, a majority, 82 per cent (strongly agree and agree responses) of respondents revealed that the intermediaries provided assistance in settlement of grievances. Only three point seven per cent of the respondents felt that the intermediaries did not assist in settlement of grievances. Remaining 14.1 per cent neither agreed nor disagreed with the statement.

As regards the statement that the intermediaries assist in settlement of claim, a majority, 80.6 per cent (strongly agree and agree responses) of respondents revealed that the intermediaries provided assistance in settlement of claim. Only three point zero three per cent of the respondents felt that the intermediaries did not assist in settlement of claim. Remaining 16.1 per cent answered negatively.

Thus, the above analysis reveals that majority of the policy holders considered that, the intermediaries assisted in the purchase of policy, provided information at the introduction of the new policy and possessed thorough knowledge about the company's policies.

Table 4.41 reveals the opinions of the policyholders of Bajaj as regards the distribution mix of the company. It is clear that, as regards the statement that the intermediaries render valuable assistance for the purchase of policy, a majority, 94.1 per cent (strongly agree and agree responses) of the respondents felt the statement to be true. No respondent felt that it was not true. Five point nine per cent of the respondents were undecided to give a clear answer.

Table 4.41 : Distribution Mix-Bajaj

Variables	Strongly agree	Agree	Neutral	Disagree	Strongly disagree
Intermediaries provide information at the introduction of new policy	59(28.8)	128(62.4)	17(8.3)	1(0.5)	—
Intermediaries assist in purchase of new policy	81(39.5)	112(54.6)	12(5.9)	—	—
Intermediaries assist in claim settlement	35(17.1)	106(51.7)	64((31.2)	—	—
Intermediaries assist in grievance settlement	41(20.0)	105(51.2)	57(27.8)	2(1.0)	—
Intermediaries have thorough knowledge of the products	68(33.2)	99(48.3)	38(18.5)	—	—

Source: Primary data
Figures in ( ) represent percentage.

Majority of the respondents, 91.2 per cent (strongly agree and agree responses) of respondents revealed that the intermediaries provided information to the policyholders about the introduction of new policies. Zero point five per cent of the respondents felt that the intermediaries did not provide information. Remaining eight point three per cent were undecided to give a clear answer.

In respect of the statement that, intermediaries possessed thorough knowledge about the company's policies, majority of the respondents, 81.5 per cent (strongly agree and agree responses) of the respondents felt the statement to be true. No respondent felt that it was not true. Eight point three per cent refused to give a clear answer.

With reference to the statement that the intermediaries assist in settlement of grievances, majority of the respondents, 71.2 per cent (strongly agree and agree responses) of respondents revealed that the intermediaries provided assistance in settlement of grievances. Only one per cent of the respondents felt that the intermediaries did not assist in settlement of grievances. Remaining 27.8 per cent were indecisive to give a clear answer.

As regards the statement that the intermediaries assist in settlement of claim, majority of the respondents, 68.8 per cent (strongly agree and agree responses) of respondents revealed that the intermediaries provided assistance in settlement of claim. No respondent felt that the intermediaries did not assist in settlement of claim. Remaining 31.2 per cent were indecisive to give a clear answer.

It can be concluded that, policyholders appeared to have a belief that the intermediaries rendered a commendable job as there is no response for strongly disagree.

Table 4.42 : Distribution Mix-ICICI

Variables	Strongly agree	Agree	Neutral	Disagree	Strongly disagree
Intermediaries provide information at the introduction of new policy	81(30.0)	129(47.8)	42(15.6)	16(5.9)	2(0.7)
Intermediaries assist in purchase of new policy	84(31.1)	136(50.4)	34(12.6)	13(4.8)	3(1.1)
Intermediaries assist in claim settlement	58(21.5)	125(46.3)	68(25.2)	13(4.8)	6(2.2)
Intermediaries assist in grievance settlement	58(21.5)	131(48.5)	65(24.1)	10(3.7)	6(2.2)
Intermediaries have thorough knowledge of the products	87(32.2)	114(42.2)	46(17.0)	11(4.1)	12(4.4)

Source: Primary data
Figures in ( ) represent percentage.

Table 4.42 depicts the opinions of the policyholders of ICICI as regards the distribution mix of the company. It is clear that, as regards the statement that the intermediaries render valuable assistance for the purchase of policy, a majority, 81.5 per cent (strongly agree and agree responses) of the respondents felt the statement to be true. Five point nine per cent of the respondents felt that it was not true. However, 12.6 per cent of the respondents were undecided to give a clear answer.

Majority of the respondents, 77.8 per cent (strongly agree and agree responses) revealed that the intermediaries provided information to the policyholders about the introduction of new policies. Six point six per cent of the respondents felt that the intermediaries did not provide information. Remaining 15.6 were undecided to give a clear answer.

In respect of the statement that, intermediaries possessed thorough knowledge about the company's policies. Majority of the respondents, 77.4 per cent (strongly agree and agree responses) felt that, the statement was true. Eight point five per cent of the respondents felt that, it was not true. Remaining 17 per cent were undecided to give a clear answer.

With reference to the statement that the intermediaries assist in settlement of grievances, majority of the respondents, 70 per cent (strongly agree and agree responses) of respondents revealed that the intermediaries provided assistance in settlement of grievances. Only five point nine per cent of the respondents felt that the intermediaries did not assist in settlement of grievances. Remaining 24.1 per cent were undecided to give a clear answer.

As regards the statement that the intermediaries assist in settlement of claim, majority of the respondents, 67.8 per cent (strongly agree and agree responses) of respondents revealed that the intermediaries provided assistance in settlement of claim. Seven per cent of the respondents felt that the intermediaries did not assist in settlement of claim. Remaining 25.2 per cent were indecisive to give a clear answer.

The policyholders of ICICI assertively stated that the intermediaries rendered valuable assistance for the purchase of the policy, they provided information about the introduction of new policies and they possessed thorough knowledge about the company's policies.

Table 4.43 : Mean Score of Distribution Mix of the Life Insurance Companies

Variables	LIC	Bajaj	ICICI
Intermediaries provide information at the introduction of new policy	4.20	4.20	4.00
Intermediaries assist in purchase of new policy	4.33	4.34	4.06
Intermediaries assist in claim settlement	4.10	3.86	3.80
Intermediaries assist in grievance settlement	4.05	3.90	3.83
Intermediaries have thorough knowledge of the products	4.33	4.15	3.94
Grand Average	**4.28**	**4.06**	**3.92**

Table 4.43 depicts the mean score of the variable distribution calculated on the basis of the response of the policy holders of the companies selected for study. LIC and Bajaj have been awarded the first rank by the policy holders in respect of the statement that intermediaries provide information at the introduction of new policy. This is evident from the fact that, they have obtained the highest mean score of four point two, as compared to ICICI that has obtained a mean score of four.

In respect of the statement that intermediaries assist in purchase of new policy, Bajaj has scored a high mean score of four point three four. A marginal difference has been noticed between the mean scores of Bajaj and LIC, the latter's mean score being four point three three ICICI has been ranked third in this aspect.

With regard to the statement that intermediaries assist in claim settlement, LIC has been ranked first by getting the highest mean score of four point one. Bajaj policy holders have ranked the company second with three point eight six as its score in this aspect and the third rank (three point eight) has been awarded to ICICI.

In respect of the statement that intermediaries assist in grievance settlement, LIC has been ranked high with four point zero five as mean score. Bajaj has bagged the second rank with three point nine as its mean score followed by ICICI which has obtained the least mean score of three point eight three.

The policy holders of LIC has awarded the highest position to the company in respect of the statement that the intermediaries have thorough knowledge of the products, by giving a mean score of four point three three. Bajaj follows LIC with four point one five as mean score and ICICI ranks third with three point nine four as its mean score.

The grand average of the mean scores calculated reveals that, LIC has been ranked first with four point two eight as its score followed by Bajaj which has scored four point zero six.

PEOPLE AND PROCESS MIX (CUSTOMER CARE SERVICES)

The fifth and sixth dimensions of the marketing mix are people and process mix. People and process mix in the present context refers to customer care services rendered by the three chosen life insurance companies namely Bajaj Allianz Life Insurance Company, Life Insurance Corporation and ICICI Prudential Life Insurance Company. The People and process mix has been analysed with reference to the customer care services namely prompt service rendered by the employees, information at policy lapse, assistance in reviving, policy, promptness in attending enquiries, promptness in claim settlement, friendliness of employees, settlement of grievances, maintenance of accurate records and promptness in document issue.

The response of the policyholders towards the enquiries made determines the effectiveness of the variable people and process mix. The opinion has been exhibited in the following tables.

Table – 47 discloses the opinions of the policyholders of LIC as regards the people and process mix (customer care services) of the company. It can be inferred that, as regards the statement that the company maintains accurate records, 92.2 per cent (strongly agree and agree responses) of the respondents felt the statement to be true. Only one point seven per cent of the respondents felt that it was not true. However, six per cent of the respondents were hesitant to give a clear answer.

It was revealed by 85.2 per cent of the respondents (strongly agree and agree responses) that the company provided information to policyholders at the lapse of the policy. Two point three per cent of the respondents felt that the company did not provide information. Remaining 12.4 were undecided to give a clear answer.

Table 4.44 : People and Process Mix-LIC

Variables	Strongly agree	Agree	Neutral	Disagree	Strongly disagree
The company is prompt in sanctioning loans	61(20.5)	162(54.4)	65(21.8)	9(3.0)	1(0.3)
Company provides information at the lapse of policy	73(24.5)	181(60.7)	37(12.4)	6(2.0)	1(0.3)
Company provides assistance in reviving policy	67(22.5)	151(50.7)	70(23.5)	9(3.0)	1(0.3)
Employees respond to the enquires of policyholders	61(20.5)	173(58.1)	46(15.4)	17(5.7)	1(0.3)
Company settles claim on time	86(28.9)	152(51.0)	46(15.4)	12(4.0)	2(0.7)
Employees maintain cordial relationship with the policyholders	59(19.8)	177(59.4)	40(13.4)	19(6.4)	3(1.0)
Company settles grievances on time	55(18.5)	160(53.7)	71(23.8)	11(3.7)	1(0.3)
Company maintains accurate records	150(50.3)	125(41.9)	18(6.0)	5(1.7)	—
Company issues documents promptly	82(27.5)	163(54.7)	24(8.1)	26(8.7)	3(1.0)

Source: Primary data
Figures in ( ) represent percentage.

In respect of the statement that, the company issued the policy documents promptly, 82.2 per cent of the respondents (strongly agree and agree responses) felt that the statement was true. Nine point seven per cent of the respondents felt that, it was not true. Remaining eight point one per cent were undecided to give a clear answer.

With reference to the statement that the company settles claim on time, 79.9 per cent of the respondents (strongly agree and agree responses) revealed that, the company settled the claim on time. Four point seven per cent of the respondents felt that, the company did not settle claim on time. Remaining 15.4 per cent were reluctant to give a clear answer.

As regards the statement that the employees maintained cordial relationship with the policy holders, 79.2 per cent of the respondents (strongly agree and agree responses) revealed that, the employees maintained cordial relationship with the policy holders. Seven point four per cent of the respondents felt that, the employees did not maintain cordial relationship with the policy holders. Remaining 13.4 per cent were indecisive to give a clear answer.

It was revealed by 78.6 per cent of the respondents (strongly agree and agree responses) that, the employees responded to the enquiries of the policyholders. Six per cent of the respondents felt that, the employees did not respond to the enquiries of the policyholders. Remaining 15.4 were undecided to give a clear answer.

As regards the statement that the company was prompt in sanctioning loans to the policyholders, 74.9 per cent of the respondents (strongly agree and agree responses) felt that, the statement was true. Only three point three per cent of the respondents felt that, it was not true. However, 21.8 per cent of the respondents were undecided to give a clear answer.

In respect of the statement that, the company took immediate steps to revive the policies issued, 73.2 per cent of the respondents (strongly agree and agree responses) felt that the statement was true. Only three point three of the respondents felt that, it was not true. Remaining 23.5 per cent were undecided to give a clear answer.

Table 4.45 : People and Process Mix-Bajaj

Variables	Strongly agree	Agree	Neutral	Disagree	Strongly disagree
The company is prompt in sanctioning loans	39(19.0)	60(29.3)	98(47.8)	7(3.4)	1(0.5)
Company provides information at the lapse of policy	69(33.7)	87(42.4)	47(22.9)	2(1.0)	—
Company provides assistance in reviving policy	72(35.1)	95(46.3)	36(17.6)	2(1.0)	—
Employees respond to the enquires of policyholders	78(38.0)	92(44.9)	34(16.6)	1(0.5)	—
Company settles claim on time	63(30.7)	71(34.6)	69(33.7)	2(1.0)	—
Employees maintain cordial relationship with the policyholders	90(43.9)	110(53.7)	3(1.5)	2(1.0)	—
Company settles grievances on time	50(24.4)	78(38.0)	77(37.6)	—	—
Company maintains accurate records	61(29.8)	133(64.9)	11(5.4)	—	—
Company issues documents promptly	68(33.2)	103(50.2)	30(14.6)	3(1.5)	1(0.5)

Source: Primary data
Figures in ( ) represent percentage.

As regards the statement that the company took steps to settle the grievances, 72.2 per cent of the respondents (strongly agree and agree responses) felt that, the statement was true. Only four per cent of the respondents felt that, it was not true. However, 23.8 per cent of the respondents were undecided to give a clear answer.

Table 4.45 reveals the opinions of the policyholders of Bajaj as regards the people and process mix (customer care services) of the company. It is clear that, as regards the statement that the employees maintained cordial relationship with the policy holders, 97.6 per cent of the respondents (strongly agree and agree responses) revealed that the employees maintained cordial relationship with the policy holders. Only one per cent of the respondents felt that the employees did not maintain cordial relationship with the policy holders. Remaining one point five per cent was indecisive to give a clear answer.

In respect of the statement that the company maintains accurate records, 94.7 per cent of the respondents (strongly agree and agree responses) felt that, the statement was true. No respondent had felt that, it was not true. However, five point four per cent of the respondents were undecided to give a clear answer.

In respect of the statement that, the company issued the policy documents promptly, 83.2 per cent of the respondents (strongly agree and agree responses) felt that, the statement was true. Only two per cent of the respondents felt that, it was not true. Remaining 14.6 per cent were not sure to give a clear answer.

It was revealed by 82.9 per cent of the respondents (strongly agree and agree responses) that the employees responded to the enquiries of the policyholders. A negligible (zero point five) per cent of the respondents felt that the employees did not respond to the enquiries of the policyholders. Remaining 16.6 were undecided to give a clear answer.

In respect of the statement that, the company took immediate steps to revive the policies issued, 84.1 per cent of the respondents (strongly agree and agree responses) felt that, the statement was true. Only one per cent of the respondents felt that, it was not true. Remaining 17.6 per cent could not give a clear answer.

It was revealed by 76.1 per cent of the respondents (strongly agree and agree responses) that, the company provided information to policyholders at the lapse of the policy. A negligible, one per cent of the respondents felt that, the company did not provide information. Remaining 22.9 were undecided to give a clear answer.

With reference to the statement that the company settles claim on time, 65.3 per cent of the respondents (strongly agree and agree responses) revealed that, the company settled the claim on time. Only one per cent of the respondents felt that, the company did not settle claim on time. Remaining 33.7 per cent were indecisive to give a clear answer.

As regards the statement that the company took steps to settle the grievances, 62.4 per cent of the respondents (strongly agree and agree responses) felt that, the statement was true. No respondent felt that, it was not true. However, 37.6 per cent of the respondents were reluctant to give a clear answer.

As regards the statement that the company is prompt in sanctioning loans to the policyholders, 48.3 per cent of the respondents (strongly agree and agree responses) answered in the affirmative. Only three point nine per cent of the respondents answered negatively. However, 47.8 per cent of the respondents were unsure of a clear answer. It may be because, loan facilities were not provided directly by the company.

It can be concluded that, the policyholders of Bajaj were very much satisfied with the cordial relationship maintained by the employees of the company with the policyholders, the maintenance of accurate records and the promptness with which the policy documents were issued by the company.

Table 4.46 : People and Process Mix-ICICI

Variables	Strongly agree	Agree	Neutral	Disagree	Strongly disagree
The company is prompt in sanctioning loans	48(17.8)	116(43.0)	81(30.0)	19(7.0)	6(2.2)
Company provides information at the lapse of policy	64(23.7)	103(38.1)	61(22.6)	38(14.1)	4(1.5)
Company provides assistance in reviving policy	66(24.4)	123(45.6)	58(21.5)	16(5.9)	7(2.6)
Employees respond to the enquires of policyholders	64(23.7)	143(53.0)	47(17.4)	11(4.1)	5(1.9)
Company settles claim on time	63(23.3)	124(45.9)	56(20.7)	17(6.3)	10(3.7)
Employees maintain cordial relationship with the policyholders	89(33.0)	129(47.8)	31(11.5)	12(4.4)	9(3.3)
Company settles grievances on time	55(20.4)	131(48.5)	71(26.3)	12(4.4)	1(0.4)
Company maintains accurate records	62(23.0)	121(44.8)	50(18.5)	29(10.7)	8(3.0)
Company issues documents promptly	69(25.6)	149(55.2)	28(10.4)	17(6.3)	7(2.6)

Source: Primary data
Figures in ( ) represent percentage.

Table 4.46 depicts the opinions of the policyholders of ICICI as regards the people and process mix (customer care services) of the company. It indicates that, as regards the statement that the employees maintain cordial relationship with the policy holders, 83.8 per cent of the respondents (strongly agree and agree responses) revealed that, the employees maintained cordial relationship with the policy holders. Only seven point seven per cent of the respondents felt that, the employees did not maintain cordial relationship with the policy holders. Remaining eight point five per cent were indecisive, to give a clear answer.

In respect of the statement that, the company issued the policy documents promptly, 80.8 per cent of the respondents (strongly agree and agree responses) felt that, the statement was true. Only eight point nine per cent of the respondents felt that, it was not true. Remaining 10.4 per cent were undecided to give a clear answer.

It was revealed by 76.7 per cent of the respondents (strongly agree and agree responses) that, the employees responded to the enquiries of the policyholders. Six per cent of the respondents felt that, the employees did not respond to the enquiries of the policyholders. Remaining 17.3 were undecided to give a clear answer.

As regards the statement that the company is prompt in sanctioning loans to the policyholders, 60.8 per cent of the respondents (strongly agree and agree responses) felt that, the statement was true. Only nine point two per cent of the respondents felt that, it was not true. However, 14.2 per cent of the respondents were undecided to give a clear answer.

In respect of the statement that the company took immediate steps to revive the policies issued, 70 per cent of the respondents (strongly agree and agree responses) felt that, the statement was true. Only eight point five per cent of the respondents felt that, it was not true. Remaining 21.5 per cent were undecided to give a clear answer.

With reference to the statement that the company settles claim on time, 69.2 per cent of the respondents (strongly agree and agree responses) revealed that, the company settled the claim on time. Only ten per cent of the respondents felt that, the company did not settle claim on time. Remaining 20.7 per cent were undecided to give a clear answer.

As regards the statement that the company took steps to settle the grievances, 68.9 per cent of the respondents (strongly agree and agree responses) felt, that the statement was true. Four point eight per cent of the respondents felt that, it was not true. However, 26.3 per cent of the respondents were undecided to give a clear answer.

In respect of the statement that the company maintains accurate records, 67.8 per cent of the respondents (strongly agree and agree responses) felt that, the statement was true. Thirteen point seven per cent of the respondents had felt that, it was not true. However, 18.5 per cent of the respondents were resistant to give a clear answer.

It was revealed by 51.8 per cent of the respondents (strongly agree and agree responses) revealed that, the company provided information to policyholders at the lapse of the policy. Fifteen point six per cent of the respondents felt that, the company did not provide information. Remaining 22.6 were undecided to give a clear answer.

It can be concluded that, the policyholders of ICICI were very much satisfied with the cordial relationship maintained by the employees of the company with the policyholders, prompt issue of policy documents by the company and the response given by the employees of the company to the enquiries of the policyholders.

Table 4.47 : Mean Score of People and Process Mix of the Life Insurance Companies

Variables	LIC	Bajaj	ICICI
The company is prompt in sanctioning loans	3.92	3.63	3.67
Company provides information at the lapse of policy	4.07	4.09	3.69
Company provides assistance in reviving policy	3.92	4.16	3.83
Employees respond to the enquires of policyholders	3.93	4.20	3.93
Company settles claim on time	4.03	3.95	3.79
Employees maintain cordial relationship with the policyholders	3.91	4.40	4.03
Company settles grievances on time	3.86	3.87	3.84
Company maintains accurate records	4.41	4.24	3.74
Company issues documents promptly	3.99	4.14	3.95
Grand Average	**4.00**	**4.08**	**3.83**

Table 4.47 exhibits the mean score of the variable process and people, calculated on the basis of the response of the policy holders of the companies selected for study.

It is clear from the table that, LIC has obtained the highest mean score of three point nine two in respect of the statement that, the company is prompt in sanctioning loans. The second rank has been secured by ICICI with three point six seven as mean score followed by Bajaj that has obtained the least mean score of three point six three. In respect of the statement Company provides information at the lapse of policy the highest mean score (four point zero nine) has been given to Bajaj. LIC has been ranked second (four point zero seven) in this aspect followed by ICICI that has been ranked third with three point six nine as the mean score.

The statement that the company provides assistance in reviving policy has been ranked high (four point one six) by the policy holders of Bajaj. LIC has been given three point nine two as mean score ranking second, followed by ICICI which was ranked third with three point eight three as the mean score.

In respect of the statement that the employees respond to the enquires of policyholders Bajaj has been ranked first with four point two zero as mean score however both LIC and ICICI have been ranked second by scoring the same mean score of three point nine three.

With regard to the statement that, the company settles claim on time, LIC has been ranked first by getting the highest mean score of four point zero three. Bajaj policy holders have ranked the company second (three point nine five) in this aspect and the third rank (three point seven nine) has been awarded to ICICI.

In respect of the statement that, the employees maintain cordial relationship with the policyholders Bajaj has been the top scorer with four point four as mean score. ICICI has bagged the second rank with four point zero three as its mean score followed by LIC which has obtained the least mean score of three point nine one.

As regards the statement that, the company settles grievances on time Bajaj has been the high scorer (three point eight seven) followed by ICICI which has obtained a mean score three point eight six the LIC has been awarded the third place with three point eight four as the mean score.

It is striking to note that policy holders of LIC have given higher ranking for the statement that, the company maintains accurate records. It is revealed by the high mean score (four point four one) obtained by the company. The policy holders of Bajaj also appreciated that statement, by giving a mean score of four point two four. However, ICICI has been ranked third (three point seven four) in this aspect.

As regards the statement that the company issues documents promptly Bajaj has been the high scorer (four point one four) followed by LIC which has obtained a mean score three point nine nine the ICICI has been awarded the third place with three point nine five as the mean score.

The grand average of the mean scores calculated reveals that, Bajaj has been ranked first with four point zero eight as its score followed by LIC with four as its score.

People And Process Mix and the Life Insurance Companies

Null Hypothesis H_{o1} : The three companies are equally preferred in respect of process and people mix.

Null Hypothesis H_{o2} : Each attribute of the Process and People mix is equally preferred.

Alternate Hypothesis H_{11} : Atleast one company is different from the other two companies.

Alternate Hypothesis H_{12} : Atleast one attribute is different from the other attributes.

Level of Significance (α) = 0.05

Table 4.48 : Anova Table

Source	Type III Sum of Squares	df	Mean Square	F	Sig.
Corrected Model	.672a	10	.067	2.719	.036
Intercept	425.068	1	425.068	17207.297	.000
Insurance Company	.304	2	.152	6.162	.010
Factors	.367	8	.046	1.858	.139
Error	.395	16	.025		
Total	426.135	27			
Corrected Total	1.067	26			

R Squared = .630 (Adjusted R Squared = .398)
Calculated p value = .010

Calculated *p* value (0.010) < 0.05 (level of significance). Hence H_{o1} is rejected and H_{11} is accepted. It is concluded that the People and process mix of at least one company is different from the other companies.

It has also been proved with the help of Duncan Test which showed the following result.

Table 4.49 : Result of Duncan Post HOC Test-Life Insurance Companies

Company	Subset Value	
	1	2
ICICI	3.8233	—
LIC	—	4.0044
Bajaj	—	4.0756

It is concluded that ICICI has been viewed differently as compared to LIC and Bajaj which are viewed similarly.

Calculated p value (0.139) > 0.05 (level of significance). Hence H_{o2} is accepted and H_{12} is rejected. It is concluded that there is no significance difference in the Customer Care Services of the Life insurance companies.

PHYSICAL EVIDENCE MIX

The last dimension of the marketing mix is the physical evidence mix. It refers to the physical evidence practices followed by the three chosen life insurance companies namely Bajaj Allianz Life Insurance Company, Life Insurance Corporation and ICICI Prudential Life Insurance Company. The physical evidence mix has been analysed with reference to convenience of location and operating hours, availability of water facilities, seating facilities and infrastructure facilities.

The response of the policyholders towards the enquiries made determines the effectiveness of the variable physical evidence mix. The opinion has been exhibited in the following tables:

Table 4.50 : Physical Evidence Mix-LIC

Variables	Strongly agree	Agree	Neutral	Disagree	Strongly disagree
Branches are located at convenient places	75(25.2)	196(65.8)	12(4.0)	15(5.0)	—
The company provides adequate water facilities	73(24.5)	153(51.3)	30(10.1)	28(9.4)	14(4.7)
The company has adequate seating facilities	46(15.4)	155(52.0)	50(16.8)	31(10.4)	16(5.4)
Operating hours are convenient	58(19.5)	196(65.8)	39(13.1)	4(1.3)	1(0.3)
The company has adequate infrastructure facilities	66(22.1)	144(48.3)	64(21.5)	22(7.4)	2(0.7)

Source: Primary data
Figures in ( ) represent percentage.

Table 4.50 discloses the opinions of the policyholders of LIC as regards the physical evidence mix of the company. It can be inferred that, as regards the statement that the branches are located at convenient places, 91 per cent of the respondents (strongly agree and agree responses) felt that, the branches were located at convenient places. Only five per cent felt that, the branches were not located at convenient places. Four per cent of the respondents were undecided to give a clear answer.

It was revealed by 84.3 per cent (strongly agree and agree responses) of the respondents that, the operating hours of the branch were convenient. A negligible one point six per cent of the respondents felt that the operating hours of the branch were not convenient. Remaining thirteen point one per cent of the respondents were undecided to give a clear answer.

In respect of the statement that the company provides adequate water facilities, 75.8 per cent of the respondents (strongly agree and agree responses) felt that, the statement was true. Fourteen point one per cent of the respondents felt that, it was not true. However, 10.1 per cent were undecided to give a clear answer.

With reference to the statement that the company provides infrastructure facilities, 70.4 per cent of the respondents (strongly agree and agree responses) revealed that, the company had provided infrastructure facilities. Eight point one per cent of the respondents felt that, the company did not provide infrastructure facilities. Remaining 21.5 per cent were reluctant to give a clear answer.

As regards the statement that the company has adequate seating facilities, 67 per cent of the respondents (strongly agree and agree responses) revealed that, the company had adequate seating facilities. Fifteen point eight per cent of the respondents felt that, the company did not have adequate seating facilities. Remaining 16.8 per cent were not sure to give a clear answer.

It can be concluded that, the policyholders of LIC showed much satisfaction as regards the factors such as, location of branches at convenient places, convenient operating hours and the provision of water facility in the branches.

Table 4.51 : Physical Evidence Mix-Bajaj

Variables	Strongly agree	Agree	Neutral	Disagree	Strongly disagree
Branches are located at convenient places	72(35.1)	115(56.1)	17(8.3)	1(0.5)	—
The company provides adequate water facilities	77(37.6)	88(42.9)	31(15.1)	9(4.4)	—
The company has adequate seating facilities	80(39.0)	84(41.0)	33(16.1)	8(3.9)	—
Operating hours are convenient	74(36.1)	114(55.6)	16(7.8)	1(0.5)	—
The company has adequate infra-structure facilities	80(39.0)	87(42.4)	36(17.6)	2(1.0)	—

Source: Primary data
Figures in ( ) represent percentage.

Table 4.51 reveals the opinions of the policyholders of Bajaj as regards the physical evidence mix of the company. It is clear that, 91.7 per cent of the respondents (strongly agree and agree responses) revealed that, the operating hours of the branch were convenient. A negligible zero point five per cent of the respondents felt that, the operating hours of the branch were not convenient. Remaining seven point eight per cent of the respondents were undecided to give a clear answer.

It was revealed by 91.2 per cent of the respondents (strongly agree and agree responses) felt that, the branches were located at convenient places.

Only zero point five per cent of the respondents felt that, the branches were not located at convenient places. Four per cent of the respondents were undecided to give a clear answer.

With reference to the statement that the company provides infrastructure facilities, 81.4 per cent of the respondents (strongly agree and agree responses) revealed that, the company had provided infrastructure facilities. Only one per cent of the respondents felt that, the company did not provide infrastructure facilities. Remaining 17.6 per cent were undecided to give a clear answer.

In respect of the statement that the company provides adequate water facilities, 80.5 per cent of the respondents (strongly agree and agree responses) felt that, the statement was true. Four point four per cent of the respondents felt that, it was not true. However, 15.1 three per cent were undecided to give a clear answer.

As regards the statement that the company has adequate seating facilities, 80 per cent of the respondents (strongly agree and agree responses) revealed that, the company had adequate seating facilities. Three point nine per cent of the respondents felt that, the company did not have adequate seating facilities. Remaining 16.1 per cent were indecisive to give a clear answer.

It can be concluded that, the policy holders were highly appreciative of the convenient operating hours, location of branches at convenient places and the infrastructure facilities. The policyholders appeared to have a belief that the physical evidence mix of the company was good as there is no response for strongly disagree.

Table 4.52 : Physical Evidence Mix-ICICI

Variables	Strongly agree	Agree	Neutral	Disagree	Strongly disagree
Branches are located at convenient places	99(36.7)	130(48.1)	22(8.1)	16(5.9)	3(1.1)
The company provides adequate water facilities	92(34.1)	130(48.1)	25(9.3)	10(3.7)	13(4.8)
The company has adequate seating facilities	98(36.3)	131(48.5)	20(7.4)	15(5.6)	6(2.2)
Operating hours are convenient	89(33.0)	139(51.5)	31(11.5)	9(3.3)	2(0.7)
The company has adequate infra-structure facilities	69(25.6)	139(51.5)	50(18.5)	7(2.6)	5(1.9)

Source: Primary data
Figures in ( ) represent percentage.

Table 4.52 depicts the opinions of the policyholders of ICICI as regards the physical evidence mix of the company. It is evident that, 85.8 per cent of the respondents (strongly agree and agree responses) felt that, the branches were located at convenient places. Only seven per cent of the respondents felt that, the branches were not located at convenient places. Seven point two per cent of the respondents were undecided to give a clear answer.

As regards the statement that the company has adequate seating facilities, 84.8 per cent of the respondents (strongly agree and agree responses) revealed that, the company had adequate seating facilities. Seven point eight per cent of the respondents felt that, the company did not have adequate seating facilities. Remaining seven point four per cent were indecisive to give a clear answer.

It was revealed by 84.5 per cent of the respondents (strongly agree and agree responses) that, the operating hours of the branch were convenient. Four per cent of the respondents felt that, the operating hours of the branch were not convenient. Remaining 11.5 per cent of the respondents were undecided to give a clear answer.

In respect of the statement that the company provides adequate water facilities, 82.2 per cent of the respondents (strongly agree and agree responses) felt that, the statement was true. Eight point five per cent of the respondents felt that, it was not true. However, nine point three per cent were undecided to give a clear answer.

With reference to the statement that the company provides infrastructure facilities, 77.1 per cent of the respondents (strongly agree and agree responses) revealed that, the company had provided infrastructure facilities. Only four point five per cent of the respondents felt that, the company did not provide infrastructure facilities. Remaining 18.5 per cent were unsure of a clear answer.

It can be concluded that, in respect of ICICI factors such as, location of branches, provision of adequate seating facilities by the company and the convenient operating hours were very much appreciated by the policyholders.

Table 4.53 : Mean Score of Physical Evidence Mix of the Life Insurance Companies

Variables	LIC	Bajaj	ICICI
Branches are located at convenient places	4.11	4.26	4.13
The company provides adequate water facilities	3.82	4.14	4.03
The company has adequate seating facilities	3.62	4.15	4.11
Operating hours are convenient	4.03	4.27	4.13
The company has adequate infrastructure facilities	3.84	4.20	3.96
Grand Average	**3.88**	**4.20**	**4.07**

Table 4.53 depicts the mean score of the variable physical evidence calculated on the basis of the response of the policy holders of the companies selected for study.

The policy holders of Bajaj have given higher ranking for the company in respect of the statement that Branches are located at convenient places by giving four point two six as mean score. ICICI has been ranked second by securing a mean score of four point one three followed by LIC which has been ranked third with four point one one as the mean score.

As regards the statement that the company provides adequate water facilities Bajaj has been the high scorer (four point one four) followed by ICICI which has obtained a mean score four point zero three the LIC has been awarded the third place with three point eight two as the mean score.

In respect of the statement that the company has adequate seating facilities, Bajaj has been the top scorer with four point one five as mean score. ICICI has bagged the second rank with four point one one as its mean score followed by LIC which has obtained the least mean score of three point six two.

With respect to the statement that the Operating hours are convenient Bajaj has scored the highest mean score of four point two seven followed by ICICI which secured four point one three as mean score. The mean score of LIC was the least (three point eight four) among all the companies.

The policy holders of Bajaj have given a higher mean score four point two for the statement that the company has adequate infrastructure facilities. ICICI ranks second with three point nine six as the mean score and LIC has been ranked third with three point eight four as the mean score.

The grand average of the mean scores calculated reveals that Bajaj has been ranked first with four point two as its score followed by ICICI which has scored four point zero seven.

Physical Evidence Practices and the Life Insurance Companies

Null Hypothesis H_{01} : The three companies are equally preferred in respect of physical evidence mix.

Null Hypothesis H_{02} : Each attribute of the physical evidence mix is equally preferred.

Alternate Hypothesis H_{11} : Atleast one company is different from the other two companies.

Alternate Hypothesis H_{12} : Atleast one attribute is different from the other attributes.

Level of Significance (α) = 0.05

Table 4.54 : Anova Table

Source	Type III Sum of Squares	df	Mean Square	F	Sig.
Corrected Model	.366a	6	.061	6.253	.011
Intercept	246.443	1	246.443	25280.492	.000
Insurance company	.259	2	.129	13.264	.003
Factors	.107	4	.027	1.747	.104
Error	.078	8	.010		
Total	246.886	15			
Corrected Total	.444	14			

Calculated p value (0.003) < 0.05 (level of significance). Hence H_{o1} is rejected and H_{11} is accepted. It is concluded that the physical evidence mix of at least one company is different from the other companies.

It has also been proved with the help of Duncan Test which showed the following result.

Table 4.55 : Result of Duncan Post HOC Test-Life Insurance Companies

Company	Subset Value	
	1	2
LIC	3.8840	—
ICICI	—	4.0720
Bajaj	—	4.2040

It is concluded that LIC has been viewed differently as compared to ICICI and Bajaj which are viewed similarly.

Calculated p value (0.104) > 0.05 (level of significance). Hence H_{o2} is accepted and H_{12} is rejected. It is concluded that there is no significant difference in the Physical Evidence practices of the Life insurance companies.

Table 4.56 : Overall Performance of the Life Insurance Companies

Remarks	Number of Respondents	Per cent
Excellent	259	32.8
Good	365	46.3
Fair	136	17.6
Poor	8	1.7
Very Poor	5	1.6
Total	**773**	**100.0**

Source: Primary data

Table 4.56 indicates the opinion of the respondents as regards the overall performance of the companies chosen for study. Majority of the respondents (46.3 per cent) have expressed that the performance of all the three companies was good. It is striking to note that 32.9 per cent of the respondents have highly appreciated the performance of the companies. The performance of the companies has been indicated as fair by 17.6 per cent of the respondents. Only three point three percent of the respondents have expressed dissatisfaction with regard to the performance.

It can be concluded that, the performance of the all the three companies chosen for study has been appreciated by the policy holders.

Table 4.57 : Table Showing the Unique Selling Proposition of Life Insurance Companies

Factors	LIC	Bajaj	ICICI
Product	1. Risk cover 2. Security	2. Security 2. Risk cover	1. Security 2. Returns
Price - Premium - Bonus	Affordable/Moderate Moderate	Affordable/Moderate Moderate	Affordable/Moderate Moderate
Promotion	1. Motivation through advertisements 2. Informative advertisemenets	2. Informative Pamphlets 2. Informative Websites	1. Informative pamphlets 2. Motivation through advertisements
Distribution	1. assistance by intermediaries in purchasing the policies 2. knowledge of the agents	1. assistance by intermediaries in purchasing the policies 2. information provided at the introduction of the policy	1. assistance by intermediaries in purchasing the policies 2. information provided at the introduction of the policy
Process and people	1. Maintenance of accurate records 2. Information at policy lapse	1. friendliness of employees 2. Maintenance of accurate records	1. Friendliness of employees 2. Promptness in document issues
Physical evidence	1. Convenient location 2. Convenient operating hours	1. Convenient operation hours 2. Convenient location	1. Convenient location and 2. Facilities at office-seating arrangement.

Table 4.57 indicates the most predominant factors in each of the elements of marketing mix namely, product, price, promotion, distribution, people, process and physical evidence. It is clear that in respect of the product mix security and risk cover where the dominating factors for LIC and Bajaj where as security and adequate returns were the predominant factors for ICICI.

In respect of the premium component of all the three companies, the policy holders had perceived it to be moderate. The same was the opinion as regards the bonus component also.

With regard to the promotion mix, motivation through advertisements and the knowledge of the agents were the predominant factors in respect of LIC. Informative pamphlets and informative websites were the dominating factors for Bajaj where as Informative pamphlets and motivation through advertisements was the predominant factors for ICICI.

With regard to the distribution mix, assistance by intermediaries in purchasing the policies knowledge of the agents were the predominant factors in respect of LIC. In case of Bajaj, assistance by intermediaries in purchasing the policies and information provided at the introduction of the policy were the predominant factors. For ICICI, assistance by intermediaries in purchasing the policies and information provided at the introduction of the policy were the predominant factors.

With regard to the people and process mix, maintenance of accurate records and information at policy lapse were the predominant factors. In case of Bajaj, friendliness of employees and maintenance of accurate records were the predominant factors. In case of ICICI and friendliness of employees and promptness in document issue were the predominant factors.

With regard to the physical evidence mix, convenient location and convenient operating hours were the predominant factors. In case of Bajaj, convenient operating hours and convenient location were the predominant factors. In case of ICICI, convenient location and operating hours and facilities at office-seating arrangement were the predominant factors

Discriminant Analysis

The researcher made an attempt to identify the factors that were more effective in the elements of marketing mix of the companies chosen for study.

In the five point scale, the options strongly agree and agree were grouped as effective and the options no opinion, disagree and strongly disagree were grouped as ineffective. Since the left hand side is a categorical variable (dichotamy) discriminant analysis has been carried out.

The suitability of the discriminant function was verified with the help of classification results. When more than 75 per cent of original grouped cases are correctly classified the model is considered to be valid and using the Standardized Canonical Discriminant Function Co-efficient, the more effective factors for each company were identified. Discriminant analysis identifying the factors that are to be concentrated more with a view to improve the effectiveness of the marketing mix elements.

The summary of the results obtained is furnished below.

Table 4.58 : Validity of the Discriminant Analysis Classification Results of Promotion Mix of the Life Insurance Companies

LIC	81.9 per cent of original grouped cases correctly classified.
Bajaj	81.0 per cent of original grouped cases correctly classified.
ICICI	77.0 per cent of original grouped cases correctly classified.

Since more than 75% of original group cases correctly classified the model is valid. This has been substantiated by Wilks' Lambda Test also which revealed the following results.

Table 4.59 : Results of Wilks' LAMBDA

Insurance Company	Wilks' Lambda	Chi-square	df	Sig.
LIC	0.700	104.329	8	0.000
BAJAJ	0.727	63.376	8	0.000
ICICI	0.701	93.829	8	0.000
Total	**0.736**	**235.329**	**8**	**0.000**

Since the Wilks' Lambda results are closer to one, the model is considered to be valid.

Table 4.60 : Effectiveness of Promotion Mix of the Life Insurance Companies

Insurance	Effective		Ineffective		Total	
Company	Frequency	Percent	Frequency	Percent	Frequency	Percent
LIC	211	70.8	87	29.2	298	100.0
BAJAJ	159	77.6	46	22.4	205	100.0
ICICI	184	68.1	86	31.9	270	100.0

Source: Primary data

It is clear from table 4.60 that majority of the respondents belonging to the chosen companies felt that the promotional strategies were effective.

In respect of LIC 70.8 per cent of the respondents considered the promotional mix to be effective while 29.2 per cent felt it to be ineffective.

As regards, Bajaj 77.6 per cent of the respondents agreed that the promotion mix was effective whereas 22.4 per cent considered it to be ineffective.

With regard to ICICI, the number of respondents who felt that the promotion mix was effective constituted 68.1 per cent of the total respondents while it was 31.9 per cent of respondents who considered the promotion mix to be ineffective.

It is concluded that of the three companies, majority (77.6 per cent) of the respondents of Bajaj, considered the promotion mix to be effective.

The percentage of respondents who considered it to be ineffective was maximum in case of ICICI followed by LIC.

Table 4.61 : Standardized Canonical Discriminant Function Co-efficient

Variables	Insurance Company		
	LIC	Bajaj	ICICI
Visual appeal of Advertisement is Good	0.387	0.014	0.297
Advertisements are informative	0.023	0.490	-0.168
Technology is useful	0.199	0.019	-0.159
Website is informative	-0.104	0.287	0.330
Advertisement is motivating	0.121	-0.125	-0.034
Posters are impressive	0.305	0.083	0.218
Pamphlets are informative	0.064	0.393	0.060
The company interacts with the policyholders regularly	0.526	0.552	0.750

Table 4.61 depicts the major contributing factors to the effectiveness of the promotion mix of the select insurance companies.

It is observed from the table that in respect of LIC factors such as policy holders meet, visual appeal of the advertisement and the impressive posters exhibited by the company were the major contributors to the effectiveness of the promotion mix.

In respect of Bajaj, policy holders meet informative advertisements and information given through the pamphlets were the predominant contributors.

In respect of ICICI the policy holders meet was the most predominant factor followed by the information provided through the website and the visual appeal of the advertisements exhibited by the company.

It can be concluded that the interactions made by the company with the policy holders, was the most predominant factor in the promotion mix of the companies.

Table4.62 : Validity of the Discriminant Analysis

Classification Results of Distribution Mix of the Life Insurance Companies

LIC	83.9 per cent of original grouped cases correctly classified.
Bajaj	75.6 per cent of original grouped cases correctly classified.
ICICI	75.9 per cent of original grouped cases correctly classified.

Since more than 75% of original group cases correctly classified the model is valid. This has been substantiated by Wilks' Lambda Test also which revealed the following results.

Table 4.63 : Results of Wilks' LAMBDA

Insurance Company	Wilks' Lambda	Chi-square	df	Sig.
LIC	0.778	73.709	5	0.000
BAJAJ	0.817	40.549	5	0.000
ICICI	0.731	83.316	5	0.000
Total	**0.667**	**309.875**	**9**	**0.000**

Since the Wilks' Lambda results are closer to one, the model is considered to be valid.

Table 4.64 : Effectiveness of Distribution Mix of the Life Insurance Companies

Insurance Company	Effective		Ineffective		Total	
	Frequency	Percent	Frequency	Percent	Frequency	Percent
LIC	229	76.8	69	23.2	298	100.0
BAJAJ	152	74.1	53	25.9	205	100.0
ICICI	184	68.1	86	31.9	270	100.0

Source: Primary data

It is clear from table 4.64 that majority of the respondents belonging to the chosen companies felt that the distribution strategies were effective.

In respect of LIC 76.8 per cent of the respondents considered the distributional mix to be effective while 23.2 per cent felt it to be ineffective.

As regards, Bajaj 74.1 per cent of the respondents agreed that the distribution mix was effective whereas 25.9 per cent considered it to be ineffective.

With regard to ICICI, the number of respondents who felt that the distribution mix was effective constituted 68.1 per cent of the total respondents while it was 31.9 per cent of respondents who considered the promotion mix to be ineffective.

It is concluded that of the three companies, majority (76.8 per cent) of the respondents of LIC considered the distribution mix to be effective.

The percentage of respondents who considered it to be ineffective was maximum in case of ICICI followed by Bajaj.

Table-68 depicts the major contributing factors to the effectiveness of the distribution mix of the select insurance companies. It is observed from the table that in respect of LIC factors such as knowledge of the agent, grievance redressal and information provided by the agents at the introduction of the policy were the major contributors to the effectiveness of the distribution mix.

Table 4.65 : Standardized Canonical Discriminant Function Co-efficient

Variables	Insurance Company		
	LIC	Bajaj	ICICI
Intermediaries provide information at the introduction of new policy	0.258	-0.009	0.175
Intermediaries assist in purchase of new policy	-0.052	0.536	-0.184
Intermediaries assist in claim settlement	0.040	0.332	0.146
Intermediaries assist in grievance settlement	0.528	0.053	0.583
Intermediaries have thorough knowledge of the products	0.638	0.641	0.509

In respect of Bajaj, knowledge of the agent, assistance rendered by the agent at the time of purchase of policy and claim settlement were the predominant contributors.

In respect of ICICI, grievance redressal was the most predominant factor followed by the knowledge of the agent.

It can be concluded that knowledge of the agent was the most predominant factor in the distribution mix of LIC and Bajaj while grievance redressal was the major contributor for ICICI.

Table 4.66 : Validity of the Discriminant Analysis Classification Results of People And Process Mix of the Life Insurance Companies

LIC	86.9 per cent of original grouped cases correctly classified.
Bajaj	88.3 per cent of original grouped cases correctly classified.
ICICI	88.9 per cent of original grouped cases correctly classified.

Since more than 75% of original group cases correctly classified the model is valid. This has been substantiated by Wilks' Lambda Test also which revealed the following results.

Table 4.67 : Results of Wilks' LAMBDA

Insurance Company	Wilks' Lambda	Chi-square	df	Sig.
LIC	0.697	105.191	9	0.000
BAJAJ	0.674	78.388	9	0.000
ICICI	0.573	146.823	9	0.000

Since the Wilks' Lambda results are closer to one, the model is considered to be valid.

Table 4.68 : Effectiveness of People and Process Mix of the Life Insurance Companies

Insurance Company	Effective		Ineffective		Total	
	Frequency	Percent	Frequency	Percent	Frequency	Percent
LIC	235	78.9	63	21.1	298	100.0
BAJAJ	174	84.9	31	15.1	205	100.0
ICICI	204	75.6	66	24.4	270	100.0

Source: Primary data

It is clear from table 4.68 that majority of the respondents belonging to the chosen companies felt that the customer care services were effective.

In respect of LIC 78.9 per cent of the respondents considered the physical evidence mix to be effective while 21.1 per cent felt it to be ineffective.

As regards, Bajaj 84.9 per cent of the respondents agreed that the physical evidence mix was effective whereas 15.1 per cent considered it to be ineffective.

With regard to ICICI, the number of respondents who felt that the physical evidence mix was effective constituted 75.6 per cent of the total respondents while it was 24.4 per cent of respondents who considered the promotion mix to be ineffective.

It is concluded that of the three companies, majority (84.9 per cent) of the respondents of Bajaj considered the people and process mix to be effective.

The percentage of respondents who considered it to be ineffective was maximum in case of ICICI followed by LIC.

Table 4.69 : Standardized Canonical Discriminant Function Co-efficient

Variables	Insurance Company		
	LIC	Bajaj	ICICI
The company is prompt in sanctioning loans	0.192	0.170	0.163
Company provides information at the lapse of policy	-0.017	0.194	-0.208
Company provides assistance in reviving policy	0.110	0.079	0.202
Employees respond to the enquires of policy-holders	0.055	0.472	0.304
Company settles claim on time	0.136	-0.132	0.276
Employees maintain cordial relationship with the policyholders	0.145	-0.212	0.253
Company settles grievances on time	0.469	0.188	-0.147
Company maintains accurate records	-0.164	0.239	0.346
Company issues documents promptly	0.585	0.436	0.496

Table 4.69 depicts the major contributing factors to the effectiveness of the people and process mix of the select insurance companies.

It is observed from the table that in respect of LIC factors such as maintenance of accurate records, prompt issue of documents, settlement of grievances and sanction of loans were the major contributors to the effectiveness of the people and process mix. In respect of Bajaj, promptness in attending enquiries, document issue and maintenance of records were the predominant contributors. In respect of ICICI, promptness in document issues was the major contributing factor followed by the maintenance of accurate records.

It can be concluded that promptness in attending enquiries was the most predominant factor in the people and process mix of LIC and ICICI while promptness in attending enquiries was the major contributing factor for Bajaj.

Table 4.70 : Validity of the Discriminant Analysis Classification Results of Physical Evidence Mix of the Life Insurance Companies

LIC	86.9 per cent of original grouped cases correctly classified.
Bajaj	89.3 per cent of original grouped cases correctly classified.
ICICI	79.6 per cent of original grouped cases correctly classified.

Since more than 75% of original group cases correctly classified the model is valid. This has been substantiated by Wilks' Lambda Test also which revealed the following results.

Table 4.71 : Results of Wilks' LAMBDA

Insurance Company	Wilks' Lambda	Chi-square	df	Sig.
LIC	0.698	105.562	5	0.000
BAJAJ	0.896	21.986	5	0.000
ICICI	0.723	86.266	5	0.000
Total	**0.762**	**208.897**	**5**	**0.000**

Since the Wilks' Lambda results are closer to one, the model is considered to be valid.

It is clear from table 4.71 that majority of the respondents belonging to the chosen companies felt that the physical evidence practices were effective.

In respect of LIC 77.5 per cent of the respondents considered to be physical evidence mix effective while 22.5 per cent felt it to be ineffective.

As regards, Bajaj 87.3 per cent of the respondents agreed that the physical evidence mix was effective whereas 12.7 per cent considered it to be ineffective.

Table 4.72 : Effectiveness of Physical Evidence Mix of the Life Insurance Companies

Insurance Company	Effective		Ineffective		Total	
	Frequency	Percent	Frequency	Percent	Frequency	Percent
LIC	231	77.5	67	22.5	298	100.0
BAJAJ	179	87.3	26	12.7	205	100.0
ICICI	202	74.8	68	25.2	270	100.0

Source: Primary data

With regard to ICICI, the number of respondents who felt that the physical evidence mix was effective constituted 74.8 per cent of the total respondents while it was 25.2 per cent of respondents who considered the physical evidence mix to be ineffective.

It is concluded that of the three companies, majority (87.3 per cent) of the respondents of Bajaj considered the physical evidence mix to be effective.

The percentage of respondents who considered it to be ineffective was maximum in case of ICICI followed by LIC.

Table 4.73 : Standardized Canonical Discriminant Function Co-efficient

Variables	Insurance Company		
	LIC	Bajaj	ICICI
Branches are located at convenient places	0.301	0.506	0.256
The company provides adequate water facilities	0.085	0.343	0.201
The company has adequate seating facilities	-0.030	-0.226	-0.006
Operating hours are convenient	0.226	0.314	-0.154
The company has adequate infrastructure facilities	0.761	0.303	0.950

Table 4.73 depicts the major contributing factors to the effectiveness of the physical evidence mix of the select insurance companies.

It is observed from the table that in respect of LIC infrastructure facilities, location of the branch and convenient working hours were the major contributors to the effectiveness of the physical evidence mix.

In respect of Bajaj, location of the branch and availability of water facility were the predominant contributors.

In respect of ICICI, infrastructure facility was the major contributing factor followed by location of the branch and water facility.

It can be concluded that infrastructure facility was the most predominant factor in the physical evidence mix of LIC and ICICI while location of the branch was the major contributing factor for Bajaj.

5

Findings, Conclusion and Suggestions

Chapter 5 is a summary of the data collected on various aspects such as, the socio-economic personal profile of all the respondents irrespective of the company chosen by them. It also presents the findings, based on the study of seven elements of the marketing mix of the chosen life insurance companies namely LIC, BAJAJ and ICICI. The attributes of all the seven elements have been identified and analysed in detail from the policy holders' point of view. The findings have been presented below:

- Maximum number (48 per cent) of the respondents belonged to the age group of 41-60. Majority of the respondents (65.1 per cent) were male.
- Graduates including under graduates and post graduates had shown greater preference for purchasing life insurance policies, than others.
- Majority of the respondents (69.6 per cent) lived in urban areas, where the business potential was high.
- The respondents employed in private sector and business men showed greater interest, in purchasing life insurance policies irrespective of the company, as one of their choices of financial planning, for reasons of safety and security.
- Maximum number of respondents who fell within the monthly income ranging between Rs. 5,001 to 15,000 in all the three companies, preferred investing in life insurance policies in order to meet all family needs such as education, marriage, illness, housing facilities and so on.
- The life insurance policy purchasing is more among the nuclear families than the joint families, to save for the future and also to assert their self confidence and potential for saving.

- With respect to decision making in the purchase of policies it was observed that, in 45.8 per cent of the families of the respondents, the decisions were made jointly by husband and wife.
- Majority of the respondents, (60.93 per cent), had selected the companies attracted by their brand image. The next important factor which had attracted people to select the company was, the security guarantee that the companies promised.
- Majority of the policy holders preferred the add-on rider – Accidental Death benefit.
- Conventionally agents are the prime movers in any service business, particularly in insurance business. The prime source of information for majority of the policyholders was through agents only.
- A consistent demand for the traditional well-known policies namely Endowment and Money Back Policies has been noticed. Unit-linked policies and pension policies which are of recent origin, were found to be gaining momentum.

The Chi-Square Test Revealed the Following Facts

- Age of the respondents has no influence in choosing a company based on the selection criteria namely brand image, prompt service, reputation and security.
- Sex of the respondents has no influence in choosing a company based on the selection criteria namely brand image, prompt service, reputation and security.
- Age of the respondents has influence in the choice of the company.
- Location of the respondents has no influence in the choice of the company.

The chief objective of the study was to elicit the opinion of respondents in respect of, various dimensions of the marketing mix of the select life insurance companies. To attain the objective the respondents were given a set of questions requiring their responses on a five point scale. The highest score in the scale meant a positive response and the lowest score meant the least response. Based on these premises, the following observations were made, the details of which are given below.

Product Mix

Six attributes of the product mix element of the life insurance companies namely, security, risk cover, adequate returns, and fulfillment of requirements, tax relief and additional benefits were identified and analyzed in a five point scale. The respondents' attitude towards the different attributes of the product mix was analyzed. The opinion based survey conducted, on a sample of 773 respondents with respect to the product mix of select companies revealed that, LIC was doing better with regard to risk cover but Bajaj was sweeping high in all the other variables.

The grand average of the mean scores calculated revealed that Bajaj has been ranked first with the four point two five as its score followed by LIC, which scored four point one seven.

The Two-way Anova revealed that, in respect of product mix, LIC and Bajaj were equally preferred while ICICI was less preferred and attributes such as, security and risk cover were viewed differently when compared to other attributes.

Price Mix

The policy holders' opinions regarding the premium charged by the companies and the bonus declared have been analyzed and it was observed that, majority of the respondents of the three select companies was of the same opinion, with respect to premium and bonus components. The premium and the bonus they felt, were neither very high nor very low.

Promotion Mix

The promotion mix has been analyzed with reference to the advertisement, technology, websites, posters exhibited by the company, pamphlets issued and the interaction with the policyholders. The respondents from all the three select companies have agreed that all the three companies gave advertisements which were very impressive and motivating.

The results of the discriminant analysis revealed that, of the three companies, majority of the respondents of Bajaj (77.6 per cent), considered the promotion mix to be effective.

Distribution Mix

The distribution mix has been analyzed with reference to, the assistance rendered by the intermediaries to the policyholders in the purchase of the policy, claim settlement, grievance settlement and information provided at the introduction of policies. Eliciting the opinion of the respondents with respect to the distribution channel of products brought to light, some interesting observations. The assistance of the agents in providing information about the introduction as well as in the purchase of the policies attracted a favourable response from the policy holders.

The results of the discriminant analysis revealed that, majority (76.8 per cent) of the respondents of LIC considered the distribution mix, to be effective.

People and Process Mix

The People and process mix has been analyzed with reference to, the customer care services namely sanctioning of loans by the company, information at policy lapse, assistance in reviving policy, promptness in attending enquiries, promptness in claim settlement, friendliness of employees, settlement of grievances, maintenance of accurate records and promptness in document issue. The respondents of the two private companies Bajaj and ICICI were highly satisfied with the customer friendly attitude which was ranked first, while the respondents of public company LIC appreciated the accurate record maintenance which was ranked first.

The results of the discriminant analysis revealed that, majority of the respondents of Bajaj (84.9 per cent), considered the people and process mix to be effective.

PHYSICAL EVIDENCE MIX

The physical evidence mix has been analyzed with reference to, convenience of location of the branches, convenience of operating hours, availability of water facilities, seating facilities and infrastructure facilities. Convenient location of the offices proved to be a positive factor, for all the three select companies, as opined by the respondents. The operating hours also seemed to be convenient, for the respondents of all the three companies.

The results of the discriminant analysis revealed that, majority (87.3 per cent) of the respondents of Bajaj considered the physical evidence mix to be effective.

The Duncan post hoc test revealed the following facts:

Duncan post hoc test revealed that in respect of product mix LIC and Bajaj were equally preferred by the policyholders while ICICI was less preferred. Similarly product variables namely security and risk cover were viewed together whereas the other variables were viewed differently.

In respect of people and process mix of LIC and Bajaj were viewed similarly whereas ICICI was viewed differently. However there was no significant difference in the people and product mix of the life insurance companies chosen for study.

In respect of physical evidence mix ICICI and Bajaj were viewed similarly whereas LIC was viewed differently. However there was no significant difference in the physical evidence mix of the life insurance companies chosen for study.

Majority of the respondents (46.3 per cent) have expressed that the performance of all the three companies was good. 32.9 per cent of the respondents have highly appreciated the performance of the companies.

An analysis of the marketing mix of LIC, on the basis of the responses given by 298 respondents, revealed the following facts:

- Majority of the respondents, (68.1 percent), were male and the maximum number of the respondents, (52.7 per cent) belonged to the age group of 41-60 years.

- Majority of the respondents, (61.4 per cent) followed Hinduism and 29.9 per cent of respondents followed Christianity.
- Thirty point nine per cent of the respondents had completed school education, followed by, 27.5 per cent of respondents who were undergraduates.
- Majority of the respondents, (67.4 per cent) resided in urban areas.
- Majority of the respondents, (29.5 per cent) were engaged in business and 23.8 per cent of the respondents were employed in private concerns.
- The income earned by 30 per cent of the respondents was between Rs. 5,001-Rs.10, 000 per month. Twenty five point five per cent of the respondents were earning a monthly income of Rs. 10,001-Rs.15, 000.
- Majority of the respondents, (59.4 per cent), lived in nuclear families and majority of the respondents (56.7 per cent) had 4 to 6 members in the family.

Produce Mix

- The policy holders of LIC were highly appreciative of the company since its policies provided security, risk cover and adequate returns.
- The mean score calculated on the basis of the response given by the policyholders also endorsed the same result. However, the mean score obtained in respect of the policy holders opinion regarding the fulfillment of specific requirement such as children's education, marriage expenses and so on was minimum.
- LIC was ranked second, next to Bajaj in respect of the product mix as revealed by the grand average score (4.25) of different variables of product mix.

Price Mix

- Majority of the respondents, (53.4 per cent) felt that the premium charged by the LIC was moderate and for 23.8 per cent of the respondents, the premium charged was low/very low.
- As regards the bonus declared by the company, 50.3 per cent of the respondents have felt that it was moderate.
- The bonus declared by the company has been considered as high by 33.6 per cent of the respondents.
- The mean scores calculated on the basis of the responses given by the policy holders of LIC for the premium and the bonus components were high.

Promotion Mix

- For the customers of Life Insurance Corporation , advertisements played an effective role as a promotional tool, since majority of the respondents highly appreciated that the advertisements were informative (82.9 per cent), advertisements were highly motivating (81.6 per cent) and had good visual appeal and the posters were also highly impressive.

- The mean score obtained by the company, as regards the various attributes of promotion mix was high in respect of the informative and motivating advertisements. It was low, in respect of the interaction with the policyholders.
- The results of the discriminant analysis revealed that, in respect of LIC, 70.8 per cent of the respondents considered the promotional mix to be effective while 29.2 per cent felt it to be ineffective.
- The predominant contributors to the effectiveness of promotion mix were the interaction with the policyholders, visual appeal of the advertisements and the impressive posters indicating that, if the company concentrates more on these aspects, it would have a much more effective promotion mix.

Distribution Mix

- Majority of the policy holders considered that, the intermediaries provided information at the introduction of the new policy assisted in the purchase of the policy and possessed thorough knowledge about the company's policies.
- The mean score calculated on the basis of the response given by the policyholders also endorsed the same result. However, the mean score obtained in respect of the policy holders' opinion regarding the intermediaries' assistance in the grievance settlement was low.
- The results of the discriminant analysis revealed that, in respect of LIC 76.8 per cent of the respondents considered the distributional mix to be effective while 23.2 per cent felt it to be ineffective.
- The predominant contributors to the effectiveness of distribution mix were the knowledge of the intermediaries, assistance in grievance settlement and the information provided at the introduction of the policy indicating that, if the company concentrates more on these aspects, it would have a much more effective distribution mix.

People and Process Mix

- Factors such as maintenance of accurate records by the company, information provided to the policyholders at the lapse of policy and prompt issue of the policy documents were highly appreciated by the policy holders of LIC.
- The mean score calculated on the basis of the response given by the policyholders also endorsed the same result. However, the mean score obtained in respect of the policy holders' opinion regarding the settlement of grievances by the company was low.

- The results of the discriminant analysis revealed that, in respect of LIC 78.9 per cent of the respondents considered the distributional mix to be effective while 21.1 per cent felt it to be ineffective.
- The predominant contributors to the effectiveness of distribution mix were the prompt issue of documents, timely settlement of grievances indicating that, if the company concentrates more on these aspects, it would have a much more effective distribution mix.

Physical Evidence Mix

- The policyholders of LIC showed much satisfaction as regards the factors such as, location of branches at convenient places, convenient operating hours and the provision of water facility in the branches.
- The mean score calculated on the basis of the response given by the policyholders also endorsed the same result. However, the mean score obtained in respect of the policy holders' opinion regarding the seating facilities available in the company was low.
- The results of the discriminant analysis revealed that, in respect of LIC 77.5 per cent of the respondents considered the physical evidence mix to be effective while, 22.5 per cent felt it to be ineffective mix.
- The predominant contributors to the effectiveness of physical evidence mix were the infrastructure facilities, location of branches at convenience places, and convenient working hours indicating that, if the company concentrates more on these aspects, it would have a much more effective distribution mix.

An analysis of the marketing mix of Bajaj Allianz Life Insurance Company on the basis of the response given by 205 respondents revealed the following facts:

- Majority of the respondents (64.9 per cent) were male and the maximum number of the total respondents (54.6 per cent) were in the age group between 21-40 years.
- Majority of the respondents, (76.6 per cent) were Hindus followed by Christians being 17.6 per cent of the respondents.
- Majority of the respondents, (45.4 per cent), were undergraduates and 20.5 per cent of the respondents were post graduates.
- The highest proportion of 74.6 per cent of the respondents resided in urban areas.
- Out of 205 respondents, 34.6 per cent were employed in private sector and 28.8 per cent were business men.
- Majority of the respondents, (56.5 per cent), were earning a monthly income ranging from Rs. 5,001-Rs.15.000.

- Majority of the respondents, (64.4%) lived in nuclear families and majority of the respondents (45.4%) had one to three members in the family.
- Majority of the respondents, (51.7%) revealed that, the decision to purchase the policy was taken jointly by husband and wife and for 25.37 per cent of the respondents, it was the decision taken by the husband.
- Brand image was the prime factor that motivated the policy holders to purchase its policy. It is evident from the fact that, 56.1 per cent of the respondents chose the Bajaj Allianz Life Insurance Company for the brand image it had created.
- Of the various add-on-riders made available to the policy holders, Accidental Death benefit was the much sought rider, for majority (41.5%) of the respondents.
- Majority of the respondents (51.7%) had received information about the policy only through the agents, followed by 27.8 per cent of respondents who had received information through the corporate agents.
- Agency system of selling the life insurance products was the dominating intermediary of Bajaj Company. However, corporate agents also have been the source of purchase for 30.7 per cent of the respondents.
- Of the various categories of policies available, unit-linked policies were favoured by 38.5 per cent respondents of Bajaj, followed by the policies meant exclusively for children's education, marriage and so on.

Product Mix

- Bajaj Allianz Life Insurance products were favoured mainly for their security aspect followed by risk cover, fulfillment of specific requirements such as children's education and daughter's marriage.
- The mean score calculated on the basis of the response given by the policyholders also endorsed the above fact. However, the mean score obtained in respect of the policy holders' opinion regarding the provision of adequate returns by the policy was low.
- The product mix of Bajaj has been considered as more effective by majority of the respondents as revealed by the grand average score (4.25) of different variables of product mix.

Price Mix

- A majority (42 per cent) of the respondents felt that ,the premium charged by Bajaj has been moderate. According to 36.1 per cent of the respondents, the premium charged was very high or high.

- As regards the bonus declared by the company, the percentage of respondents who felt that the bonus was very high/high was 55.1 per cent and 40 per cent of the respondents felt that it was moderate.
- The premium charged by the company has been considered as reasonable whereas the bonus declared has been considered as high.

Promotion Mix

- The sales promotional activities of Bajaj Allianz Life Insurance Company were appreciated due to the issue of informative pamphlets, provision of information through website and interactions with the policy holders. However, advertisements made through the posters and hoardings have been less attractive.
- The mean score calculated on the basis of the response given by the policyholders also endorsed the above fact. However, the mean score obtained in respect of the policyholders' opinion regarding the provision of impressive posters was low.
- The promotion mix of the company has been considered as more effective for Bajaj as revealed by the highest grand average (4.05) obtained by the company.
- The results of the discriminant analysis revealed that, as regards Bajaj, 77.6 per cent of the respondents agreed that the promotion mix was effective whereas 22.4 per cent considered it to be ineffective.
- The predominant contributors to the effectiveness of promotion mix were the interaction with the policyholders, informative advertisements and the informative pamphlets indicating that, , if the company concentrates more on these aspects ,it would have a much more effective promotion mix.

Distribution Mix

- The distribution mix of Bajaj Allianz was highly appreciated by the policy holders. According to them, the intermediaries rendered valuable assistance for the purchase of policies, provided information about the introduction of new policies and possessed a thorough knowledge of the company's policies.
- The mean score calculated on the basis of the response given by the policyholders also endorsed the same result. However, the mean score obtained in respect of the policy holders' opinion regarding the intermediaries' assistance in claim settlement was low.
- The results of the discriminant analysis revealed that, as regards Bajaj, 74.1 per cent of the respondents agreed that the distribution mix was effective whereas 25.9 per cent considered it to be ineffective.
- The predominant contributors to the effectiveness of distribution mix were the knowledge of the intermediaries, assistance rendered

by them in the purchase of policy and in the claim settlement indicating that, if the company concentrates more on these aspects, it would have a much more effective distribution mix.

People and Process Mix

- The employees of Bajaj have been highly appreciated, for maintaining cordial relationship with the policy holders as revealed by majority (97.6%) of the respondents. The services of the company were highly appreciated with regard to the maintenance of accurate records and for the prompt issue of policy documents.
- The mean score calculated on the basis of the response given by the policyholders also endorsed the same result. However, the mean score obtained in respect of the policy holders' opinion regarding promptness of the company in sanctioning loans was low. This may be because the company did not grant loans directly to the policy holders and the policy holders had to raise loans from outside sources on the strength of the policy.
- The results of the discriminant analysis revealed that, in respect of Bajaj 84.9 per cent of the respondents considered the distribution mix to be effective while 15.1 per cent felt it to be ineffective.
- The predominant contributors to the effectiveness of people and process mix were the employees' response to the enquiries of the policyholders, prompt issue of policy documents, indicating that, if the company concentrates more on these aspects, it would have a much more effective people and process mix.

Physical Evidence Mix

- The physical evidence mix of Bajaj was highly appreciated by the respondents, who revealed that the operating hours were convenient, the branches were located at convenient places and that the company had provided adequate infrastructure facilities to the policy holders.
- The mean score calculated on the basis of the response given by the policyholders also endorsed the same result. However, the mean score obtained in respect of the policy holders' opinion regarding the water facilities available in the company was low.
- The results of the discriminant analysis revealed that, as regards Bajaj, 87.3 per cent of the respondents agreed that the physical evidence mix was effective, whereas 12.7 per cent considered it to be ineffective.
- The predominant contributors to the effectiveness of physical evidence mix were location of branches at convenience places, availability of water facilities and convenient working hours indicating that, if the company concentrates more on these aspects, it would have a much more effective physical evidence mix.

An analysis of the marketing mix of ICICI Prudential Life Insurance Company on the basis of the response given by 270 respondents, revealed the following facts.

- Majority of the respondents, (61.9 per cent) were male and 38.1 per cent of the respondents were in the age group between 36-50 years.
- Majority of the respondents (73 per cent) were Hindus.
- Majority of the respondents (36.3 per cent) were undergraduates and 21.1 per cent of the respondents had completed their Higher Secondary course.
- Majority of the respondents (68.5per cent), resided in urban areas.
- The respondents employed in private sector constituted 40 per cent of the total respondents, followed by 18.1 per cent of respondents who were businessmen.
- The monthly income of majority of the respondents was Rs.10,000 to Rs.15.000 (31.5 per cent) and Rs.5,001-Rs.10,000 (28.1 per cent).
- The number of respondents living in nuclear families was more, (63.3 per cent), when compared with the number of respondents living in joint families (36.7 per cent). Majority of the respondents (54.1 per cent) had 1-3 members in the family.
- The decision to take life insurance policy was made jointly by husband and wife (58.5 per cent).
- For the policy holders of ICICI, Brand image was the first reason that motivated them to purchase the policy followed by the security factor.
- Majority of the respondents, (52.2 per cent), preferred the Accidental Death Benefit compared to the other benefits.
- Majority of the respondents (68.5 per cent) of ICICI Prudential Life Insurance Company, had knowledge about the policy only through the agents and 14.8 per cent of the respondents through banks.
- Agents were the prime source of purchase for 71.1 per cent of the respondents of ICICI. Banks had sold the life insurance policy to 15.9 per cent of the respondents.
- The policy holders of ICICI had a preference for the unit-linked policies followed by the policies designed exclusively for children.

Product Mix

- ICICI products were favoured since they provided security and adequate returns.
- The mean score calculated on the basis of the response given by the policyholders also endorsed the above fact. However, the mean score obtained in respect of the policy holders' opinion regarding the provision of adequate risk cover by the additional benefits was low.

Price Mix

- The premium charged by the company was considered to be very high/high by majority (55.9 per cent) of the respondents. However the premium charged was considered to be moderate, by 25.9 per cent of the respondents and 18.1 per cent of the respondents have felt that the premium was low/very low.
- The bonus offered by the company was considered to be high by 48.1 per cent of the respondents. According to 34.4 per cent of the respondents, the bonus declared by the company was moderate while, for 17.4 per cent of the respondents it was very low or low.
- For majority of the respondents the premium charged was high and the bonus declared was also high.

Promotion Mix

- ICICI Prudential Life Insurance Company has been recognized well by the policy holders, for its informative pamphlets and motivation of customers through advertisements.
- The mean score obtained by the company as regards the various attributes of promotion mix was high in respect of the informative pamphlets. It was low in respect of the impressiveness of posters.
- The results of the discriminant analysis revealed that, with regard to ICICI, the number of respondents who felt that the promotion mix was effective. constituted 68.1 per cent of the total respondents while it was 31.9 per cent of respondents who considered the promotion mix to be ineffective.
- The predominant contributors to the effectiveness of promotion mix were the interaction with the policyholders, visual appeal of the advertisements and the informative website indicating that, if the company gives more emphasis on these aspects, it would have a much more effective promotion mix.

Distribution Mix

- The policyholders of ICICI assertively stated that, the intermediaries rendered valuable assistance for the purchase of the policy, they provided information about the introduction of new policies and they possessed thorough knowledge about the company's policies.
- The mean score calculated on the basis of the response given by the policyholders also endorsed the same result. However, the mean score obtained in respect of the policy holders' opinion regarding the intermediaries assistance in the claim settlement was low.
- The results of the discriminant analysis revealed that, with regard to ICICI, the number of respondents who felt that the distribution mix

was effective constituted 68.1 per cent of the total respondents while it was 31.9 per cent of respondents who considered the promotion mix to be ineffective.

- The predominant contributors to the effectiveness of distribution mix were the assistance rendered by the intermediaries in the grievance settlement, knowledge of the intermediaries and information provided by them at the introduction of the policy indicating that, if the company gives more emphasis on these aspects, it would have a much more effective distribution mix.

People and Process Mix

- The policyholders of ICICI were very much satisfied as regards, the cordial relationship maintained by the employees with the policyholders, prompt issue of policy documents by the company and the response given by the employees of the company to the enquiries of the policyholders.
- The mean score calculated on the basis of the response given by the policyholders also endorsed the same result. However, the mean score obtained in respect of the policy holders' opinion regarding promptness of the company in sanctioning loans was low. This may be because the company did not grant loans directly to the policy holders and the policy holders had to raise loans from outside sources on the strength of the policy.
- The results of the discriminant analysis revealed that, in respect of ICICI 75.6 per cent of the respondents considered the distributional mix to be effective, while 24.4 per cent felt it to be ineffective.
- The predominant contributors to the effectiveness of people and process mix were the prompt issue of policy documents, maintenance of accurate records and employees' response to the enquiries of the policyholders indicating that, if the company gives more emphasis on these aspects, it would have a much more effective distribution mix.

Physical Evidence Mix

- In respect of ICICI factors such as the location of branches, provision of adequate seating facilities by the company and the convenient operating hours were very much appreciated by the policyholders.
- The mean score calculated on the basis of the response given by the policyholders also endorsed the same result. However, the mean score obtained in respect of the policy holders' opinion regarding the infrastructure facilities available in the company was low.
- The results of the discriminant analysis revealed that, with regard to ICICI, the number of respondents who felt that the physical evidence

mix was effective constituted 74.8 per cent of the total respondents, while it was 25.2 per cent of respondents who considered the physical evidence mix to be ineffective.

- The predominant contributors to the effectiveness of physical evidence mix were the infrastructure facilities, location of branches at convenience places and availability of water facilities indicating that if the company gives more emphasis on these aspects, it would have a much more effective physical evidence mix.

Conclusion

The life insurance sector which is the most promising sectors in India has become a very attractive destination for global insurance players. Increased dynamism in the external environment in the form of growth in competition has made its imperative to bring about transformation in the life insurance market. A key issue for the insurance players is to recognize the relevant marketing dimensions reaching out both new and existing customers.

Due to the privatization process initiated by the central Government several life insurance players have come into the fray. The life insurance companies vie with each other to capture a significant share in the life insurance markets. An effective marketing mix comprised of innovative products, pricing strategies, attractive promotional tools, well designed distribution strategies, people-oriented quality service mechanisms and physical evidence practices providing better infrastructure facilities has been facilitated by the companies. In this context, an attempt has been made by the researcher to analyze the marketing mix of three major life insurance companies namely the Life Insurance Corporation of India, Bajaj Allianz Life Insurance Company and ICICI Prudential Life Insurance Company.

The attributes of each component of the marketing mix were identified and analysed by obtaining the opinion of the respondents about each attribute. The socio-economic profile of the respondents was analysed and, it was found that majority of customers falling under the age group of 41-60 gave preference for purchasing the life insurance policies; in most of the families purchase of life insurance policy was the joint decision of the husband and wife; customers earning a monthly income of ranging from Rs. 5,000 to Rs. 15,000/- had purchased the life insurance policies. Respondents belonged to the three major religions namely, Christianity, Hinduism and Islam.

Two important factors were identified during the study. Brand image was the prime criteria adopted by majority of the respondents for the selection of the company. Agents played a pivotal role in providing information about the policies and were also the major intermediaries in the life insurance market. Their commendable service was highly appreciated by majority of the respondents.

Various attributes of product mix were analysed and it was revealed that risk cover and security factors of LIC and Bajaj and security and returns factor of ICICI were the predominant factors in determining the product mix. The premium charged by all the three companies was considered to be moderate and the same was the opinion with regard to the bonus declared by the companies. Of the various promotional tools employed by the three companies, it was identified that in respect of LIC, motivation through advertisements and informative agents; in case of Bajaj, pamphlets and websites and in case of ICICI, pamphlets and motivation through advertisements were the predominant promotion tools. The analysis of the various attributes of the distribution mix made it clear that in respect of all the three life insurance companies, assistance rendered by the intermediaries in taking policies and knowledge of the intermediaries were the major contributors to the distribution mix. The study on the customer care services (people and process mix) brought to light that in respect of LIC, maintenance of accurate records and information at policy lapse; in respect of Bajaj, friendliness of employees and maintenance of accurate records and in respect of ICICI, friendliness of employees and promptness in document issue were the major contributors to the people and process mix. The analysis of the physical evidence practices revealed that in respect of LICand Bajaj, convenient location and convenient operating hours; and in respect of ICICI, convenient location and convenient operation hours and adequate seating arrangements in the office were the major contributors to the physical evidence mix.

Likewise, Bajaj was considered to be the best in respect of product mix, promotion mix, people and process mix and physical evidence mix. LIC ranked first in respect of distribution mix as well as the premium and bonus components of price mix and occupied second place in respect of product, people and process mix and stood third in respect of physical evidence mix and the promotion mix. ICICI was ranked second in respect of the physical evidence mix, the bonus component of price mix and promotion mix. It was ranked third in respect of all the other components of marketing mix. The statistical tools applied also indicated the same results.

Of all the three companies namely, Life Insurance Corporation, Bajaj Allianz Life Insurance Corporation of India and ICICI Prudential Life Insurance Company, Bajaj was sweeping high in respect of four major components of marketing mix followed by LIC which occupied the dominant position in respect of two components. As per the result of the study, ICICI had to improve in almost all the elements. In most aspects of the marketing mix Bajaj has been dominating, perhaps indicating Bajaj stands for the best. This fact has been proved by the statistical records released by the IRDA which state that Bajaj was number one in respect of the number of policies underwritten by the life insurance companies during the year, 2007-2008 (Annexture-2).

Life insurance companies can grow from strength to strength by changing their limited focus and looking for positive outcomes through progressive ideas. The companies should strive hard to transform their creative vision into dynamic action through committed mission of genuine customer service

In keeping with the proverbial saying that,

"THE JOURNEY OF A THOUSAND MILES BEGINS WITH ONE STEP"

The insurance companies can start their promising march into the future with the first step of a strong foundation to serve the customers and through them the nation by excellent service in providing security for the future and risk cover along with timely payment of returns.

Suggestions

Based on the facts revealed by the study conducted by the researcher, the following suggestions are made.

LIC

- LIC the pioneer life insurance company has been ranked high by its policy holders for its valuable services rendered in providing life insurance cover for all sections of people especially to the rural masses. But it is still regarded as a conventional insurance organization. It should be revamped and given a modern focus and approach that is adaptable to the present societal needs.
- LIC can concentrate more on Unit linked products which seem to give more returns in a short span of time.
- More short term policies or policies that would fetch the policyholders, financial returns at regular intervals for children's educational needs and medical purposes as in the case of money back policies.
- In this competitive scenario technology plays a vital role in promoting the sale of any product. LIC by making effective use of the technological advancement can capture a wide market through facilitating on line payments, on line tracking, on line delivery and so on. The pamphlets of LIC should provide detailed information about the policy to the policy holders.
- LIC should improve upon its infrastructure facilities. Improved physical ambience of the LIC would result in more customer satisfaction .

Bajaj

- Products which would fetch more returns are expected more by the policy holders of Bajaj. It would be advisable for the company to look into this expectation to provide customer satisfaction.

- Loan facilities are not offered by the company directly to the policyholders. It is suggested that the company should directly grant loans to the policyholders on the strength of the policy.
- Advertisements through posters could be more impressive using the advanced technology to create a more dynamic and lasting impact.

ICICI

- The physical evidence practices of ICICI have been appreciated by majority of the policy holders. But the other dimensions of marketing mix have been considered less effective. But recent developments that have taken place in the company reveal that the defects have been rectified.
- To create a more dynamic and lasting impact advertisements through posters could be more impressive using the advanced technology.
- The company should introduce more products for the rural masses and the low income group prospects at minimum affordable prices.
- The company should try to focus on the add on riders more.
- Loan facilities are not offered by the company directly to the policyholders. It is suggested that the company should directly grant loans to the policyholders on the strength of the policy for, it would attract more policy holders.

Suggestions to the Insurance Companies

- There is a welcome shift in the product offering of the life insurance companies. Traditional products which have a long-term commitment and fetch returns after a long time have been replaced by unit linked policies with short period commitment and guaranteed returns within a short period of time. However, it is suggested that due care should be exercised by the life insurance companies to provide products with assured safety of funds as well as returns.
- With the breakdown of joint family system in the present social set up, there is increase in the nuclear families giving rise to demands for children's plan. With increase in the cost of education, expenses incurred in settling the children, it is expected that there would be huge potential for children's plans. Hence it is suggested that the insurance companies should come up with a variety of children's policies which would be of use for their future education, marriage and other requirements. The companies could come out with creative short-term policies for children that if taken at the time of child's birth, would yield monetary benefit every four or five years which would support the child's education even at the initial stages.
- The statistical report released by the IRDA reveals that the policy taking is concentrated mainly to the last two or three months of the financial year. Therefore it is suggested that policy taking should be

done in a phased-out manner throughout the year and not just in one or two months towards the close of the financial year. Incentives in the form of rebates may be announced by the companies for the policy holders who invest their money in the life insurance policies during the initial months in the year.

- If a life insurance company has the various essential factors such as product mix, price mix, promotion mix, distribution mix, people and process mix and physical evidence mix in a highly promising manner for the policy takers such a company is sure to be in the fore front because it has also the highly effective marketing strategies. The company should in the product and pricing give top priority to security and risk cover along with affordable premium with good bonus. With regard to promotion the dominant factor of the company should be on motivation through effective and highly informative advertisements. The company should, with regard to distribution, especially focus on effective agents with thorough knowledge of policies and willingness to provide valuable assistance to the customers while purchasing the policies. In connection with customer service – process and people – a company that strives to be on top should provide customer friendly employees, along with maintenance of accurate records. A company which desires to excel should also give importance to physical evidence by providing convenient location and convenience time for transaction.
- A blend of all these essential factors in the motor satisfactory proportion will definitely result in the life insurance company being rated the first and the best.

Suggestions to the Government and Policy Makers

- India lives in the villages. With 70 crores of people living in rural areas, the rural market has a good potential for life insurance market. However, this market can be tapped only with the introduction of low premium life insurance products. A committee may be constituted having the panchayat board members (president and members), the village administration (village administrate officer, and the office assistants) and the staff of the primary health centres (doctors, nurses and the anganwadi workers) as the members. A life insurance company may join with this committee and take initiatives to create awareness among the rural masses about the advantages of purchasing a life insurance policy.
- Each insurance company must be asked to identify a village with maximum number of policyholders and adopt it. As an incentive, it may be asked to transform the village so adopted chosen into a model village consisting of :

Better transportation facilities with frequent bus facilities and well laid road facilities; water and sanitation facilities by procuring pipeline connection, constructing water tanks for the benefit of the villagers, taking initiatives for the construction of government-aided toilet facilities and so on; electricity services may be provided to each house by obtaining such facilities from the government; mini-libraries may be opened for the benefit of the villagers; steps may be taken to improve the health care facilities – medical facilities may be made available for 24 hours to meet the emergency requirements and organizing self employment training programmes for the village youth.

- Children are the wealth of the nation. The life insurance company may take initiatives to improve the education facilities by providing better infra structure facilities such as: Well protected compound facilities, library facilities, class rooms with adequate seating facilities, water and sanitation facilities – pollution free environment, employing the unemployed youth in the village for conducting coaching classes for the slow learners; encouraging the students to take part in the sports events at the district, state level, national, and international level competitions, providing e-learning facilities with minimum one computer in schools, arrange for the supply of free books, study materials and stationary articles. This would reduce the number of dropouts from schools.
- It is suggested that apart from conducting exhibitions, fairs, by banner display and rallies and by conducting door to door campaigns for motivating the rural people to go in for such policies that would yield good returns besides providing life cover, the insurance companies should make use of the Non Government Organisations, and agents of post offices and banks. The Public relations officers of the life insurance companies can work with the village administration and give video presentations through info-tainment techniques.
- The Government sponsored National Rural Employment Guarantee Scheme (NREGS) should include a family insurance policy for a minimum period of five years as part of the employment scheme so that, the workers who have to pay the minimum premium for one hundred days will be motivated to continue the policy. This would procure more business for the life insurance companies, as there is a proposal with the Central Government, to increase the guaranteed working days from 100 to 150.
- Agents who are not the employees of the company play a vital role in promoting the sale of life insurance policies. What would be the position of the insurance companies without these tied agents is a serious question to be thought of by the insurance companies. In this context, it is advised that Direct marketing technique which would be much beneficial to the policy holders (agent's commission is nil) and the Bancassurance model which would procure the business of the bank customers could be adopted by the companies.

BOOKS

Bodla, B.S., Garg, M.C. and Singh, K.P., (2003), Insurance Fundamentals, Environment and Procedures. New Delhi: Deep & Deep Publications Pvt. Ltd.

Chhabra, T.N. and Grover, S.K. (1999). Marketing Management – concepts and Practice. New Delhi : Dhanpat Rai & Co.

Jha, S.M. (2003). Services Marketing. New Delhi: Himalaya Publishing House.

Julia Holy Oake / Bill Weipers. (2002). Insurance. New Delhi: A.I.T.B.S. Publishers and distribution.

Karam Pal. (2004). Insurance Management : Principles and Practice. Deep & Deep Publication.

Kotreshwar, G. (2005). Risk Management Insurance and Derivatives. Mumbai: Himalaya Publishing House.

Kottler, P. & Armstrong. (2005). Marketing Management: Analysis, Planning, Implementation and Control. New Delhi: Prentice Hall of India Pvt. Ltd., Ed.7.

Mathew, M.J. (2005). Insurance Principles and practices. Jaipur: RBSA Publishers.

Mehr and Gustavson. (1984). Life Insurance Theory and Practice. University of Georgia, Texas:. Business Publication.

Mishra, M.N. and Mishra, S.B. (2007). Insurance Principles and Practice. New Delhi: S. Chand & Company Ltd.

Mishra, M.N. (1979). Insurance – Principles and Practices. New Delhi : S. Chand & Company Ltd. p.5.

Mishra, M.N. (1999). Insurance Principles and Practice. New Delhi: S. Chand & Company Ltd.

Motihar. (2004). Insurance Principles practices. Management and Salesmenship. Allahabad: Sharda Pustak Bhawan.

Nalini Prava Tripathy . and Pal .(2004). Insurance Theory and Practice. Mumbai: Prentice Hall of India.

Palande, P. S., Shah. R.S. and Lunawat, M.L. (2007). Insurance in India, Changing polices and emerging opportunities. New Delhi: Sage publications.

Periyasamy, P. (2005). Principles and Practice of Insurance. Mumbai : Himalaya Publishing House.

Pillai, R.S.N. and Bhagavathi, (2000). Modern Marketing Principles and Practices. New Delhi: S.Chand and Company.

Ronald C Horn. (1964). Subrogation in Insurance Theory and Practice. Published for the S.S Huerbrer Foundation.

Sajit Ali., Riyaz Mohammad. and Masharique Ahmed. (2007). Insurance in India. New Delhi: Regal Publications.

Srivastava, D.C. and Shashank Srivasta. (2003). Indian Insurance Industries Transition and Prospects. New Delhi: New Century publication.

Stanton, W., and Furtell, C., (2006). Fundamental of Marketing. New York: Mc Graw Hill Road, Company.

Surender Manola, (2004). Insurance Management. New Delhi: Vishvabharathi Publications.

Sushil Chandra Pal, Insurance Industry in New Millennium (A Case of LIC : Challenges and Response). New Delhi : Rajat Publications.

Tryst with Trust – The LIC Story - Life Insurance corporation of India. New Delhi.

Varshney, R.L. and Gupta,S.L. (2004). Marketing Management, An Indian Perspective. New Delhi: Sultan Chand and Sons.

Vasanthi Venugopal. and Raghu, V.N. (2006). Services Marketing. Mumbai: Himalaya Publishing House.

JOURNALS

Abhishek Agarwal. (2002). Distribution of Life Insurance products in India. *Journal of Insurance Chronicle*, 2(8), 53-55.

Alagar, R.(2005). Retailing with Supply Chain Management. *Journal of Insurance Watch*, 3(4), 50-51.

Alok Mittal. and Akash Kumar. (2001). An Exploratory Study of Factors Affecting Selection of Life Insurance Products. *Journal of Insurance Chronicle*, 1(4), 23.

American Marketing Association, (1960). Report of the definitions committee of the American Marketing Association. Chicago, p.13.

Amita Fatterpekar. (2007). Measuring customer loyalty-A New Marketing Research tool. *Journal of Yogakshema*, 51(7), 40, 42.

Anand, M. (2002). Indian Insurance Industry – Channelising growth. *Journal of Insurance Chronicle*, 2(12), 66-67.

Anand Adhikari.(2005). Five Years After Privatisation. *Journal of Business Today*, 25(8), 110-112.

Anand Pejwar. (2008). Bancassurance in India Potential Unlimited. *IRDA journal*, 6(10), 23-28.

Anil Chandhok.(2004). Emerging issues in the distribution of life insurance products. *Journal of Insurance Chronicle*, 4(12),28-32.

Anil Chandhok. and Mittal,R.K. (2004). Critical study of the first year lapsation ratio of Life Insurance business. *Journal of Insurance Chronicle*, 4(9), 76-79.

Anil Chandok. (2005). A comparative study of the performance of life insurance players. *Journal of Insurance Chronicle*, 5(4), 75-77.

Anuradha Sharma. (2008). Life insurance evaluation and current perspectives. *Journal of Asia Insurance Post*, 8(9), 22-25.

Anurika Vaish. and Pallavi Dixit. (2007). Insurance Companies in the Present Global Scenario. *Journal of Insurance Chronicle*, 7(1), 32.

Anuroop Singh. (2004). Challenging opportunity. *Journal of Asia Insurance Post*, 5(1), 28-29.

Apparao Machiraju. (2003). A Distribution Odyssey. *IRDA Journal*, 1(10), 25-27.

Bijal Mehta. and Shubhra Anand,. (2007). Study of the Need Analyser Tools used by LIC for the insurance markets. *Journal of Insurance Chronicle*, 7(4),66-74.

Bodla, B.S. and Sushma Rani Verma.(2004). Life Insurance Policies in Rural area: Understanding buyer behaviuour. *Indian Journal of Marketing*, 34(5), 6-8.

Capgemini and European, (2007). Financial Management and Marketing Association, Market Training Centre of L,I,C, India.

Case Studies in Insurance.(2005). Hyderabad : ICFAI Centre for management.

Chari, V.G. (2005). Insurance–A relook at the distribution strategy. *Journal of Insurance Chronicle*, 5(3), 28-36.

Chinnadorai, K.M., Kalpana, B. and Sadana, B. (2007). A study of motivational factors and level of satisfaction of agents and development officers of LIC of India. *The ICFAI Journal of services Marketing*, 5(1), 45-53.

Customers' choice, *Asia Insurance Post*, 6(4), 20-22.

Darling selvi, V. (2005). Insurance Industry–A source for investment and employment. Kissan World, 32(12), 15-16.

Devarakonda, VS. Ramesh. (2008). Redefining Distribution, The changing paradigms in insurance intermediation. *Journal of Insurance Chronicle*, 8(1), 28.

Dilip Maitra.(2008). Life insurance is essential for everyone. *Journal of Banking and Finance,5(3),22.*

Divya Gupta. and Bajaj,S,Polygamous. (2008). Bancassurance, A boon or bane. *Journal of Insurance Chronicle*, 8(6), 20-25.

Geethanjali Mehlwal. (2006). The face of the Insurance Industry in India. *Journal of Insurance chronicle*, 6(1),59-64.

Ghodeswar, B.M. (2008). Customer connections: A key advantage in life insurance sector. *Journal of Yogashema*, 52(9), 22, 24, 50.

Giresh Kumar, GS. and Eldhose, KV.(2008). Customer perceptions on Life Insurance services-A Comparative study. *Journal of Insurance Chronicle*, 8(8), 65-74.

Gopal,V.V.(2005). Indian Insurance Industry, embracing the CRM Philosophy. *Journal of Insurance chronicle*, 5(9), 35-39.

Gopala Krishna, G. (2008). Customer relationship management in Insurance. *Journal of Insurance Chronicle*, 8(1), 23.

Govardhan, N.M.(2008). Relevance of distribution channels, Emerging Insurance markets. *IRDA journal*, 6(11), 7-10.

Gupta, P.K. (2004). Pricing of insurance products- actuarial to managerial. *The Management Accountant*, 39(2), 96-101.

Hasanbanu, S. and Nagajothi, R.S. (2007). A study of the insurance perspective in Uthamapalayam taluk. *Indian Journal of Marketing*, 37(5), 10-15, 155.

Hydrey A Rehmanje. (2002).The challenges before insurers today. *Journal of Insurance chronicle*, 2(12), 64-65.

Insurance Marketing. (2005). Hyderabad : ICFAI Centre for Management, p. 196.

Jawaharlal,U. and Kumar, K.B.S. (2004). Branding Insurance: An Indian Perspective. *Journal of Insurance Chronicle*, 4(12), 23.

Jawaharlal, U. (2005). Indian Life Insurance Industry – A retrospect. *Journal of Insurance chronicle*, 5 (9), 15-17.

Jawaharlal, U. (2006). Indian Insurance Industry – A comprehensive Analysis. *Journal of Insurance Chronicle, 6(5)*, 61-65.

Jawaharlal, U. (2008). Providing product flexibility- Riders in insurance. *IRDA journal*, 6(11), 6.

Jawaharlal, U. and Sarthak Kumar Rath, (2005). Customer – centricity in the Insurance Industry. *Journal of Insurance Chronicle*, 5(6), 20-24.

Jean Pierre Lepaud. (2008). Unit linked business product development. *IRDA journal*, 5(2), 12,13.

Jimmy John. (2002). Private companies still upbeat. *Journal of Asia Insurance review*, 2(2), 30-32.

Kaushlendra Maurya. (2005). Business Strategies and IT solutions. *Journal of Insurance Chronicle*, 5(3), 62-68.

Kishorem, R.B. (2006). A Holistic view of the Insurance Reforms and a Blue print for strengthening LIC. *Journal of Insurance Institute of India*, 38 , 35.

Kishore, R.B. (2006). Life Insurance and Affluent Segments of Market. *Journal of Insurance Chronicle*, October, 6(10), 40-45.

Krishna Kumar. and Kannan,R. (2005). LIC–Countering threat from private players. *Journal of Insurance Chronicle*, 5(2), 24-26.

Krishnamurthy, R. (2003). Blueprint for Success – Bringing Bancassurance to India. *IRDA Journal*,1(8), 20-23.

Krishnamurthy, S. (2005). Bancassurance is the most cost effective channel to make insurance products available to masses. *Journal of Asia Insurance Post*, 6(1), 28-29.

Krishna Kumar. (2005). LIC making inroads to rural India. *Journal of Insurance Chronicle*, 5(7), 42-45.

Kumar Jagendra. (2005). Innovative enviraonment in rennovated insurance industry. *Insurance Times*, 25(4), 20.

Layman's Guide to Life Insurance, 2008, New Delhi : Outlook Publishing (India) Private Limited.

Life Insurance Guide, 2007, Mumbai: Insurance Institute of India.

Life Insurance Corporation Survey (2004), *Magarantham - Life Insurance Journal*, 22.

Madhusudana Rao., *et al*. (2002). Job satisfaction of employees-A survey of LIC employees. *Indian Journal of Marketing*, 32(10), 28-34.

Malabika Deo. (2005). Bancassurance: A win-win solution for banks and insurers. *Journal of Facts for You*, 31(6), 39-42.

Marketing Study course, The Chartered Insurance Institute, 2000

Mckinsey and Company. (2008). Report on Indian Life Insurance. *Journal of Yogashema*, 52(1), 9-11.

Manchanda, S,M. (2005). Importance of the Need to Cover the Death Risk. *Journal of Insurance Chronicle*, 5(9), 23-28.

Mekala Mary Selwyn. (2004). An Evaluation of Distribution Channels in Life Insurance: Agents Vs Bancassurance. *Journal of Insurance Chronicle*, 4(3), 46-48.

Mittal, R.K. and Anil Chandhok. (2005). Privatisation of Life Insurance Services in India – Impact and Perspective. *Journal of Insurance chronicle*, 5(3),24.

Mittal, R.K. (2002). Privatization of Life Insurance sector in India. *Indian Journal of Marketing*, 22(6), 5.

Mishra, K.C. and Simita Mishra. (2000). Global Insurance Market structure. *Journal of The Management accountant*, 35(3), 23.

Mishra, K.C. (2000). The game is changing, Bancassurance. *Journal of The Management Accountant*, 35(6), 374.

Mony, S.V. (2003). Life insurance, private players Initiatives. *The Hindu Survey of Indian Industry*, 78-80.

Mukesh KumarBaura. (2006). Bancassurance in life insurance in India: The brick and mortar model. *The ICFAI Journal of Risk and Insurance* , 6, 42-52.

Narayanan Krishnamurthy. (2000). From the Sidelines. *Advertising and Marketing Journal*, 18(5), 110

Nalini Prava Tripathy. (2006). Bancassurance in the New Millennium. *Journal of Insurance Chronicle*, 6(9), 18.

Nalini Prava Tripathy. (2006). An Application of factor analysis approach towards designing Insurance Products in India. *Journal of Insurance Chronicle*, 6(2), 84-90.

Namasivayam. N., Ganesan, S. and Rajendran, S. (2006). Socio,economic Factors Influencing the Decision in Taking Life Insurance Policies. *Journal of Insurance Chronicle*, 6(8), 65-67.

Naren N, Joshi. (2002). Rural Insurance Issues Challenges and opportunities. paper presented at National Workshop on Insurance– Growth Prospects of Emerging Insurance Market: Challenges and Opportunities.

Naren N, Joshi. (2002). Developing a Rural Distribution Strategy for Insurers paper presented at National Workshop on Insurance– Growth Prospects of Emerging Insurance Market: Challenges and Opportunities.

Neelam Jain. (2000). Liberalisation of Insurance in India: Opportunities and Challenges. *Journal of Southern Economist*, 39(3), 7-11.

Neera Banzal. (2004). New tool for developing life insurance marketing - Policy holders Meet and Bouquet. *Insurance Watch*, 3(9), 23.

Pandey, K.C.(2004). Insurance sector changing with time. *The Management Accountant*, 39(2), 102-104.

Parakala, V.S. and Nagaraja Rao. (2004).Alternative channels of India Sixth Global Conference of Actuaries. 18, 19.

Paromita Goswami. (2007). Customer satisfaction with service quality in the Life Insurance Industry in India. *ICFAI Journal of services Marketing*, 5(1), 25-30.

Pillai, VNS. (2007). Simple Approach to Life Insurance and Pension- When I am not there – While I'm there. *Journal of Insurance Chronicle*, 7(2), 23-28.

Prabhakara, G. (2007) Creating consumer awareness-Life Insurance. *IRDA journal*, 5(12), 36.

Prakasa Rao. and Venkateshwara Rao, B.L.(2005). Buoyant Rural Markets Immense potential for Insurance. *Journal of Insurance chronicle*, 5(8), 47-49,

Prasuna, DG. and Nidhi Joshi. (2005) Rest Assured. *Journal of Charted Financial Analyst*, 23(4), 14-16.

Rajendra Prasad, T.(2007). Emergence of new players in Indian insurance sector.

Journal of Southern Economist, 46(7), 31-34.

Rajendra Prasad, T.(2007). Emergence of new players in Indian insurance sector.

Journal of Southern Economist, 46(7), 31-34.

Rajesham, Ch. and Rajender, K. (2006). Changing Scenario of Indian Insurance Sector. *Indian Journal of Marketing*, 36(7), 9-15.

Rajesh,J,Jampala. and Venkateswara Rao, C. (2005). Sales promotion in the insurance sector, A Study of LIC. *Journal of Insurance chronicle*, 5(4),48-50.

Rajesh C Jampala. (2005). Insurance Sector: Emerging Distribution Channel. *Indian Journal of Marketing*, 35(7), 24-27.

Rajesh J Champala. and Venkateswara Rao, C. (2005). Claim settlement, the key success factor of LIC. *Journal of Insurance Chronicle*, 5(7), 20-22.

Rajesh C Jampala. and Venkateswara Rao, B.H. (2005). Impact of Liberalization on LIC. *,Journal of Insurance Chronicle*, 5(2), 37.

Rajesh C Jampala and Polavarapu Adilakshmi, (2006). Scale up for Success – The Mantra for Private Insurance in India, *Journal of Insurance Chronicle*, 6(11), 26-31.

Rajesh C, Jampala. and Polavarapu Adi Lakshmi. (2006). Emerging Markets, Changing the Landscape of the Insurance Sector. *Journal of Insurance Chronicle*, 6(3), 39-43.

Ramamurthy, A. (2003). LIC Advantage of strong base. *The Hindu Survey of Indian Industry*, 81.

Ramakrishnarao, TS. and Samuel B Sekar. (2008). Shopassurance, New kid on the block. *Journal of Insurance Chronicle*, 8(8),17-20.

Ramamurthy, P. (2008). Selling life insurance art or science?. *Journal of Yogakshema*, 52(5), 7- 8.

Ranjan Kumar. and Koushal Vaidhya. (2004). Differentiation strategies of Insurance companies. *Journal of Insurance Chronicle*, 4(3),27.

Rao, G.V. (2003).What Brokers are . *IRDA Journal*, 1(10),19.

Rao, G.V. (2005). Emerging Trends in the Asian Insurance Scene – Impact of Global Trends. *Journal of Insurance Chronicle*, 5(6), 13-19.

Rao, G.V. (2008). Retail shift. *Journal of Asia Insurance Post*, 6(3), 37-39.

Rao, G.V. (2004).Liberalized Customers: A Challenge for insurers. *IRDA Journal*, 2(5), 24.

Richard Holloway. and Rajagopalan Krishnamurthy. (2006). Insuring rural India. *Journal of Insurance Chronicle*, 6(12), 47-51.

Ravi Kumar Sharma. (2005). Insurance Perspective in Eastern Up – An Empirical Study. *Indian Journal of Marketing*, 35(6), 14-20.

Ravi Prakash, S., Satyanarayana, T. and Shyam Sundar, C. (2003). Globalisation – It's impact on insurance industry. Indian Journal of Marketing, 33(10), 5,6,9.

Ravi Kumar, VV. (2005). The Emerging Structure of Bancassurance in India. *Journal of Insurance Chronicle*, 5(9) , 35.

Reddy, C.R. and Vidyasagar Reddy, G. (2008). Reforms of Insurance Service Sector: Strategic approach. *Southern Economist*, 47(14), 19-22.

Rengachary, N. (2003).Life Insurance –Vision for the future. *The Hindu Survey of Indian Industry* , 39-41.

Rudra Saibaba., *e.,al.* (2002). Perception and attitude of women towards life insurance policies. *Indian Journal of Marketing*, 32(12), 10-12.

Rumeer Shah. (2003). What makes Bancassurance Happen. *IRDA Journal*, 1(11), 18-19.

Rumki Banyopadhyay. (2006).Role of Private Players - Opportunities and Challenges. *Journal of Business Toda y, 40(3), 20.*

Ramakrishna Rao, T.S.(2006). Unit Linked Insurance Product – The Big Leap. *Journal of Insurance Chronicle*, 6(3), 15-18.

Rama Krishna Rao, T.S. (2006). Private insurers come of age. *Journal of Insurance chronicle*, 6(4), 13-16.

Ramesh, D.V.S.(2006). Retaining a life policy, Distributor's ethics. *IRDA journal*, 5(1), 18-19.

Rao, R.V.S.(2003). Life Insurance Private Players initiatives. *The Hindu Survey of Indian Industry*, 78.

Rao,C.S. (2007). Indian Insurance Industry, a Remarkable journey. *Journal of Insurance Chronicle*, 7(8),32.

Rajat Gera. (2004). Life Insurance Marketing in India – The missing product. *Journal of Insurance watch*, 2(6), 25.

Ravi, Kumar, V.V. (2006). Bancassurance in India, An emerging concept, *Journal of Insurance chronicle*, 6(4),35-37.

Ravikumar, V.V. (2005).Emerging structure of Bank assurance in India. *Journal of Insurance chronicle*, 5(12), 35-41.

Sai Kumar. (2006). Life Insurance Products in India- Issues in Distribution. *IRDA Journal*, 5(1), 22-23.

Samuel B Sekar., (2007). Know your policy holder. *Journal of Insurance Chronicle* , 7(5) 35-38.

Samuel B Sekar. (2008). Indian Insurance Industry poised for growth. *Journal of Insurance Chronicle*, 8(6),39-45.

Samuel B Sekar. (2006). Demand Driven Innovation in Insurance Products. *Journal of Insurance Chronicle*, 6(1), 32-36.

Sethi, S.K. (2008). Role of intermediaries in Insurance, Importance of brokers. *IRDA journal*, 6(11), 45.

Sesha Ayyar. (1999). New Insurance products in the next century. *Journal of Insurance Institute of India*, 21(1), 47-50.

Sharma, NC. (2008). Performance Paradox, *Journal of Asia Insurance Post*, 8(6), 21-23.

Sharma,N,C.(2004).Top Gear., *Journal of Asia Insurance Post*,4(6),35-38.

Shekar Chandra Sahoo. (1998). Future Marketing strategies for Life Insurance. *Journal of Insurance Industry of India*, 13, 81-84.

Sheela,P.and Arti, G.(2007). A study on the awareness of Life insurance policies in Vishakha patnam. *Journal of Insurance Chronicle*, 7(9) 25.

Shesha Ayyer,V. (2002). Life Insurance in India: Opportunities, challenges and pitfall. *Journal of Insurance Chronicle*, 2(11), 57-61.

Shesha Ayyar. (2000). Insurance Reforms – What are the implications. *Journal of Insurance Institute of India*, 15, 63.

Shikha Sharma. (2002). Changing face of Life Insurance in India. *Journal of Insurance chronicle*, 2(12), 41-43.

Shikha Sharma. (2004). Growing with customers. *IRDA Journal*, 2(5), 21.

Shikha Sharma. (2002). Life insurance – The challenges ahead – Paper presented at the 7th Insurance Summit – 'Deepening Penetration from 1,5% to 5%'", conducted by Confederation of Indian Industry.

Shikha Sharma. (2004).Benefits of competition.The Hindu Survey of Indian Industry, 59.

Sithapathy, V. (2008). What has been and what will be? Role of an insurance broker. *IRDA journal*, 6(11), 42.,

Shilpi Malaiya. and Jain, V.K. (2007). A study of policy purchasing behaviour and situations for settlement of claims – A customer's perspective. *Journal of Insurance watch*, 5(2).

Shobhit. and Sanjay, (2004). An Empirical study and analysis of failure of private players rural areas. *Journal of Insurance chronicle*, 4(5), 30-32.

Shobit. and Sanjay. (2004).An Empirical Study & Analysis of Failure of Private Insurance players in Rural Areas. *Journal of Insurance chronicle*,4(5), 56-62.

Siva Kumar., et.al. (2007). Insurance Industry: A Changing Scenario. *Journal of Insurance Chronicle*, 7(3), 19.

Snekha Shukla. (2008). Insuring the bottom of the pyramid. *Journal of Insurance Chronicle*, 8(9), 27-29.

Sri Jyothi, T. (2008) CRM Practices in Indian Insurance sector. *Journal of Insurance Chronicle*, 8(3), 16.

Sridevi Lakshmikutti. and Sridharan Baskar. (2005). Insurance Distribution in India – A Perspective. *Journal of Insurance Chronicle*, 5(6), 17-22.

Sree Lakshmi,V. (2005). How Indian Insurance Industry should go. *Journal of The economic Challenger*, 7(1), 67.

Srinivas, S,S. and Anand,V. (2005). Unit Linked Investor Guidance Note. *Journal of Insurance chronicle*, 5(12), 42-51.

Srinivas Subbarao, P. (2006). Bancassurance – Challenges and Strategies. *Journal of Insurance Chronicle*, 6(8),27.

Stuart Purdy. (2004). Selling Insurance Products – A challenge for players. *The Hindu Survey of Indian Industry* , 73.

Stephen Wylie. (2005). Agency Management Trends. *Insurance Watch*, 3(7)), 42-43.

Stuart Purdy. (2003). Huge opportunity. *IRDA Journal*, 2(1), 30.

Subhash Lakhotia. (2003). How to sell more life insurance products. Journal *of Insurance watch*, 3(5), 26.

Subrahamanya Sarma,M. and Kalyani, V.(2006). C.R.M. in LIC – Some Reflections. *Journal of Management Accountant*, 41(9), 707-713.

Sukanya Praveen. (2005).Bancassurance in India. *Journal of Insurance Chronicle*, 5(7), 75-78,

Sumit Khana. (2004). *Journal of Insurance Chronicle*, 4(12), 26.

Sunder Ram Korivi. (2004). Insurance sector in India- Challenges ahead. *Journal of Insurance chronicle*,4(1), 39.

Suresh , K.(2003). Innovations in Indian Insurance Distribution. *Journal of Insurance chronicle*, 3(12),41-44.

Swiss Reinsurance Company. *Journal of Insurance Chronicle*, 3(12), 25.

Tripathy, NP. (2004). An Application of Multidimensional Scaling Model Towards Brand Positioning of Insurance Industries: A Study of Private Players. *Journal of Insurance Chronicle, 4(7),25-28.*

Tanuja R Kumar. (2005). Insightful intermediary. *Asia Insurance Post*, 5(5), 38-39.

Tarun Kapoor. (2003). Issues and challenges facing the insurance industry. *Journal of Insurance watch*, 2(5), 25.

Tarun Kapoor. (2004). Marketing of Insurance product. *Journal of Insurance watch*, 3(6),27.

Vasantha, P. (2008).Life Insurance – The Hot Investment. *HRD Times*, 20-21.

Venkateswara Rao, BH. (2005).LIC Agents – Are they all Productive?. *Journal of Insurance Chronicle*, 5(9), 39-42.

Venugopal, R. (2008). Bancassurance in India- Problems and potential. *Journal of Yogashema*, 52(3),9-11.

Vijay Srinivas, K.B. (2000). How returns linked insurance products can be popularized. *Journal of Insurance Institute of India*, 12, 67.

Vijayakumar, A. (2004).Globalization of Indian Insurance sector- Issues and challenges. *The Management Accountant*, 39(3), 195-198.

Vinayagamoorthi, A. and Gopi, R. (2005). Life Insuranace in rural India. Kisan World, 32(11), 14-15.

Vinayagamurthy. (2006). Indian Insurance: Modern Marketing Approach. *Southern Economist*, 45(12), 17-19.

Viswanathan. (2008). Bancassurance The modern fable of hare and tortoise. *Journal of Yogashema*, 52(9), 22-24.

REPORTS

Naren, N. Joshi (2002), Rural Insurance Issues Challenges and opportunities. paper presented at National Workshop on Insurance – Growth Prospects of Emerging Insurance Market: Challenges and Opportunities'

Naren, N. Joshi (2002), Developing a Rural Distribution Strategy for Insurers paper presented at National Workshop on Insurance – Growth Prospects of Emerging Insurance Market: Challenges and Opportunities.

NEWSPAPER

India's share of world insurance rises, *The Economic Times*, June 2008.

WEBSITES

Amit Shrivastava, et al. (2008). Effect of demographic factors in consumer buyer behaviour: A study with specific reference to Indian Life Insurance Industry. Accessed 24 March 2008. www.indiamba.com/Facultycolumn/FC604.htm.

Anurag. (2008). Innovative channel strategies on life insurance. Accessed 15 March 2008. ENG.com.

Bala Krishnamohan, R. and Muralidhar, K. Accessed 18 April 2008.

http://www.oecd.org/dataoecd/40/11/1857811,pdf

Bala Krishna Mohan,R. and Muralidhar,K. CRM Mantra for life insurance industry. Accessed 18 April 2008. http,www.oecd.org.dataoecd/40/10/18578.pdf.

Deva Senathipathi. et al. (2008). A study on the consumer preference and comparative analysis of life insurance companies. Accessed 25 March 2008.

http://www.iupindia.org/1207/IJCB.Focus.asp 26

Gregory A. Kuhlemeyer. and Garth H. Allen.(2008).Consumer satisfaction with Life insurance - A Bench mark survey. Accessed 25 March 2008.

www.afcpe.org/doc/vol1024.pdf.

Marketing Decision making. (2007). Accessed 2 April 2009. http://www.londremarketing.com

Nalini Prava Tripathy.(2007).Brand Positioning of Insurance Industries – A study on Private Players. Accessed 25 March 2008. www.Bimaonline.com ,

NCAER, (2006). Categories of income, Accessed 16 March 2009. http://www.indianplanning commission.com.

Nitin Tanted. (2006) Growth and survival strategy for Indian Insurance companies in the era of emerging global competition. Accessed 20March 2008. http://www.indianmba.com/Faculty_Column/ FC349/fc349,html

Ramkumar,D. (2007).Relationship Marketing- The new mantra for Life insurance sector. Accessed 18 April 2008. http://www.indiabschools.com/marketing.

RNCOS-Indian Insurance Industry Forecast 2007-2009, Accessed 18 September 2008. www.mcos.com. 2008

Service sector in the Indian Economy (2009). Accessed 4 April 2009.

http://www.indiaonestop.com/economy-macro-view.html.

Thompson Report (2007). Urban and Rural Insurance, Accessed 18 March 2009. http://in.reuters.com/article/businessNews/idINIndia- 29442620070910?pageNumber=2&virtualBrandChannel=0&sp=true

New Encyclopedia Americana. (1978), pp.295.

http://www.economywatch.com, Accessed 12 January 2009.

http://www.international insurance.org. Accessed 15 March 2006.

http://www.irdaindia.org, Accessed March 27, 2009.

http://www.irdaindia.org. Accessed 15 June 2006.

http://www.in.reuters.com/article/business news/id/ndia. Accessed 18 March, 2009.

www.niapune.com, Accessed April 28, 2009.

http://www.statistics.com. Accessed July 20, 2009.

http://www.trichycitycorporation.com/tiruchirappalli. Assessed on 10 May 2009.

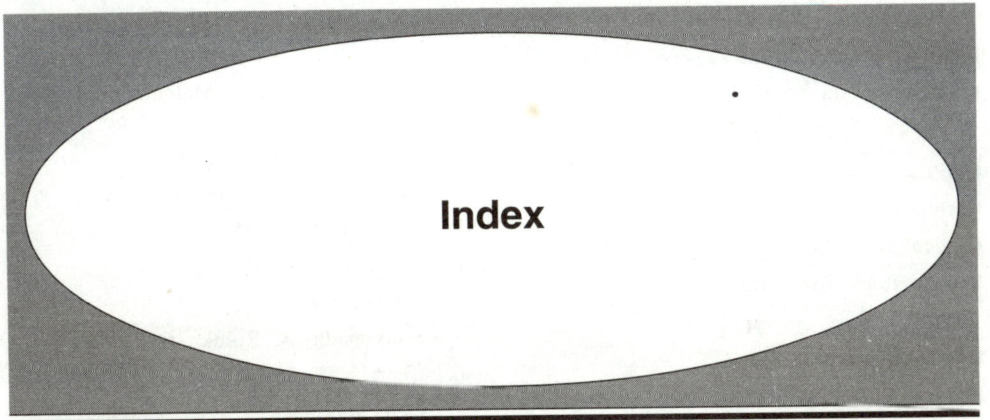

Index